PRAISE FOR BOOKS BY RICK ANTONSON

Walking with Ghosts in Papua New Guinea

"*Walking With Ghosts In Papua New Guinea* is among the best travel narratives I have read. Rick Antonson beautifully creates a sense of the environment in New Guinea as well as the local people he encountered. He effortlessly weaves in the dramatic wartime history of the Kokoda Trail as his party treks across rushing streams and up and down the mountainous terrain. I highly recommend this book to armchair travelers anxious to experience life in a truly wild, and in many ways, primitive world."

—James P. Duffy, author of *War at the End of the World*

"A wild and forbidding terrain reveals its dramatic history. Vancouver-based travel writer Antonson vividly recounts a two-week, 60-mile journey on the formidable Kokoda Trail in Papua New Guinea, a rugged terrain marked by jungle, bogs, gullies, cliffs, malarial mosquitoes, rigorous ascents, and steep, slippery descents . . . An absorbing account of a physically and spiritually challenging journey."

—*Kirkus Reviews*

Full Moon over Noah's Ark

"It's not just about the journey, or standard travel writing. It's about story-telling, and Rick takes us on a magical, almost mystical adventure to destinations once only shrouded in mythology."

—Peter Greenburg, travel editor, *CBS News*

"A book filled with the enthusiasm of discovery, the delight in accomplishment, and the relief of return."

—*Kirkus Reviews*

"This is one of those rare books, full of emotion and insight, the work of a true traveler."

—Dina Bennett, author of *Peking to Paris*

To Timbuktu for a Haircut

"Rick Antonson's classic travel memoir."

—*Chicago Tribune*

"Anyone planning a trip to Africa should put Antonson's book on their packing list right after malaria tablets."

—*National Post*

"In the magical-travel-names-department, Timbuktu undoubtedly holds the trump card—Marrakesh, Kathmandu, or Zanzibar are mere runners-up—but Rick Antonson's trek to the fabled desert city proves that dreamtime destinations are found in our minds just as much as on our maps."

—Tony Wheeler, co-founder of Lonely Planet and author of *Bad Lands: A Tourist on the Axis of Evil*

"The remarkable combination of Rick Antonson exploring the ancient mysteries of Timbuktu matched with the rich culture of Mali that he captures so well . . . makes a page-turner from start to finish."

—Jerry W. Bird, editor, *Africa Travel Magazine*

Route 66 Still Kicks

"One of the best books of the bunch."

—*The New York Times* 2012 round up of holiday travel books

"A must for Route 66 aficionados."

—*Chicago Tribune*

"The most impressive account of a road trip I have ever read."

—Paul Taylor, publisher of *Route 66 Magazine*

"A middle-age Woodstock in motion, an encounter with an America that isn't as lost as we think . . . in the end Antonson proves that Route 66 indeed still kicks—as does America."

—Keith Bellows, editor in chief, *National Geographic Traveler*

WALKING WITH GHOSTS IN PAPUA NEW GUINEA

⅂ GHOSTS
IN PAPUA NEW GUINEA

Crossing the Kokoda Trail in the
Last Wild Place on Earth

RICK ANTONSON

Skyhorse Publishing

Skyhorse Publishing books may be purchased in bulk at special discounts for sales promotion, corporate gifts, fund-raising, or educational purposes. Special editions can also be created to specifications. For details, contact the Special Sales Department, Skyhorse Publishing, 307 West 36th Street, 11th Floor, New York, NY 10018 or info@skyhorsepublishing.com.

Skyhorse® and Skyhorse Publishing® are registered trademarks of Skyhorse Publishing, Inc. ®, a Delaware corporation.

Visit our website at www.skyhorsepublishing.com.

10 9 8 7 6 5 4 3 2 1

Library of Congress Cataloging-in-Publication Data is available on file.

Hardcover ISBN: 978-1-5107-0566-1
Ebook ISBN: 978-1-5107-0568-5

Cover design by Brian Peterson
Cover photograph by Andrew Peacock
Interior maps by Eric Leinberger
Pages xiii, 57, 100, 110, 163: photograph by Glen "Monk" Thompson
Pages 116, 218: photograph by Tori McCarthy
Page 208: photograph by Michael Bowles
Page 237: photograph by Rick Antonson
Page 241: photograph by Janice Antonson

Printed in the United States of America

For my wife, Janice—
whose career working abroad has brought the wonder of adventures,
the blessing of new friends, and a world of eye-opening experiences
I'd not have had without her.

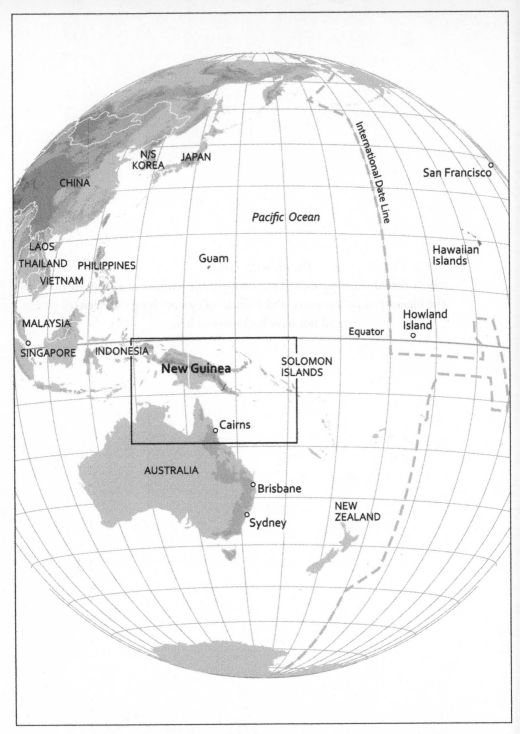

The Asia Pacific region as it is today. New Guinea is said by some to be "the last wild place on earth." The *western half* is part of Indonesia. The *eastern half* is the country of Papua New Guinea—a name by which the entire island is frequently, and erroneously, referenced. The Kokoda Trail is shown here as a thin line on the eastern portion of the island.

Contents

The Kokoda Trail is on the island of New Guinea, in today's country of Papua New Guinea (PNG), which was formed in 1975. The island has been called "the last unknown." In 1942, American General Douglas MacArthur called it "green hell." Action there during World War II took place within the context of a regional theater of war. The place names shown are circa 2019.

Pacific Ocean

Solomon Sea

Rabaul

SOLOMON ISLANDS

Lae

Wau

Kokoda Trail Gona

Buna

Port Moresby

Milne Bay

Guadalcanal

Coral Sea

N
W · E
S

Cairns

0   200 miles

0   200 kilometers

What I regard as the most important single element in the physical act of walking: rhythm. But the fact remains that although you must change gear in an almost literal sense at the bottom and top of a steep hill you can maintain the deeper continuity of the old rhythm.

—Colin Fletcher, *The Complete Walker*

There are a dozen bridges over creeks and rivers along the Kokoda Trail. They are frequently damaged by weather and water, requiring replacement. Each bridge, whether an assortment of logs and branches shoved together or vine-lashed architectural beauties, is designed for locals and used by trekkers.

It's all a strange history, and histories never end, but go on living in their consequences.

—Henry James

ONE

Miles from Nowhere

"I have come from 50,000 years."
—Kumalau Tawali, Papuan poet

Who can resist serendipity? Surely not a traveler . . .

It was August in Australia, their southern winter. I'd flown there from North America's summer, the climatic juxtaposition accented by Queensland's tropical setting. My wife Janice was in airport management and a new posting had brought her to Cairns a few months before my visit, giving her time to settle into work responsibilities while temporarily living out of an apartment. On the afternoon I arrived, we moved fourteen miles north of Cairns Airport to Clifton Beach and into our leased house, one with Balinese architecture. Waves from the Coral Sea pounded to shore in the background. As evening arrived that first night, the moving crew finished unloading the furnishings, and took away cardboard packaging for recycling. Our new home was beginning to feel comfortable.

A gruff voice shouted over the neighbor's fence: "Who are you?"

"Come over and find out," Janice replied.

Within two minutes, they were at our place. The movers had left the front door ajar. A man and wife, whose ages paralleled our own, walked in.

Wens's smile made its own welcome. She was a dozen years younger than her partner. "Glen," he said, one hand reaching out to shake mine while the other clasped two beer bottles by their necks. He passed me one. "Friends call me the Monk." He was a walking fitness regimen, four inches shorter than my six feet and without the paunch.

"Hope you're staying longer than the last renters," said Wens.

Janice assured her that the work visa was for three years.

Monk returned to the open doorway where he retrieved a case of cold Fosters and a bottle of Jim Beam. "We'll only stay awhile," he said.

As the hours marched on, our lives entwined. We told each other our (undoubtedly embellished) life stories as takeout pizza topped with bacon and egg and crocodile spring rolls arrived by delivery and quickly disappeared, washed down with ale and wine.

By midnight, there was little verbal jousting left unsaid in the new friendship between Monk and me. He was self-made, self-educated, and self-sufficient. He could fix anything with moving parts. He'd built houses, and once owned a fleet of mobile mechanic shops that moved around Australia delivering parts and providing mechanical expertise. That'd made him financially independent.

Monk recounted his escapades in Southeast Asia and it made my travel envy rise. He owned a restaurant in Bali, where he had a part-time home. Wanting to offer anecdotes to rival his, I told him of my recent ascent of 17,000-foot Mount Ararat in eastern Turkey, and an Outward Bound expedition to a summit in Canada. When hearing those, his mood shifted noticeably, and his face took on a gleam of seriousness that I misinterpreted as respect. He pursed his lips as if debating with himself. He guzzled yet another beer.

I detected a slight nod of his head, as though he'd reached an internal decision. He moved his left shoulder into mine in a nudge I took to be a dare.

"I'm going to do *the Kokoda*," he said. "Do you wanna come?"

"Absolutely," I said, without hesitation, emboldened by a few hours of liquid courage. He held out his hand and I grasped it in firm commitment.

Wens gave a warning smile to Janice, who simply laughed. This kind of rash behavior was not surprising to her.

"Agreed, then." A smirk in Monk's eyes cemented our quest.

There was just one thing I wasn't one hundred percent sure about.

"What's *the Kokoda*?" I asked.

Monk played to my ignorance. "It's a walk across the country."

"Which country?"

"Papua New Guinea."

The American writer Peter Matthiessen wrote of a first Papuan who was the earliest human to arrive on the island of New Guinea. "How many years, or centuries of years, this man had wandered out of Africa and Asia may never be known, for he traveled lightly, and he left no trail." Papuan poet Kumalau Tawali narrowed Matthiessen's speculation with his own understanding: "I have come from 50,000 years." Archaeologists agree.

The first Papuan people arrived by sea, landing on the island's northern shores. Contingents crossed the equator in rudimentary craft, pushed southward by currents and winds. They found a place with abundant seafood, lush jungles and welcoming beaches (with seasonal inlets), open plains (with swampy floods), and mountains (with roiling rivers). In our modern calendar's vernacular, we show that time as 50,000 BCE.

Those Melanesians were of Southeast Asian descent. This was the same period when Australia, the barren continent south of New Guinea, also received its first immigrants. At one time there existed a 100-mile land connection between these two landmasses, but as the last Ice Age started to recede, circa 15,000 BCE, its melt raised sea levels globally and this dry breach was eventually lost as the rising waters turned higher ground into hundreds of islands. By 6,000 BCE, ocean waters had formed yet-to-be-named landmarks: Australia, and this new island of New Guinea, with the Torres Strait in between them and the Coral Sea to the east.

More people continued to arrive and took up isolated habitats, each claiming a valley, a hillside, or a shoreline as their own. They seldom interacted with other established groups. Their self-reliance required neither trade nor war. The island became home to highland cliques as well as jungle clans and coastal dwellers, each tribe developing its own parlance and subsistence lifestyle.

Of course, I didn't know any of this yet on the morning after meeting Monk, when I awoke hungover with Papua New Guinea on my mind. Sipping coffee brought a first reference point. I remembered a thick, flavorful brew with a nice reputation sourced from that country.

My scant knowledge about the place was, frankly, embarrassing. For anyone living in Europe or North America, "PNG," as Monk called it, is about as far away from home as you can get. It is tucked unceremoniously above Australia. After World War II it was largely ignored in world affairs unless a foreigner went missing or an explorer mentioned a "lost tribe." Forgotten, perhaps, but not gone. I wondered about the country's people. What brought them together as a nation? I could not visualize their flag nor hear their music. No native language came to mind.

My next thought was of Amelia Earhart; hadn't she made her final takeoff from there, never to be seen again?

Into my thinking crept the name Rockefeller. The son of a famous US governor went missing in New Guinea in the 1960s. He'd fallen off a boat—and was thought to have swum into a tribe of headhunters who killed him and, quite possibly, ate him.

I was somewhat aware of a current unease in PNG. In the months before I arrived in Australia, Janice had twice been to PNG on airport business, staying within Port Moresby's business community, a protective zone of landings, consultations, and takeoffs. She told me, "I went from one meeting to another escorted by a guard with a shotgun and a dog named Gangster." Along with that had come stories of *raskols*, gangs whose bad behavior provided cover for what was wrong with the country (high unemployment, poor economy, rampant crime, and perceived lack of benefits for communities hosting mining or logging operations). Monk reinforced what Janice conveyed when he said, "Every Aussie who heads to PNG has the risk of *raskols* in the back of their mind."

In one of his travel books, *Running Away to Sea*, writer George Fetherling observed the early days of the *raskols* phenomenon in Papua

New Guinea, decades ago. He wrote, "Anthropologists and others would have you believe that the best time to visit PNG is always yesterday, before it was exposed to western daylight." The plight that spawned the *raskols* movement continues to flourish today. Squatter settlements grew as families were drawn to larger towns and Moresby. Employment was hard to find. As the number of disenfranchised residents increased, the percentage of angry ones grew as well. More young men sought out the drug trade. The problem spread throughout the islands, exhibiting itself in kidnappings, assaults, and robberies—often for minor financial gain. The brazen *raskols* became synonymous with the image of the country, staining the PNG brand. They have been blamed for deterring tourists. *Raskols* came to be seen as the reason for, not the result of, 60-plus percent unemployment in urban areas. One result: façades of prickly steel wire wrap around anywhere comfortable in Port Moresby while also securing the town's ranking among the world's most unlivable cities. One such survey's 130-city listing placed Lagos in Nigeria, Dhaka in Bangladesh, and Karachi in Pakistan ahead of Port Moresby, which came in at last place.

The view of omnipresent danger in PNG was one that my travels would cure, but prior to meeting Papuans personally it was prudent to consider one's safety at risk when there.

Other matters surfaced as I pondered my new destination. Many years ago, my first fascination with travel writers came from reading Peter Matthiessen's *The Snow Leopard*. Entranced, I sought out his earlier writing and spent time with *Under the Mountain Wall*, about his time in New Guinea. Unlike the first book, that one didn't stick. I couldn't digest his intense writing or the complexity of the society about which he wrote. I gave up on the book, though his writing left a marker in my memory; he'd contrasted starkly those people who lived there and those who chose to visit. As I would soon be one of the latter, I realized it best to review Matthiessen's narrative as a more mature reader.

Only later would I find the numbers to inform another piece of trivia I tried to recall that morning: of the 6,800 "living languages" that survive in our world, 832[1] of them are found in Papua New Guinea, making it "the most linguistically diverse place on earth."

Monk arrived on our front porch. A cup of coffee hung in the grip of two fingers and his other hand scrunched a sheet of paper. "Thought we should talk about the Kokoda Trail, mate, since you'll be coming along."

He smoothed the paper on the kitchen countertop, revealing a map. "We start here," he said, pointing to the city of Port Moresby[2] on the southeastern coast of New Guinea. "Moresby's the capital of PNG." His finger traced a jagged northeastern arc from there across the country, moving over a razorback range of mountains. "That's the Kokoda Trail. We'll walk it." His finger continued toward ocean beaches on the northern coast. "Then to here." He tapped the map as a punctuation mark. "Two weeks all in."

"Remind me again why we're doing this," I asked.

"You said you wanted to."

I wondered about Monk's motivations for such a dramatic trek. Was he hiding something from me? He pivoted to another topic as though he sensed my question. "In World War II, the Japanese landed heaps of soldiers on Papua's northern beaches in July 1942," he said. "They meant to cross the Kokoda Track and attack Moresby. With control of that, they'd be set to invade Australia. Can't have that now, can we, mate?"

I was learning about such places as the Owen Stanley Range, mountains named after a Royal Navy captain who surveyed there in the mid-1800s. They stretch for 200 miles in an east-west slant along the geographic tail of

---

1   Papua New Guinea's languages represent 12% of living languages worldwide, while the PNG's population represents only 0.1% of the population worldwide. By comparison, India has a similar number of living languages but 18% of the world's population.

2   Early visits from European explorers brought with them presumptuous "Naming Rights." British Captain John Moresby sailed to this port in 1873, ignoring designations the Motuan people had already given this trading center. Instead, he deemed it the namesake of his father.

Papua New Guinea. The range is 55 miles wide where Monk and I would be. In places the peaks rise to 9,000 feet. "Our walk"—he still called it a walk—"will reach 7,000 feet altitude." The journey would take us through awe-inspiring foliage. We'd visit dozens of out-of-the-way sites familiar only to Papuans and trekkers. Locals would be open to our arrival and just as happy to see us leave. We'd listen to music not heard anywhere else. The vistas would be breathtaking. If the demands of the trek didn't kill us (as they had others in recent years), we'd have the trip of a lifetime.

Later, as I was unpacking Janice's books and putting them on a shelf in the den, I arranged *Snakes of Australia*, *Australian Crocodiles*, the less alarming *Birds of Australia*, and two bush cookbooks. There was an atlas that oriented me: Port Moresby was a two-hour flight north of where I stood.

I would learn more about this mysterious land in books I borrowed, online, or in conversations, feeling awkward with how little I knew about one of the world's most enchanting places, replacing that ignorance with facts. New Guinea's pocket tribes had lived in a nameless place for its unwritten history. Portuguese spice- and slave-seeker Jorge de Meneses was the first European to poke about the west coast of the island in 1526. Upon seeing dwellers with coil-like hair, he designated the area as *Ilhas dos Papuas*. His "Island of the Papuans" was based around the Malay word *papua*, meaning frizzy-haired.

Nearly 20 years later, the Spanish explorer Inigo Ortiz de Retes sailed along the north coast of the island, scouting locations for a colony. The terrain reminded him of Guinea in Africa, so he named it *Nueva Guinea*.

Spanish man-about-the-seas Luís Vaz de Torres, in 1606, was the first recorded European to make his way through the passage between today's Australia and New Guinea, leaving his name for the Torres Strait. He staked claim on the island, as one would in those days, in the name of the Spanish King. His arrogance was indifferent to the possibility that others might have preceded him, and paid no mind to the concept of indigenous peoples and their traditional lands.

When British Captain James Cook made his first voyage charting the Pacific Ocean, he visited New Zealand and Australia. Then he sailed through the Torres Strait (he called it Endeavour Strait) but didn't make landfall. His journal in August of 1770 showed the ship's location as "off New Guinea." Following on through the Torres Strait in 1789, not at all willingly, was Lieutenant William Bligh, freshly adrift off the HMS *Bounty* and making what is still the longest-ever ocean voyage in an open launch, some 4,000 nautical miles to Timor.

The last century of political evolution has been complicated for New Guinea, which is the world's second-largest island. (Greenland's the answer you're looking for . . .) With the end of World War I, Australia accepted a protective role over the newly-named Territory of Papua and Territory of New Guinea. Ambiguity was such that many Japanese soldiers invading the country in 1942 believed they were invading Australia, and in a sense they were correct, as Papua was an Australian territory with almost the same legal connection as Australia's Northern Territory of the time.

Today the island's western half (formerly Dutch New Guinea) confuses nomenclature for references in my text, as it includes both the Indonesian provinces named Papua (known as Irian Jaya as recently as 2002) and West Papua. The island's eastern half, along with a number of islands, forms Papua New Guinea's 178,700 square miles (slightly larger than California and slightly smaller than Texas). Its population is over eight million, half of them children.

Travel that is too premeditated steals *ah-ha* moments from a journey, and dampens discovery. Yet I was hungry to understand our walk's historic context. Perspective came in the parallel of two warmongering nations in Europe and Asia, both plotting to expand their power in 1939. Germany occupied Poland, with their eyes on the Netherlands and Belgium; they also planned to invade France, Britain, and elsewhere. Also that year, in Asia, Japan extended its hold on China, and ruled the Korean Peninsula (North and South Korea did not exist separately until 1945) with their eyes on Indochina (today Cambodia, Laos, and Vietnam); they also planned to invade Thailand, Singapore, and elsewhere—notably Papua New Guinea, which would secure their southern perimeter and poise them to attack Australia, should they wish.

Port Moresby was the only place on the island geographically suited to base an army division of 20,000 or more. As the historian Dr. Peter Williams put it: "It had an excellent anchorage for a large fleet, an airfield and lots of flat land to build others, docks and storage space for the equipment armies need, and a reliable supply of fresh water." Port Moresby in Japanese hands would also remove the American and Australian ability to base aircraft there within striking distance of the Japanese fleet.

Over six months in late 1942, Papua became the lynchpin that fell loose from the Asian aggressor's planning wheel, changing everything.

As I learned of PNG's pivotal position in that world conflict, I also learned about the country's inhospitable terrain. The physical requirements of our journey caught my attention. My ascent of Mount Ararat was a few years earlier, at a time when I was extremely fit. Since then, weight had been gained, not shed. I needed to drop my newfound Aussie affection for beer, and get into shape. The arduous nature of our trek was not new to me, but it was nevertheless intimidating.

I'd moved to Australia about a year out from the date Monk and I had set for our walk. To prepare, Monk and I made hill hikes in the Australian rainforest. One morning, we took on Earl Hill near Cairns, as had become our practice. It was a steep climb for 30 or 40 minutes, followed by a jarring decent. We'd been told its one-hour circuit replicated one hour on the Kokoda Trail, and that one day on the Kokoda could be equivalent to five or six times up and down Earl Hill.

On those jaunts, I'd taken to spouting short questions on the hike up, conserving my energy. Monk, never short of breath, would expound on whatever topic I'd raised. I listened to his history buff responses, and huffed behind him. This is how I learned that, for Australians, their soldiers' defense of Papua New Guinea had come to symbolize World War II, similar to how Gallipoli[3] symbolized World War I for them: a defining moment in the country's coming-of-age during international conflict.

I also understood that Japan lusted after the precious resources such as iron, natural gas, and oil that would be available to them if they moved southward to Indochina.[4] As Monk put it, "The territories Japan coveted were protectorates of European nations occupied by Hitler. They were vulnerable." The Netherlands was unable to protect the Dutch East Indies, which supplied much of the world's rubber. France, its Vichy government cooperating with Germany, was not about to provide support for its Indochina colony. Britain, threatened by a German invasion, could not ensure protection for Hong Kong, Singapore, or Malaya.

As we hiked that day, I tripped on an Earl Hill stump and tottered along the trail. Monk put a steadying hand on my pack. We stopped for a rest, drinking from our water bottles. Monk opened a chocolate bar, and talked on. Clearly, he was intrigued with the war's greater causes and nearby effects: "Imperial Headquarters in Tokyo viewed US trade and military outposts in the Pacific as exporting American values like democracy, particularly in the Philippines."[5] To watch over those inter-

---

3 In 1915, during World War I, Australian and New Zealand forces made a famously futile fight against the Ottoman Empire (today Turkey). While the plan of attack was a fair one, the Gallipoli Campaign was a failure. For Australia and New Zealand, out of failure arose a national consciousness, which was both confident and independent of Britain.

4 In 1939's pre-war atmosphere, embargoes and sanctions were the US's diplomatic tool of choice. Eighty percent of Japan's oil was imported from the United States. The US restricted shipments and froze Japanese assets and banking transactions. Japan gambled they could replace those imports as part of their vision for a Greater East Asia Co-Prosperity Sphere.

5 In 1939, the Philippines was a US territory (annexed in 1898 with the Treaty of Paris ending the Spanish-American War). A large contingent of US forces was based there, a strategic holdover from World War I.

ests, in 1940 the American Pacific Fleet had been deployed from San Diego to Pearl Harbor.

This had become clear: if Japan were to successfully invade the Asia Pacific region, first it must compromise US presence there. Japan's plan called for six months—from start to finish—to achieve control over their targeted territory.

When Monk and I finished our first loop of Earl Hill that day, I drew deep breaths, gulping for a rest. He looked me in the eyes, nodded to the slope, and muttered, "Mate." Then he bolted back up the incline. I wondered: why such determination?

That evening Monk phoned me. "Did you see tonight's TV news?"

I hadn't.

"A guy hiked Earl Hill this afternoon, less than an hour after we left. Had his camera with him. TV showed his video of a twelve-foot python snaking across the trail. Right where you tripped and we rested." I wondered if the dangers of training for the Kokoda Trail might be greater than the dangers of trekking it.

On December 7, 1941 (going by US time zones—it actually overlapped with December 8 on Asia's calendar), Japan swept to war in the Pacific, inflicting losses on the US Navy hardware, first attacking Pearl Harbor in Hawaii. Over the next seven hours, they hit Guam, Wake Island, Malaya, and Thailand, and targeted Shanghai and British Hong Kong.

Canada, with troops stationed in Hong Kong, was the first Western country to declare war on Japan. The following day, the US, New Zealand, and Britain joined them. In the immediate aftermath of the Pearl Harbor travesty, Australia's prime minister said: "From one hour ago, Australia has been at war with the Japanese Empire."

Ten hours after they attacked Pearl Harbor, the Imperial Japanese Navy had destroyed the infrastructure of American-led forces in the

Philippines. US Army General Douglas MacArthur[6] was forced to retreat from there to Australia.

The strategic town of Rabaul, east of New Guinea on the island of New Britain, was under Japanese control, just as they'd planned. Soon, Singapore surrendered, with 20,000 Australians and many British and Indian soldiers taken into captivity. Within days after the fall of Singapore, part of the same Japanese squadrons that attacked Pearl Harbor raided Darwin, Australia. Fronted by 188 carrier aircraft, both fighters and bombers, they were followed within the hour by 55 high-flying bombers from Japanese-controlled airfields in the Dutch East Indies. This attack sank ten ships including the USS destroyer *Peary*, and incapacitated harbor infrastructure, airports, and the town. In two bombing waves they dropped more bombs on Darwin than they'd used striking Pearl Harbor. The Australian population was startled and unnerved. The Japanese next targeted the Dutch holdings of Timor, Java, and Bali.

By early 1942, the key missing land piece in Japan's Pacific Campaign was the territory of Papua on the island of New Guinea, specifically Port Moresby. Consequently, in March the Japanese army stormed the northeastern town of Lae in Papua to anchor its upcoming moves.

In response to all this, the 62-year-old MacArthur was appointed Supreme Allied Commander, South West Pacific Area, based in Brisbane. In the words of author James Duffy, the Australians "wanted an American commander who would ensure that the fight to save Australia from invasion would become an American fight."

MacArthur's nemesis was the seasoned 54-year-old Lieutenant-General Harukichi Hyakutake, the Seventeenth Army's commander responsible for overseeing actions of the Japanese Imperial forces on

---

6   Having retired a four-star general in the United States, Douglas MacArthur was retained by the Philippines' president to command that country's forces. As war clouds gathered in summer of 1941, President Roosevelt insisted the Philippine Army come under formal US control. MacArthur was reinstated as Commanding General of US Army forces in the Far East, coincident with his Philippine Army responsibilities.

Guadalcanal in the Solomon Islands as well as their Moresby offensive in New Guinea. Hyakutake was based in Rabaul.

One morning a month before our trek, Monk and I were out for a power-walk on the beach, using the sand's unpredictability to strengthen our ankles and calves in preparation for the Kokoda Trail's foot-twisting root structure. Beautiful shores stretched along Clifton Beach and Palm Cove, where we lived. The ocean we trained alongside that morning was the Coral Sea.

"Maybe 600 miles northeast of here is where American and Aussie ships intercepted the Japanese navy," offered Monk. His hand pointed generally to the nearby Great Barrier Reef, and northward.

When the Japanese navy left Rabaul, heading southward for their assault on Port Moresby, the flotilla was comprised of three aircraft carriers escorting transport ships carrying the Nankai Shitai (South Seas Force). These soldiers had fought in China for several years. Their record of winning land-based battles was 100 percent. Monk always made sure I understood the relevance of his training talks. "If the Japanese had won the Battle of the Coral Sea, then the Battle of the Kokoda Track would never have happened. And we wouldn't be heading out on our walk."

It wasn't just our walk that wouldn't have happened. Had Japan won the Battle of the Coral Sea, and then been able to take Port Moresby by sea, the US would not have invaded Guadalcanal in the Solomon Islands, or they would have done so on a different timeline and almost certainly faced a much larger Japanese defense. Until we got talking about Guadalcanal, I didn't realize the US invasion occurred coincident with the Papuan Campaign,[7] with major ramifications for both conflicts. Although they were 800 miles apart, Monk reflected a popular sentiment

---

7   Guadalcanal fighting was from August 7, 1942, to February 9, 1943. The Kokoda Track and Northern Beaches battles were July 22, 1942, to January 22, 1943. A tipping point for each conflict was in the second week of September '42.

that the two campaigns took place almost within sight and sound of each other. There was a shared cause and effect between the Australians winning along the Kokoda Track and the Americans winning in the Solomon Islands. The combined Australian and American successes set on course the geopolitics of the contemporary Asia Pacific region.

In Cairns, the dark comes clean near 6 p.m. year-round, similar to nightfall in Papua New Guinea. Janice arrived home early from work the day Monk and I had gone for our beach workout. She suggested we take a just-before-dusk walk along the same beach.

Janice asked about our morning training, verbalizing the question that always hung at the back of my mind: "Do you feel you'll be ready?" My answer to myself was always less confident than the one I gave to her. "Oh, of course. We're in great shape, and Monk's attitude will get us both through the difficulties."

It was her other question that evening that took me by surprise. Pointing to a metal contraption in the creek near the beach where we were walking, she asked, "That wasn't there yesterday, was it?"

"No, it wasn't," I said. The massive crocodile trap set in place by wildlife experts alarmed me. There must have been a reported sighting. "And it wasn't there when Monk and I were here this morning."

That evening, in the safety of home and with a glass of wine underway, I read more about the Nankai Shitai landing on the Northern Beaches of Papua. Their planners envisioned crossing the Kokoda Track unnoticed and uncontested. They would attack Port Moresby and swiftly take control. But they met resistance from a smattering of Australian soldiers posted in support of native policemen near Buna, Sanananda,[8] and

---

8 Papuan village names are pronounced phonetically as spelled, though their spoken language has an engaging, relaxed lilt, different from Aussie or American talk.

Gona. Soon, Japanese forces overwhelmed those villages, but word had made its way back to Moresby and Australia that a Japanese invasion was underway.

Swiftly, Japanese soldiers moved inland and snared Kokoda Station (the village of Kokoda)[9] with its airfield at the northern terminus of the Kokoda Track. Strategically, it would be the most advantageous property during the coming conflict, for whoever controlled it. The Japanese pushed the small contingent of Australian and Papuan soldiers back toward Isurava Village in the Owen Stanley Range. Meanwhile, Japanese engineers built up the Buna-Gona port and airfield, establishing a bustling supply base.

To counter these sudden moves by the Japanese, Australian militia were dispatched. A militia brigade—that's three infantry battalions of approximately 600 soldiers each—was already in Moresby and available. They trudged north toward Isurava to reinforce the Australian and Papuan soldiers fending off the Japanese assault. Elements of the Australian Imperial Force (AIF), veterans who had fought German General Rommel in the North African desert, were rushed from Australia to Port Moresby and hustled up the track after the militia.

In August 1942, the stage was set for the Battle of the Kokoda Track. Some 75 years after that fateful month, Monk and I readied to walk, literally and figuratively, in the footsteps of those Australians, Japanese, Papuans, and Americans who were all part of the Papuan Campaign.

In many ways it mattered not on which side of the war you fought. Confrontations were vicious and hideous. Grounds were littered with remains of the dead. Any minor body scratch could turn septic. The

---

9 The Village of Kokoda and Kokoda Station (where a government office was located) are separate places nearby one another. Given overlapping references to Kokoda as a trail, track, road, plateau, village, airfield, and battle name, Kokoda Station is used herein to identify the northern terminus of the trek today, as well as the location of the wartime airfield and site of frequent fighting in 1942.

Kokoda Track itself became a revolting sight, the conditions intolerable, even if those who were there *had* to tolerate them.

The best way I found to explain the wartime situation to friends was emailing a description I'd come across. It is from Colonel Frank Kingsley Norris, a medical officer who kept a diary of his time along the Kokoda Track in 1942. His autobiography is aptly called *No Memory for Pain*.

Here's what Norris wrote:

Imagine an area approximately one hundred miles long; crumple and fold this into a series of ridges, rising higher and higher until seven thousand feet is reached, then declining again to three thousand feet; cover this thickly with jungle, short trees and tall trees tangled with great entwining savage vines; through the oppression of this density cut a little native track two or three feet wide, up the ridges, over the spurs, around gorges, and down across swiftly flowing mountain streams. Where the track clambers up the mountainsides, cut steps, big steps, little steps, steep steps, or clear the soil from the tree roots. Every few miles bring the track through a small patch of sunlit kunai grass or an old deserted native garden, and every seven or ten miles build a group of dilapidated grass huts as staging shelter, generally set in a foul, offensive clearing. Every now and then leave beside the track dumps of discarded, putrefying food, occasional dead bodies, and human foulings. In the morning flicker the sunlight through the tall trees, after midday and throughout the night, pour water over the forest, so that the steps become broken and a continual yellow stream flows downwards, and the few flat areas become pools of putrid mud. In the high ridges [. . .] drips water day and night softly over the track and through a foetid forest, grotesque with moss and glowing phosphorescent fungi and flickering fireflies. Such is the [Kokoda] track . . .

Papua had a tradition of tribal battles all their own, long before foreigners brought war to them in 1942. Often the originating reason for their fighting was no longer remembered, yet they fought anyway.

Author Mitchell Zuckoff explained New Guinea village rivalries this way: "They had always been enemies, and so they remained enemies." He went on to say, "When compared with the causes of World War II, the motives underlying native wars were difficult for outsiders to grasp. They didn't fight for land, wealth, or power. Neither side sought to repel or conquer a foreign people, to protect a way of life, or to change their enemies' beliefs. Neither side considered war a necessary evil, a failure of diplomacy, or an interruption of a desired peace. Peace wasn't waiting on the far side of war. There *was* no far side. War moved through different phases . . . It ebbed and flowed. But it never ended. A lifetime of war was an inheritance every child could count on . . . The inexhaustible fuel for war was the need to satisfy spirits or ghosts . . ."

Packing for a jungle trek is an art. There are stupid ways to do it that look good: for instance, if you bought a stylish rucksack for show. And there are smart ways to do it that prove efficient: use of waterproof containers around vulnerable goods, avoiding duplicate equipment except backup batteries, proper selection of footwear, and so forth.

Uppermost in our minds was the trekking companies' comments about proper weight of packs. No hiker knowingly overweighs his or her pack, because of the back strain and other dangers, but it still happens if you aren't careful. Likewise, for those engaging a Papuan porter, your porter's pack should never be overweight.

The afternoon before we embarked, Monk and I got together in my garage to discard stuff: too many extra shorts and extra jerseys. We even set aside two zip-lock bags from the dozen each that Janice had packed with weighed portions of nuts and goodies. We kept a selection of bowel medicine, bite salves, lip balm, and scrape ointments, though we limited sunscreen to one tube between us as we expected more closed jungle than open sunlight in the days ahead.

We'd be with experienced guides, so this wouldn't be an orienteering mission. Still, I put a compass in my daypack alongside a candle, waterproof matches, and assorted paraphernalia I always took hiking; survival preparation is a personal responsibility.

"Got your gaiters?" Monk asked.

"Right there," I said, taking them from a bench top where I could have accidentally left them behind. Known as spats to fashionable Brits, ours were breathable polystyrene wraps to cover our bootlaces, ankles, and over six inches of lower pant leg. They'd keep out mud and twigs and rocks, and importantly guard against leeches.

Oddly, that day was the first time we'd queried one another about vaccines, each presuming that the other had been diligent. Even though it was one of the Southern Hemisphere's cooler months (mid-80s °F), August in PNG could be withering in its humidity (muggy conditions over 60 percent of the time), and ripe with bugs bent on bothering us.

"Hepatitis B?" I asked.

"Yup, got that shot for Indonesia."

"Encephalitis?"

"Yup, had to for Laos."

"Typhoid?"

"Had recently for Vietnam."

"Malaria dose?"

"Wouldn't leave home without it."

That evening we got together with Wens and Janice for a farewell dinner. Similar questions came up during drinks, voiced by nervous spouses double-checking.

Not long after the steaks were off the barbecue and off our plates, Monk and I drifted into a selfish pre-trip zone of our own. Monk told me the Kokoda Track had been home to "the worst fighting conditions any-where in World War II." He winced at the killings. "Their ghosts must still haunt the jungle," he said.

We were standing around his dining room table. Monk and I cleared plates and glasses and rolled open our now-familiar topographical map, pinning the corners down on the tabletop with empty Carlton Draft bot-tles. I'd sensed Monk's unease since he'd spoken about the ghosts, but I didn't understand it. He glanced from my eyes to where he'd marked our trail in red ink on the map. He took a long pull on his beer and said, "My father served on Kokoda."

I stared at him. The only previous time he'd ever spoken about his father was once referring to the man as "a bag of misery."

Monk looked as though he didn't know what to say next. Confessions lumbered out of his mouth. "Dad joined the army at twenty-one. Never talked about it. Scared to, I bet. That's why people don't talk about bad things, right?"

I felt hushed by his question.

"When I was ten years old, he made me promise to go to Papua one day."

Hearing for the first time this motivation for Monk's trip, I stuttered, "What did your dad do in the war?"

"I don't want to talk about that bastard," he said. And with that, the conversational door slammed shut.

Monk shifted his stance, seeking a diversion by concentrating on the map. His fingers, his mind, and his talk moved east of Kokoda's path. He traced the contour of another track through the Owen Stanley Range. "See that trail? It's called Kapa Kapa." It was the first time I'd heard the name. "American troops went north over it to shield the Aussies' eastern flank. MacArthur sent them that way to get to the Northern Beaches and fight at Buna and Gona."

Monk's bantering lore steered us away from thoughts of his dad and onto musings about this paradise in wartime. He put a finger on the map at the northern end of Kapa Kapa, and circled it where the route ended. He reminded me, "We're making for the Northern Beaches after we get through the mountains. Just like the Aussies did to meet up with the Americans for battles there with the Japanese."

"What's the Kokoda?" I'd asked Monk during our first meeting, three years earlier. Now, I realized the answers were to become overwhelmingly clear during the following weeks, as Monk and I took our walk across Papua New Guinea.

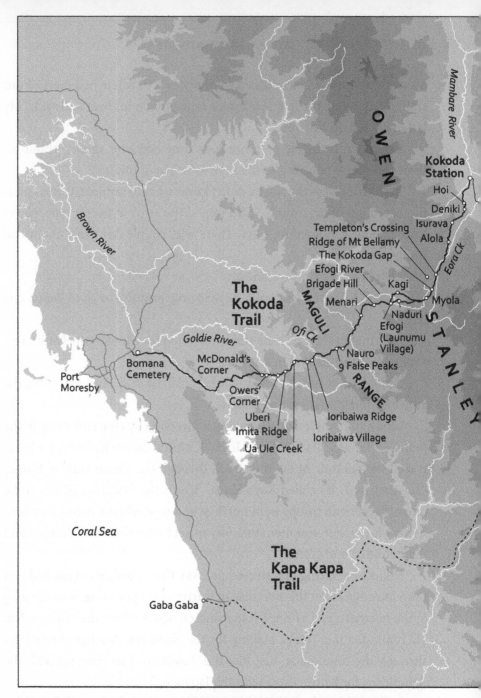

Map of the author's journey (additional landmarks provided on the map on pages 68 and 69). Buna-Sanananda-Gona, where the Japanese landed on the Northern Beaches, as well as their target, Port Moresby on the southern shore, plus the Kokoda Trail (essentially McDonald's Corner to Kokoda Station), and Milne Bay at the eastern tip where the US Corp of Engineers was building an airstrip, were all within the Territory of Papua in 1942. War scholars refer to the conflict as the Papuan Campaign.

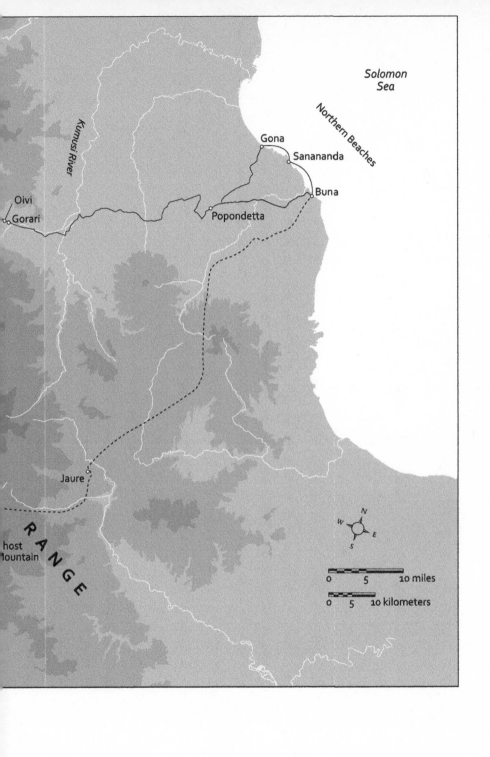

TWO

Coffee at the End
of the World

"There's more to life than being a passenger."
—Amelia Earhart

The lobby of the Palm Hotel in Cairns offered the last air conditioning we would feel for two weeks in the tropics. The hotel's aura was dank when Monk and I arrived for the pre-Papua New Guinea briefing. Our departure and that of fellow trekkers was coordinated for early the next morning. The guides deemed this evening's get-together and overnight stay mandatory.

"Mate, many Augusts we've talked about this," said Monk, looking my way while clicking his credit card on the hotel's check-in counter. Now, we were heading out within hours. His grin confirmed our staying the course was about to be rewarded. We'd trained hard. We'd packed smart. We were prepared for anything.

"There's no reservation in your name," said the clerk, snapping me back to the present.

"Gotta be," barked Monk. "Room for two. Made it through the trekking company." He tacked on, "We're expected."

"As I said—"

Before the attendant could complete his claim, a tall man broke into the conversation. "I'll take care of it," he said to the clerk, then turned to Monk and me with an extended hand. "Brett. I'm your Second Guide for Kokoda. Fixing this will be the least of your problems over the coming days."

He scrawled an authorization note and, in response, the attendant slid keys to Monk and me. Brett left us while tossing a directive over his shoulder: "Ten minutes to briefing. Outside. Hotel's empty except for us. You'll find it."

Monk and I hauled our packs to a room with four beds. "I'll do a last checkup," I said, lifting my bag onto an unused berth.

"You can't repack too often, mate," Monk said.

We'd spent weeks getting the right stuff—but as a trip nears you can always jettison something, and light packs were in order.

Monk pulled a bag of gummies from my open pack. "I'll take these to the meeting so you don't have to carry the weight."

Monk had found the trekking company through a friend's recommendation. Anyone headed for the Kokoda Trail needs to be accompanied by professional leaders and is expected to retain local packers. There are important reasons to engage guides. First off, it would be easy to get lost venturing among the many offshoot trails. Additionally, much of the land is tribally owned. Most places you're in someone's back yard, and the chief expects a payment. Companies make such arrangements in advance. Since ownership of the land is not always clear, nor titled, the guides smooth over disputes.

The company chosen by Monk proved stringent on what to pack, and they provided a three-month program to ensure your legs, lungs, and mindset were in shape. "If you can't make it, they don't want you along," Monk told me. Requirements included a doctor's note signed within 30 days of departure. Monk's knee was a hardship, weakened from a youth playing tackle sports. He was set for repair surgery the month after we returned from PNG. Regrettable timing, but there you have it.

"You're here, so I take it your doctor signed off on the knee," I said.

"Not exactly," replied Monk. "My own doctor declined. Said to wait until the surgery is done and healed. So I went to a different doctor." He laughed. "Told him my story, most of it. He could tell my heart's healthy, and that's what really counts. Right? Got sign off this morning."

Our final weeks of training had included hiking three or more days a week. Guidelines stipulated once a week with a pack on for five hours. We'd tackled Earl Hill twice in the last few days, maintaining our program: repeat circuit three times and then go for beers. Our least favorite training was on the rocky outcrops of Pyramid Mountain, because of its steepness and abrupt changes. With regularity, we worked the Blue Arrow trail that snakes for miles along a mountainside overlooking the Cairns airport.

"Insurance all good then?" I asked Monk, knowing the doctor's letter was mandatory in order to secure coverage. No one would be at tonight's briefing unless they provided "proof of insurance" for emergency helicopter retrieval from the middle of the jungle.

"Check," he said. "I read we'll hike by memorials for hikers whose hearts gave out. I don't want my own plaque."

Talking to previous trekkers had washed away our innocence with a thud of knowledge. Monk and I knew the Kokoda Trail could be described as most anything except a walk. It was up, up, up. Down. Up, down, up. The trail gasped over a mountain range, as would we. We'd be wobbling through rock-bottomed rivers. Slipping in mud, sliding on moss. Climbing backwards down waterfalls, some without water (if we were lucky).

I found the Kokoda Trail listed among "the 10 toughest and most dangerous treks in the world." As Monk noted, a number of people have died from natural causes while trekking the trail—four in a single year, two in the same week. When I asked Monk what had happened, he said, "They ran out of breath." Simple as that. (Love your heart; make sure *your* cardiac muscle tissue is fit for the trek, or don't step on the trail.) The country's image as a place where death and discovery entwine is off-putting to some. The image of the Papua New Guinea jungle deters people. If you're not Papuan, you pretty much have to be a hard-assed Aussie to endure it, something I was admittedly not.

The Kokoda Trail has belatedly become a symbol for Australian guts and nationhood. "Over 90 percent of those who hike Kokoda are Australians," Brett would tell us. "Proximity's one factor. Relating to the saga is another." It was a comment that caught my attention when I learned that the number of Japanese trekking the Kokoda Trail had increased in recent years as well. The trek is gruesome for winners and losers, and each side had enough occasions of both in '42. Relating to the saga for the Australians and Japanese is acknowledging "this is the ground" where their two societies (plus the Papuans, and eventually the Americans on the Northern Beaches) sacrificed. Trekking there makes it more real for post-veteran generations without tangential relationships to the war, let alone to Papua New Guinea.

Brett would add, "And it's hazardous." That explained the allure for trekkers of any nationality who seek out perilous paths the planet has on offer. They make their way to PNG in search of daunting days and nights on a trek you may not be able to complete, or could die trying.

Monk and I walked into a group of hikers; ten men and three women seated on cheap lawn furniture around four plastic tables. It was the best the hotel could provide—that and undrinkable coffee. I craved the real thing, and dreamed of PNG-grown coffee percolating around a campfire the following night.

Six middle-aged men sat together in the jocular fashion of mates on a mission, each muttering directions to the others. Three more men and a woman were at one table; I thought maybe contemplation of retirement age drew the four together. A man and woman sat off to the side. One young woman sat alone. Soon, a sixty-ish man called Jim and his two sons, Simon and Kieran, showed up and took position to the side of the assembly, watching on as a family unit. All wore ball caps. Thin faces and sturdy legs seemed to be in their genes. They looked relaxed, confident, and easy to get along with.

Brett arrived alongside another man, bald and fifty. "This is Mark Yeoman," Brett said. "Guide One." Yeoman was our leader. He was British, living in Australia, and, we would soon discover, he had a disciplined bent.

Yeoy, "Yo-eeee" as Aussie slang would have it, took over. He headed to PNG often, a chosen respite from running a financial management business. Over the years he'd earned his way to the front of the pack. His manner was to the point; a permanent style punctuated by bare, push-up arms outside a singlet that showed wear and pumped the name of the trek company. He put on a ball cap he'd been holding, arranging it so the brim faced backward. His tongue pressed inside his lower lip before he spoke. "We'll go around, names only. And where you're from. Let's get this done."

First off was Whitey from the six-pack of 50-ish mates. He exuded a comfort from having trekked the Kokoda Trail a few years before, but said that the experience had been rain-drenched. He "hoped for better circumstances this time." So did all of us, heading to a place where it can rain 200 inches in one year, sometimes eight inches in a day. Whitey told us that "rain there comes down in straight lines."

"I'm Mark," said the tall fellow beside him. Even when he sat, he had a calmness one suspected came from business success matched with an unwillingness to boast, complemented by sly one-liners. "We six are friends lured by Whitey's warning how difficult it'll be. Are we here on a dare? You bet."

Martin took up Mark's laugh as if it was a baton pass. He acknowledged a communications background, and cupped his left hand over his ear as though receiving a message. He mimicked a 1920s radio announcer: "Treacherous trail ahead." His voice went lower: "Only for the brave." And an octave lower: "Danger in every step."

Their camaraderie was clear. It'd be grand to have them along, as long as the joshing didn't wear thin. Anthony, next in seating, offered a self-assuredness that one likes to hear in a fellow adventurer, perhaps honed during his years as an automotive industry executive. He followed on with a simple assessment. "If Whitey made it in the rain, we can make it in good conditions." It was our reminder that the weather forecast was for dry, humid air pulsating under emerald canopies.

"You'll be able to count the raindrops that fall on you, as they'll be fat ones," said Brett.

Darren didn't look the hiker part. The heftiest of any on the trek, he carried the weight of a man enjoying his current decade at least as much as his buddies. A rock band guitarist, he had a well-considered air about him. There was nothing accidental in his thinking. He explained they were all from Melbourne. "We've been together since school days. I wouldn't stay behind," he said, offering one more rationale to escape the business world.

"None of you is here by accident," said Yeoy, assuaging anyone's concern about the others. "You've each checked out." He let it sink in as a reason to trust one another. His tongue pressed his inner lip. "You're going to need one another. The next week is going to be unhappy and tough. You'll love it."

Those among us who didn't give a nervous laugh at least gave a nervous smile.

"We believe each of you will make it," said Yeoy. "You're going to be dumbfounded by the tangled jungle," he warned. "If it rains, the ground turns to shit. It'll suck your boots off. If it doesn't rain, you'll sweat gallons. Either way, your jersey will be soaked all day, every day. And it won't dry at night."

"Stay liquid," accented Brett, patting dual water bottles strapped to his hips.

There was no smile from either Brett or Yeoy.

"People have died trekking Kokoda," Brett cautioned. "Pace yourselves."

Yeoy doubled down on the warning. "Tell me of anything that's off with you, hear that? Anything! If you're feeling faint, if your breathing is off, I need to know." Then he gave his first smile. "Your heart will pound like a piston."

I looked at Monk. "Maybe we should have made a few extra climbs up Pyramid Mountain," I muttered.

"Are there panthers along the trail?" This came from one of the six mates.

"None. Not now. Not ever. Not in PNG," said Yeoy.

I'd expected the Melbourne Six would blend in my mind as I struggled to keep their names clear in the days ahead. Now, I had a nickname for one of them: Panther.

"But I read about the Black Cat Track . . ." offered Kristy, a public practice accountant. She looked to be the fittest among us, even more than the similarly-aged hikers leaning against the wall with their father. Her smile meant she was serious about everything she said; independent.

"That's a dangerous trail," said Yeoy. "It's a hundred miles from the Kokoda."

Months ago, with beers and Monk nearby, I'd seen it on the topographical map he and I were reviewing. I liked the implication of a wild, stalking animal, but alas, Black Cat Track takes its name from an Australian mining company that was part of the vicinity's gold rush in the 1920s. That 42-mile hike is connected with another Australian campaign during the war, the Wau-Salamaua. At the time I'd asked Monk, "What about adding on a week, taking six days to hike the Black Cat Track if we can get porters and permission?"

But tragedy struck and made the decision for us. A few days after I'd broached the subject, an eight-member expedition was ambushed at their night's camp along the Black Cat Track. The group of seven Australians and one New Zealander, all men, were led by a highly competent Australian/PNG woman and escorted by 19 porters. Three aggressive natives wielded machetes, and while the foreigners avoided physical harm, two porters were hacked to death at the camp; a third died later from his wounds. Other porters were cut across their torsos, and slashes targeted their legs with crippling wounds to their Achilles tendons.

The assault was treated as robbery (the bandits made off with $5,000 in village fees and the porter payroll carried by the guide). Speculation focused on the century-old "reciprocal violence"; ongoing revenge within tribal feuds, land ownership conflicts, and unresolved wars a century old that often trigger payback. Such retribution needs little provocation other than opportunity for roving *raskols*. Investigators determined that the lonely campsite, set up away from the protection of villages, had created this occasion for inter-tribe revenge.

Government euphemisms appeared on a website: "The track is not managed for tourism at this stage." A specter of danger is the traveler's companion in Papua New Guinea.

Our conversation at the hotel moved on. Interspersed with the pre-trek briefing were tidbits about the country only two of the trekkers had ever been to. I lapped up the trivia.

"The movie *Mister Pip*, based on a book by someone named Jones, is set in PNG. Bougainville Island," said Michael, lanky and learned, the last of the Melbourne six to have been introduced, a commercial advisor for businesses in transition.

"PNG's the most diverse nation in the world," offered Deirdre, one of three women trekkers, and with a health industry professional's matter-of-fact manner, graced with a smile. Her full head of red hair looked like it didn't need a hat to keep the sun off her scalp as she had the hair tied back. She looked determined, patient, and readily likeable.

Darren said, "I have friends who swear PNG has the most spectacular scuba diving anywhere." It made me realize how little of contemporary PNG's appeal I'd be exposed to, given our narrow pathway.

"The imaginary island in Golding's *Lord of the Flies* is said to be New Guinea," said Tori, more to her husband Rod, but we all heard. No one nodded; none of us had known this. She had a ready smile, and wore a sun visor that popped her blond hair out in a bulge above her head. Everyone liked hearing Tori was a nurse, as Rod told us. He ran his hand through thin hair, grinned more than smiled, and left it at that.

Incongruously, someone said, "For many Stone Age tribes there, the first wheel they saw was on an airplane."

More on the practical side was the contribution by Robert, looking out from under a grey soft-rimmed hat that never left his head in all the times I saw him. "Half the hundred snake types in PNG are venomous." To top that cheerful note, he scratched at a short beard that matched the color of his hat. "There's this one called the Papuan Black—"

"Jungles are heaven to insects, scary spiders, and such," added Brett. "But we don't get many reports of snake sightings along the trail. A reminder though, don't head into the bushes beside the trail, keep to the clearings. Eyes open."

The three family members took to chairs, swinging them around in unison and all sitting astride, arms over the chair backs. The father, Jim, introduced himself by saying they were Aussie plumbers, all; Jim, Simon, and Kieran.

My own scrap to contribute emerged from a black-and-white television documentary on land diving, seen when I was a youngster— the same age as the boy featured in the ritual. Footage showed villagers building a high structure out of tree limbs. This was followed by measuring a jungle vine, the exactness explained by a commentator as "making the difference between life and death." The boy climbed the formation. Elders tied his ankles with the vine, knotting one end secure at his feet and the other to the tower. Only one outcome for the pubescent diver would bring acceptance into adulthood, the other a broken neck. The boy plunged headfirst toward the ground. The rope yarded tight and up, his head inches away from crashing the ground. Surely this was from Papua New Guinea. I blurted my claim to our assembly.

Martin's radio announcer voice-over began, "Bungee jumping originated centuries ago on Pentecost Island in Vanuatu." Then, in companionable terms, he said, "Rick, you're only off by a few hundred miles." I decided then to listen more and talk less while others augmented our collective understanding.

Whitey, evidently the most sincere of the Melbourne six, said, "Betel nut is everywhere. Mostly you'll see where it's been spat. It's on floors at the airport near pails meant to catch it. Or it'll be right beside a tree root you grab climbing a hill on the trail. Your porters will smile red with their lips and tongues. They chew it all the time."

Mark, tall even as he sat, had the eyes of a practical man and thought we should all know that, "Copra's their export—coconuts, or at least the oil."

A gentleman spoke next. His name was Michael, making him Michael S in my notes. Wire-rim glasses had the effect of suggesting that he was the oldest among us, and indeed, the ocean kayaker displayed the confidence of a vigorous man in his eighth decade, confirmed by his Tilly hat. "Kina's their currency—some coins have holes in them, with the intention they could wear their wealth around their necks." He told us, "Think three kina as one Aussie dollar, or that two and a half kina is one US dollar."

Robert became more forthcoming. He was Australian, originally from South Africa. His words were those of an engineer. "The language spoken all over is Tok Pisin, a pidgin English," he said. "You'll hear it often and get used to it. Maybe you'll even start to speak it," he laughed. "I toiled in PNG for a couple of years, mining."

Anthony, with a businessman's demeanor, said, "I've read that PNG's the most anthropologized country on earth."

"I knew none of this stuff," said Simon, the honesty spouting what most of us were feeling. He was one of the plumbers, exhibiting the attributes of a trickster, quick at kibitzing.

Kieran, the youngest on the trek in his late twenties, completed the trio of plumbers. He pulsed energy. We all had reason right there to envy his trail stride even before we saw it. He had the candor of youth. "Where'd all this history come from?"

"Ever hear of the hooded pitohui?" asked Michael S. "It's the only poisonous bird in the world. And it's found only in the country we're about to visit." I valued the open banter, the lack of one-upmanship, and the varied spits of information.

"They've butterflies with twelve-inch wing spans," said Deirdre, displaying a jaunty disposition.

"I hope to see the bird-of-paradise," said Phil, sounding skeptical about his chances. He was sitting with Deirdre, and had a year or more on her. This medical administrator confessed, "I am a last-minute addition to the trek, pulling up a little short on my training." He'd joined at the urging of his colleague Deirdre. Readiness seemed his priority, despite feigned Aussie indifference.

"I want to see the PNG flag," said Kieran.

"It's a beautiful flag," said Brett. "The Southern Cross is on it with white stars on black. There's a golden bird-of-paradise on a diagonal." Brett had the clipped delivery of a schoolteacher. He told us the flag's design "came from the mind of a 15-year-old-girl" and has flown for 45 years.

I looked around. Each trekker appeared to be prepared. The size of the gathering was my only concern. Monk and I had requested a trek with fewer than eight participants, and this had been confirmed. Then we heard another group had shrunk and its remaining members amalgamated with ours. We overcame that disappointment. But at the last minute, Panther and friends had appeared. We were now too many at seventeen trekkers and two guides. Trekkers by nature want individual experiences; they eschew anything that smacks of touring. But as our group size was not changeable at this point, I put aside my hesitation.

"Two pairs of footwear, everyone?" Brett jumped our attention to a concern. He wasn't going to wait for the trail to discover such a deficiency. "Keep one pair dry. Look after your feet. You'll have other reasons to regret coming along."

Our time together gave us a cadence. We were not yet a group of friends, but, except for our leaders, we saw one another as peers.

Brett grasped at history with gusto. A former officer with the Victoria Police, he dined with Melbourne veterans and listened to their stories. "Before they started to die off, I involved veterans in the Kokoda

Challenge Youth Program I ran for at-risk youth," he told us. "They were members of the Thirty-Ninth Battalion."

Monk whispered to me, "The Thirty-Ninth! That was my old man's battalion."

We'd worked our way through self-introductions when Brett leaned into the mismatched tables for a history primer. Already we realized he time-released details. His left knee kept a beat, as though a movie soundtrack was running in his mind as he spoke. "Australia's food basket and resources could have fueled the Japanese war machine long-term." He added: "Once they had the necessary resources, the bastards intended to go back to Pearl Harbor. Battles in the South Pacific were a planned prelude to Japan's full invasion of the Hawaiian Islands."

"The Americans needed the Aussies," said Rod.

"And the Aussies needed the Americans," Jim added.

Darren added, "May '42, Japanese submarines got into Sydney Harbor."

"Sunk an Aussie ship, the *Kuttabul*, but missed what they were after, the USS *Chicago*."

Brett continued filling in the neglected potholes of history. "Under orders from President Roosevelt, MacArthur escaped the Philippines." This "relocation of headquarters" to Australia included MacArthur's family, its pet monkey, and the president of the Philippines, Manuel Quezon. MacArthur was greeted with an overarching Aussie belief that the war was theirs to be won. He was arrogant at inopportune times, and his style soon grated on the Australian commanders. Later, his impatience with Australian advances along the Kokoda Track would lead him to make insulting comments about those soldiers. We can picture MacArthur's judgment being influenced by his defeat in the Philippines, concerned that a second defeat could result in his command being preempted. The senior Aussie, 58-year-old Commander Thomas Blamey, said, "The best and worst you've heard about MacArthur are true." For his part, MacArthur called Blamey "a non-professional Australian

34

drunk." Monk laughed at that last line. "The Aussie public, particularly the women, liked the American soldiers, or so I've heard," he said. "It was the Aussie men who called the Americans 'overpaid, oversexed, and over here.'"

Phil spoke: "Aussie soldiers believed loved ones—daughters, mothers, wives—were in imminent danger from the Japanese. It's why the Aussie diggers were ruthless fighters."

"The first men arriving on the Kokoda Track were militia," Brett said. "Poor uniforms, poor preparation, poorly armed. They'd not been trained for battle, but they had great courage."

"Koalas," joked Yeoy.

"Koalas?" I asked.

"Australian of origin; not to be exported or shot at," he said. "They weren't seen as up to the tests of a real fight."

Proper Aussie troops[10] were in Europe, the Middle East, and Africa, or lodged in Singapore. Initially, the militia was all the country had for the Kokoda defense.

Everyone had by now formed a circle, a presaging of nightly campfires to come. Phil was at the coffee pot, pouring and stirring. He turned and retook our attention. "Eventually MacArthur made good on his 'I shall return'[11] pledge to the Philippines in October of '44, 31 months after leaving."

---

10 Churchill maneuvered to keep a "Europe First" warfront. He wanted the Japanese restrained until Germany was defeated. In 1942, a reluctant Churchill dispatched three troopships to return battle-experienced Aussies from the Middle East, wanting them redirected to defend Dutch East Indies or Burma—his priorities above Australia. When Singapore fell under siege while they were en route, Churchill argued to turn the ships to the Asian tip. Australian Prime Minister John Curtin said no. Had Churchill got his way, a plausible scenario is that those Aussie troops would have been incarcerated in Singapore. Without those troops as reinforcements, the Aussie militia would have been annihilated on the Kokoda Track. And the Japanese would have secured Moresby. It would have been a different war.

11 In draft this famous line read, "We shall return." Given his ego, MacArthur changed it to "I shall return."

Kieran nodded in agreement, though he said, "So much of this history is news to me." But Brett was where he wanted our story to be, a cliffhanger set in the land where we would trek.

Yeoy chimed in: "But they underestimated the Maroubra Force, code name for our boys."

Kieran said, "They sound like opposing rugby squads."

Martin's announcer imitation took it from there. "Home Team Maroubra Force versus the visiting Nankai Shitai . . ."

Yeoy said, "It all happened in the last wild place on earth. You'll see for yourselves tomorrow. Good night."

A few of us remained behind. "Australians were convinced that they were pitted against overwhelming odds. That myth endured throughout the campaign," said Brett, referencing a note.[12] He told us that when the war was over, Japanese documents showed they, too, had fought under the assumption that better-armed Australians[13] outnumbered them. Brett also quoted MacArthur: "New Guinea itself is as tough and tenacious an enemy as the Japanese."

Yeoy reappeared and stood behind Brett. He finally interrupted with, "Tomorrow you're going to see what Americans and Europeans call 'the end of the world.'"

"Can't wait," I heard Monk say.

Yeoy got down to business. "Most of us are on the Qantas flight to

---

12 At his encouragement, I traced Brett's source for his observations to Peter Williams's book *The Kokoda Campaign 1942: Myth and Reality*, finding further facts. Australian forces were initially outnumbered by the Japanese, which contributed to their withdrawal and rearguard fighting. However, when the Japanese eventually retreated to Buna-Gona, the pursuing Australian forces had swelled, with two Aussies to every Japanese on the Kokoda Track.

13 Australians benefitted from the Papuan Infantry Battalion guerillas using Lee-Enfield rifles left over from World War I. Japanese endeavors included both willing and coerced Papuan and New Guinean labor, as well as conscripted Chinese, Taiwanese, and Koreans.

Moresby departing at ten in the morning." He looked over a page of names. "Glen—or is it Monk?"

Glen said, "Monk."

"Okay," Yeoy continued. "Monk and Rick, you're on Air Niugini an hour after our departure. So is Brett. Be in the lobby before sunrise."

I'd listened to the interplay of "track" and "trail" during the briefing session. In a dialect spoken by the Orokaiva people, the name Kokoda represents *koko* (skull) and *da* (place or village), reasonably translated as the "place of skulls." As with so many things regarding the Kokoda, the Japanese interpretation of the name was different: *koko* is Japanese for *here* and *da* means *it is*. One can imagine that Japanese troops anticipated something more elaborate than the muddy fields, muggy jungle, and smelly villages they found at the place marked "here it is" on their maps. Wartime references and monuments often stipulate the "Kokoda Trail." Australian soldiers ("diggers") called it the "Kokoda Track," a reflection of survey maps issued by the army. News outlets used both in 1942. Local dialect suggests the Kokoda was a "road," though not intended for vehicles. The Kokoda "way" suggested the entire route from the southern shore to the northern beaches. As to "trail" versus "track," the PNG government makes common usage of both. I've tended to use "trail" when referencing our trek and "track" when referencing wartime. However designated—trail, track, road, or way—the path has existed for hundreds of years as a means of arriving or fleeing.

Monk and I took dinner with the other walkers. Everyone talked like mates while harvesting the last restaurant menu we would see for two weeks. Enjoying grilled fish, fresh vegetables, fried chicken, and barbeque beef, we shared anticipations for the trip. Rod allowed that, "We don't get much time without our two kids unless we go out of sight." To which Tori said, "And this'll be outta sight." Rod, computer programmer by day, father by night, nodded. A marathon runner, he actually admitted, "I like hills."

When Darren turned the conversation to his personal motivation for being along on the trek, it struck me as the most novel. "Since I was a kid, I've been fascinated by the remoteness of Papua New Guinea, all because of Errol Flynn," he said.

It has been suggested that no one did more to promote Papua New Guinea's adventure and danger-as-romance than the Australian-American Flynn. Before the term swashbuckling was appended to his image as a Hollywood actor in the latter half of the 1930s, Flynn already played that role to the New Guineans. PNG was where he'd chosen to shed the embarrassments of his teenage turmoil in Tasmania. It was in 1927, when he was 18, that Flynn first found Port Moresby. Once there, he would stay in the country on and off for six years, living as an unreliable rogue. When his years of film stardom arrived, New Guinea was defined by his personal portrayal of the country as charming and alarming.

It was not Flynn's activities in New Guinea that identified him; it was the adjectives that accompanied them. *Careless* adventurer, *reckless* opium smuggler, *sloppy* gambler, *effortless* womanizer, *incautious* street fighter, *negligent* debtor, *sporadic* pearl diver, *artless* administrator, and *impractical* patrol officer. New Guinea provided Flynn with big apprenticeships but little career traction as he recruited slaves, dynamited fish, trapped birds, castrated sheep, and managed a tobacco plantation. Reputedly, he was also a police officer, diamond smuggler, and newspaper journalist, though apparently those roles were not coincident. An enthusiastic fighter, he was fond of saying, "The Good Lord gave you a fist so you could clench it."

A year after arriving in New Guinea, and unfamiliar with the territory but having made some money managing a coconut plantation, Flynn became part owner of a schooner. With his trademark bravado in the face of inexperience, he hired on as boat captain and outfitter for an American film crew making a documentary about headhunters in an area Flynn called "a human graveyard."

As a gold seeker, Flynn hiked on the Black Cat Track, and wrote about it in *My Wicked, Wicked Ways*. His memoir recalled trying to sleep in a tent and fearing "whether that crawly sound you heard a few feet away might be a snake, a cassowary, or maybe only a wild boar." Nearly a century later, his descriptions of fighting off giant roaches and night bloodsuckers made armchair travelers stay in their armchairs. He wrote, "I have seen Central Africa, but it was never anything like the jungle of New Guinea."

In the movie business, Flynn was cast as characters as varied and unbelievable as his real-life escapades in New Guinea. Whether playing mutineer Fletcher Christian in the Australian film *In the Wake of the Bounty*, starring in the English movie *Captain Blood*, or as the lead in American-made *The Adventures of Robin Hood*, Flynn was dashing and adored—at least for most of his sixty-one films. He never outgrew his image as impetuous, immature, and irresponsible. Philandering was his most consistent trait, resulting in the phrase, "In like Flynn." After becoming an American citizen in August 1942, while war raged along the Kokoda Track, he never returned to his home country of Australia, nor his adopted Papua New Guinea. Trailed by financial difficulties, and being a drug addict and seasoned alcoholic, Flynn died in the arms of a teenage actress in Canada. His death was attributed to cirrhosis of the liver. The year was 1959, a week after his fiftieth birthday. Throughout his career, Errol Flynn took pains to ensure fans knew that the wilds of Papua New Guinea were the key source of influence for his reputation as an intrepid risk-taker and troublemaker.

As I later lay on the bed, an unattributed snippet quoted over dinner wrought the impression that peril was synonymous with Papua New Guinea. Likely a century old, it still seemed tailored to me: "Headhunters lie in ambush for the tenderfoot prowler." Was I really up for this?

Monk was slinking around his side of the hotel room. He sorted his final pack-up, brushed his teeth, and crawled into bed. He spoke as much to his canvas rucksack as to me when he muttered, "My old man's been a ghost most of my life. Maybe that's what I'm looking for."

The phone rang beside Monk's bed, jarring us awake at 5 a.m. Saturday—our first Kokoda wake-up call. The other trekkers had already left the Palm Hotel for the airport. In a few hours, we'd meet them in a country of improbable greens. At the Cairns airport, Monk scuffed our packs along the floor toward Air Niugini check-in. Brett's pack looked the lightest, showing his experience. It was also a reminder that he would be carrying his own gear. Hoisting ours onto the scales reaffirmed the wisdom of hiring porters. "Your trek can be more enjoyable if your gear is carried by a packer," previous trekkers had told us. "But give them no more than 35 to 40 pounds. That's firm."

"I get it right because it's my sixth time over the Kokoda," Brett said.

Monk and I would each carry a daypack weighing 20 pounds. That backpack included a water container with a tube that looped over our shoulders, and gravity fed the water from the reservoir as we sucked while hiking. They're called hydration packs or water-bottle backpacks.

Once through customs, Monk bought us warmed croissants oozing cheese and ham. "I'm sure meals on the trail will be as gourmet as this."

Brett was behind him, carrying coffees for each of us. "It'll be instant coffee from now on," he said. "New Guinea is famous for coffee, but not where we're headed. We'll pack in everything needed for our three meals a day. Powdered milk it is. Freeze-dried food is our staple. So is Spam."

"Spam?" asked Monk.

"Today's bully beef," Brett said, reminding us of the canned corned beef foisted upon the diggers during the war. It sounded awful.

Brett was right in front of us on the plane, with no one beside him. Once in the air, he leaned over the back of his seat to talk with us. "One Japanese name to keep in mind is Major General Tomitarō Horii. He was responsible for the Nankai Shitai, and present for most of the Papuan Campaign. It's a name you'll hear about on the trail." He said Brigadier Arnold Potts[14] countered him early with the Maroubra Force at Isurava. Both names went into a blurry corner of my mind.

"Monk's father fought on Kokoda," I told Brett, hinting at a story that was not mine to tell.

Brett looked to Monk. "Did you give him respect for what he did?"

"I wouldn't give him the steam off my piss," said Monk.

The first contingent of trekkers greeted our arrival at Jackson's International Airport in Port Moresby with a grudge. The humidity had already spread sweat across their neckline and armpits. It also lent that distinctive tropical cringe that made breathing labored, so it felt less like an impulse and more like a chore. We stepped out of the relatively organized, if scruffy, terminal and into the chaos of greeters and grafters.

In the reverse of a visitor hailing a cab, the cab drivers hailed visitors, visually intruding on our space, wanting our business. I tried not to judge body odors and the spit from red lips. We commandeered a minibus and tossed packs up top or crammed them in a rear space. The first among us to board clenched daypacks to their chests or kicked them under seats. Trekkers crowded three to a two-person bench. Kristy and Tori sat on the floor. The bus chugged away from the curb and wound past the airport's spiky wire fence that separated airport arrivals from rundown neighborhoods. PNG's reputation for inhospitable social elements is, unfortunately, true. Whether the danger is ubiquitous or not,

---

14 In addition to Brigadier Potts, Japan's Horii faced a range of capable Aussie leadership, including Basil Morris, Sam Templeton, William Owen, Selwyn Porter, Tubby Allen, Cyril Clowes, Sydney "Syd" Rowell, Edmond "Ned" Herring, Ken Eather, and George Vasey. Their cohorts in achieving Australian victory were the likes of Captain Bert Kienzle, known as "the Architect of Kokoda," and ever-present medic "Doc" Vernon. Commander Blamey and/or MacArthur replaced some of those in the Allies hierarchy unceremoniously; others died in action.

the impression of it certainly is. We rolled along a roadway for ten minutes, then into the wire-rimmed compound of the Laguna Hotel. We piled out of the coach. Hotel staff pulled hiking gear off the bus and threw it onto the verandah.

Yeoy barked: "See the doorman. Get a voucher. Tag it to your leave-behind stuff. You'll be back here in two weeks. Toss everything you have for the porters into one bag. You'll meet them in half an hour." As an afterthought: "Fill up your water here. It's reliable."

Soon after, Brett shouted, "Back on the bus."

Minutes later, our vehicle swung into a full-fledged bus depot with primetime tour busses parked in waiting. Across the pavement stood a gang of Papuans. They were not *raskols*. They waved. Not one or two of them; all of them waved. These were our porters. They sported the uncertain smiles of people leery of matchmaking.

"We're about to meet new friends," Monk said, moving toward the shade as we got off the bus. We lined out. They lined out. A husky man with wooly hair, curly sideburns, and a reddish glow to his smile stepped to the front and reached a huge hand toward Yeoy's.

"This is Woody," said Yeoy, looking our way. "He's the boss. Don't screw with him." Woody held a clipboard. He tilted it to Yeoy's view and flipped two pages. Yeoy scanned them. Once Yeoy nodded, Woody walked toward us, the gang of Papuans[15] on his heels. Now we could take the measure of the men. They were of varying sizes. All wore shorts that revealed mountain-climbing calves. No one wore a top more formal than a T-shirt, though some had sleeves. A few wore hiking boots. Many had on canvas runners. Three wore flip-flops. Two were barefoot. One was in slippers.

---

15 One role for Papuans assisting our trek was *packer*, taking the camping goods necessary to support our trek—tents, tarps, cooking gear, and foodstuffs. The other was *porter*, the soon-to-be friend hired to carry our personal kit. During the war, the term *carrier* best described the Papuans' support role for the Australians. All terms meld herein as *porter*. Their unannounced role was that of protectors if awkwardness arose.

And they could take the measure of us. Trekkers, too, varied in size. We all wore short pants that revealed a range of leg strength. Some of us were in trekking company jerseys designed to wick sweat from one's body. All of us wore sturdy hiking boots. To us, the porters looked reticent. Maybe they were a little nervous. By contrast, we were wonderstruck.

Woody called out to Jim, who moved toward the Papuans. "Meet George," he said. And so pairing began. Jim looked around at the rest of us before walking over to porter George, who sported a large empty backpack made of sturdy nylon. Each porter had a similar one. These were standard issue from the organizers. They looked well used (the packs, not the porters) and had ample space. The porters would gauge the weight of our belongings and close off the container if packing them reached too much. I watched other trekkers retesting their pack weights, realizing the porters took this seriously. Before further introductions were made, George stuffed Jim's goods into his bag, then topped it up with his own possessions, a tenth of Jim's. He flipped the flap, tied it down, and lifted it onto his back. "Good," he said, shrugging this first word to the man he'd walk beside, behind, or in front of for the next eight days.

Yeoy turned to the rest of us. "Woody will read two names. One of you, one of them. If he thinks you need a more experienced porter, that's what you'll be assigned. Some of these guys have hiked Kokoda a dozen times and a few have done it over 50 times, though two of the porters are on their first trip."

Woody's eyes were quick and judgmental as the porters met the female trekkers one by one.

"Tori, meet Jonathan," and "Deirdre, meet Gerald." These were grizzled men, twice as old as the women they would care for. Yeoy looked to Kristy; she should have been on the list. She lifted her full pack onto her back without a fuss. She came across as professional, firm of body and disposition. Her pack looked to be 40 pounds. "I can probably carry my own pack," she said. Yeoy encouraged otherwise. Kristy met her porter who went by the name of Lawrence. He looked to be one of the youngest, and well matched to Kristy in physique.

Simon and Phil would carry their own gear.

Woody shrugged and continued: "Mark, meet Mike." Each Papuan porter had been given an Anglicized name, grafted onto his patrimony so as to help us pronounce and remember their names, which diluted a uniqueness I'd hoped to find. When Woody called out "Rick, meet Charles," a soft-spoken face looked at me as I stepped forward. He was shorter than me, half my weight and a third my age. The fuzz of a beard around his chin suggested he was in his late teens or early twenties. He was wiry and tightly muscled. Charles wore a T-shirt, red shorts, and plastic flip-flops.

I asked if he had a Papuan name. "Bowrie," he answered. "For you, Charles."

"Can I call you Bowrie?"

"Is my name," he said.

"Bowrie, I think I have the right weight for you."

"Is okay," he said, even before testing.

"How long have you carried on Kokoda?"

"Is first trip."

"Well, to start, this is for you. Share with the others." I handed him two of the bags Janice had packed with almonds, raisins, and chocolate squares. A smile lit his face.

My clothes and extra footwear were in a sturdy plastic bag that exhaled air when pressed so I could cap it and keep it airtight and small. Everything else, from utensils to Band-Aids, fit in another condensable bag. My gummies, energy bars, and more nuts showed through its clear cover. The bags did not take much room, though this masked their true weight. Bowrie stowed them into his pack without any sign of concern and topped in his meager personal items. When he lifted the pack, he tilted to one side. Another porter put out a hand and caught him. It was not the weight of the pack but the distribution of the weight. Woody's pairing of Bowrie and me was intended, it seemed, to underline that the pair of us had a lot to learn from one another.

We were on a bigger bus now, and the trekkers spread out. Most sat alone. The porters were on their way with our goods in separate transport. They'd meet us at Owers' Corner along with the porters hired to carry camp provisions for the coming nights. From there, we'd all head north on the trail, bound for Goodwater, our first camp. Our troupe of trekkers, packers, and porters now numbered 60.

The bus windows were open and brought in the smell of leaves drying from last night's rain. I tried to ease the nauseous headache caused by the bumpy ride. I kept my eyes synced with the horizon, which meant looking into the bushes. The hills were not intimidating and the roadway was wide. It looked quite nice for a walk. The only other person I'd read about who referenced his adventures in Papua New Guinea as a "walk across the country" was the Australian Mick Leahy, who forever changed beliefs that New Guinea's interior was unpopulated. But his discovery of "Stone Age tribes" was far from his original intentions. In the 1920s, he set out to find gold. What he found instead shocked the world.

Following hundreds of years of colonials poking about the shoreline, deeper explorations of New Guinea ("intrusions," from the indigenous people's viewpoint) accelerated in the early 1900s with gossip of gold. Like men struck by gold fever here or elsewhere, Mick Leahy spontaneously left his home to join the rush of fortune-seekers. The year was 1926, and the Queenslander would be among the earliest Westerners to venture inland of this country. The anthropologist Jane Goodale referred to him and his ilk as "young and independent, courageous and ambitious, self-confident, and above all intelligent." Leahy's legacy has little to do with finding gold, or with the fact that he went on to homestead in his adopted country. That he kept extensive field notes during his most active years (1930 to 1935) makes us all more fortunate. They provide a respectful record of tribes happily hidden from the outside world.

Without his journals, there is much we would not know. Leahy also took over 5,000 photographs and hours of movie film, irreplaceable visual documentation. His respectful approach toward native peoples should have been an example to those who followed, though this was not always the case.

Our bus turned off the road and rounded a parking lot, coming to a stop. Being in a sulk, I wasn't paying attention. I felt dismay with the size of our crowd as we stepped from the coach. What had started in my mind as Monk and me and a few porters on the Kokoda Trail was now ten times that. I wanted to feel independent, not clustered. I pulled Monk aside. "Monk, do you think there are too many of us?" He looked around. "Mate, what we are, we are." I said, "Don't you wish we were alone on Kokoda?" He said, "Really?" The somberness in his tone implicated that I was being selfish. His gregarious nature had already made him popular with the group. He was pleased to have everyone along, and felt I should be too. He stared past me at the field beside us.

I turned to follow his gaze. What I saw shocked me. Grave markers crowded the acres of grass, crosses of white on green, sorrow upon calm. We were at Bomana War Cemetery and each of us wandered through it. There were many rows of solitary graves. My urge to be alone crept away in shame. There were thousands of sites. Name upon name. Many of the dead were only 21, some were merely 16. A soldier of 67 seemed to have been the oldest. The only woman was a nurse. I froze in front of one tribute. Carved in stone was "Known Unto God." Another marker, same words. And another and another and another.

There were stones for 267 unknowns. My notion of being "alone on the Kokoda Trail" was something I would no longer crave.

On other plaques, the fallen soldier's name was followed by a single sentence without a period—words without an ending: "His duty nobly done"; "He died that we might live"; "Greater love hath no man than this."

Monk looked as disjointed as I felt when we met at the end of a row of crosses marking men killed during battle and hurriedly buried elsewhere, later retrieved and reinterred here beneath the grass.

"I knelt at the headstone at Bruce Kingsbury's grave," he told me. "Man won the Victoria Cross. Bloody hero."[16] He said that Kingsbury's grave looked like all the others. All together, there were 3,824 heroes buried there.

Everyone's emotions were hushed when we left Bomana. War tourism felt like an odd term, but an important one. People visit the sites of tragedy to pay respect, to address a curiosity, to contemplate their personal situation in a larger context—perhaps attempting to be deserving of their own good fortune, often gained through the sacrifice of unknown others. Bomana is a project of the Australian government. Among those who call this place home, in addition to Australians, are 443 Allies, many from New Zealand and the Netherlands. Among them are sailors, airmen, soldiers, and personnel, including members of the Royal Artillery from the United Kingdom, all killed in this region and buried here with honor. There are no Americans buried at Bomana, as it's a Commonwealth War Graves Commission cemetery.[17]

The rotunda at Bomana is a memorial "to the missing," an additional

---

16 The United Kingdom, which in World War II included Commonwealth countries such as Australia and Canada in its honors and awards system, bestowed the Victoria Cross as its highest honor for bravery, gallantry, and selflessness "in the face of the enemy." The US Medal of Honor, or France's Legion of Honor, is of similar prestige.

17 In the battles for control of New Guinea—taking into account the big island and numerous smaller ones in the region, thousands of indigenous Papuans died. So did 7,000 Australians and 7,000 Americans. Over 100,000 Japanese died. If one were to focus on just the Papuan campaign (mainly the Kokoda Track and Northern Beaches), not all of the 27,000 men the Japanese sent eventually went home. Nor did many of the 56,000 Australians who came to this land. Fully 29,100 of them were evacuated with tropical maladies. They suffered 5,560 casualties (those who died or were injured in battle). The United States Army suffered 8,259 casualties; 2,947 of them evacuated sick. The US Army's Air Force registered 525 killed or missing.

703 Papuans and Australians known by name but missing in action during the Papuan campaign. Brett told us that a helicopter of Japanese visitors recently tried to visit here, as part of a fly-in Kokoda tour, but the locals would not let them land. Brett knew a twist on this. "The Japanese call such visitors *irei-dan.*" As with many short Japanese words, it has a long meaning. These visitors were "trying to console the spirits of the dead."

The odds of surviving that war without personal injury were appallingly slim. I realized if the ratio was applied to our group, it would mean only three of the Melbourne guys would have returned home unharmed. Of Monk and me, one of us would have either died or come home with a debilitating illness.

What had been puzzling to me pre-trip was made less so once we were on the ground in this strange country. The Kokoda Track's context became evident on the bus leaving Bomana. Having witnessed the end result of it all at the gravesite, the sequence of events became coherent. Finally, I had my bearings on the complex storylines.

The Papua Theater of War[18] had Three Acts, so to speak.

Act I opened in July of '42, on the Northern Beaches.

Scene One: Japanese land on the Northern Beaches (Buna, Sanananda, Gona). Australian troops in Port Moresby are sent over Kokoda Track to fortify Kokoda Station and airfield, but fail when the Japanese advance pursues them back to the village of Isurava.

Scene Two: Australia sends veteran troops (AIF) to bolster the militia holding Isurava. The veterans arrive just as the militia is about to be annihilated.

---

18 The term "Theater of War" may have originated with the Coliseum of Rome, and has come to identify a geographic area of combat (even one within a larger conflict): its air, marine, and land components.

Scene Three: Ten days in late August and early September, coincident with fighting on the Kokoda Track, marked the Battle of Milne Bay on the eastern coast, where a Japanese assault was unsuccessful (as a start: they landed in the wrong location). This was the first land defeat of the Japanese in World War II, said to have "broke the myth of the invincibility of the Japanese army."

Scene Four: Battles along the Kokoda Track ensue throughout August and early September as the Japanese advance southward, forcing the Australian withdrawal to Imita Ridge where they are commanded to make a final stand. The Japanese, in full control of the higher Ioribaiwa Ridge nearby, prepare to strike the encamped Australians. Instead, it would end up being the furthest point south on the Kokoda Track for the Japanese.

Act I closes on September 16, 1942, with that standoff between Japan's Nankai Shitai and Australia's Maroubra Force, each believing the other army is larger and better equipped.

Act II opens mid-September on Imita Ridge.

Scene One: Aussies on Imita Ridge mount a northbound offensive to retake Ioribaiwa Ridge from the Japanese—only to find the Japanese gone, having begun a strategic retreat.

Scene Two: Australians continue their advance northward over ground they'd previously fought for and lost—this time chasing a Japanese fighting retreat.

Act II closes as the Maroubra Force retakes Kokoda Station and its airfield from Nankai Shitai on November 3rd. Kokoda Track is now under Australian control.

Act III opens during November on the Northern Beaches.

Scene: American forces arriving overland by the Kapa Kapa Trail, as well as by air and sea from Milne Bay, align with the Aussies. In a complicated situation with high fatalities, the Allies decimate Japanese positions during the battles of Buna, Sanananda, and Gona, forcing the Japanese, for the most part, out of Papua.

Papuans were forced to host the adversaries in the Papuan Theatre of War. During the conflict they had 18,000 of their countrymen fighting, supplying, or carrying the wounded for other countries that battled within their own, assisting both sides. Long called Fuzzy Wuzzy for their frizzy hair, the Papuan carriers earned an accented name. The Aussies appended a noun of admiration for the indefatigable role of those helping Australians, calling them "Fuzzy Wuzzy *Angels*."

Not far after we left the cemetery, a roadside display drew our attention. It designated the formal beginning of the Kokoda Track. Troops marched miles from here at McDonald's Corner to where we would soon begin our trek, at Owers' Corner. Captain Sam Templeton and his "B" Company began here in July of 1942, miles and weeks before war cast its devastating pall over them and they responded with heroics. "Those soldiers left this checkpoint in '42 with more confidence in themselves than we carry today, mate," Monk said.

I thought, but did not ask, "Even your old man?"

With trepidation, we were about to begin walking into a mad and surreal history. Muggy. Hellish heat. There was an intimidating backdrop of mountains. In the distance was Imita Ridge. Surely I was not the only one wondering whether all of us would make it all the way. We milled about.

A party of trekkers and porters came out of the forest, having just completed their north-to-south trek. They were quick to express relief, open about the varying opinions: "It's hell, sometimes." "It's really hell most of the time." "It's hell, period."

I preferred our northward trek for its historic flow, which followed the Aussie advance to victory. The jungle's spell coaxed me forward.

Nervously, I shivered. Every walker wants to feel worthy of the path ahead.

Jim was nearby, and told us he'd learned his porter's name was not really George. "It's Kipling," he said. Simon, realizing the weight of the load he'd brought along, asked his dad if Kipling might have room for some of his stuff. Jim replied a firm no.

Woody stood apart from us, close but not talking with anyone. His craggy face looked like a map of the gullies, cliffs, and broken trails he would soon guide us through. Then his smile broke and smoothed out the map-face. His eyes caught mine and made no effort to avert my stare. He took me in and moved along, locking eyes with each trekker in turn. Seeing that nonverbal exchange, Monk said, "Serious bloke." Woody carried a spade tall enough to double as his walking staff. A red ribbon was wrapped just below the shovel's handle. "He'll dig you steps when you need them," Yeoy said. "Or he'll fill potholes if they break up the trail." "Maintenance Man," Monk called him.

"This trail is never the same two days in a row," Yeoy claimed. "It self-destructs with rain and wear. You carve what you need when you need it. Fill what you must."

"Is it that temporary?" asked Kieran.

"Whatever you do in PNG is temporary."

Pointing at Woody, Brett advised, "We have a front porter and an end porter. Nobody goes ahead of the front, and nobody goes behind the end. If you find a need to go into the bushes, leave your pack on the trail, so we can find you."

"Two minutes," shouted Woody. At this first announcement of the call-to-ready, not all the trekkers took the refrain seriously. Three kept talking about the coming days. Daypacks sat idle on the ground beside them while everyone else prepped. Porters lifted trekkers' belongings onto their own backs. The nylon rigs looked comfortable on them, sometimes outsized. The porters' nonchalance and their acceptance of work had given the beginning of our journey an infectious self-confidence. They were eager to be off with their heavy responsibilities. Woody stepped onto the trail and, with long strides, set our departure's pace. The three chattering trekkers shut up, grabbed their stuff, and hustled after us.

Monk was off like a shot, full of anxious energy. Bowrie stepped behind Monk in order to be ahead of me. Kipling did the same with Jim.

The waterproof map I carried was from Bill James's *Field Guide to the Kokoda Track* that Janice had brought back from one of her trips to Moresby. I'd skimmed the book itself before this journey; it was too heavy to cart along. Now the map was indispensable. It rated elevation profiles simply as steep, very steep, or steeper. Other cautions used were "slippery" or "leeches" or "nine false peaks." The term *level* never appeared. Heading where we headed, away from the Sogeri Plateau to Goldie River, read "slope," and the trail fell away respectfully.

Most of us had walking sticks. They'd been recommended as they could telescope out for a long descent, or be shortened for steep ascents. I saw Monk propped on his, one hip against a hillside rock, taking a picture. He adjusted his walking poles. One he pointed down and ahead, as a brace. We'd trained for this on Earl Hill, practicing the bend that shifted body weight and downhill stress off our knees and onto our quads. You have to keep it top of mind or you forget. The trail narrowed or spread as the cleft allowed. The coniferous trees were tall and their leafy branches merged far above us. The forest hampers sunlight from getting through to the base plants, stalls GPS systems, and thrives on precipitation. And we weren't yet in sight of impassable jungle.

We moved ever downward on straightaways and switchbacks. Our strung-out look was colorful, scrubbed, and orderly. Everyone could see most everyone else, ahead or behind. This looked set to last but, like many other things on the Kokoda Trail, it was an illusion.

I limbered up as I walked, testing my own situation. My boots felt right, the toes not crammed at all. The weeks of wearing in new gear proved beneficial. The backpack was snug across my back. I sucked on the waterspout from the container. The cross-chest strap buckled nicely. It was too early to tell if these things were right for the longer hike, but it was not too early to tell if they were wrong and were going to be problematic. They were okay.

Sharp-edged kunai grass (home to snakes, one could imagine) covered the ground near us. The path was clayish, smoothed by rain running along it the day before and packed down by the southbound hikers we'd just met. There was a bitterness you sensed when breathing. It was laced with a woody smell, more leaf than bark. When I gulped at the air after stepping fast, it left an aftertaste on the back of my tongue—and it felt green, as though the color before me influenced how I thought about the taste.

Talk among the porters sounded unfamiliar, and I asked, "Bowrie, what do they say?"

"It is our language. Tok Pisin."

"What do the words mean?"

"That packer pointed a bird for your friend," he said. "Word is *balus*." His shyness overcome, he asked, "You know Pidgin?"

I responded overconfidently. "The bird? Yes, of course. So your *balus* means pigeon?"

"No, Rick," he said patiently. "Pidgin. It is how we say we speak." He added the explanation I needed: "Pidgin English."

Brett brokered an understanding. "Rick, *pisin* is another word they use to say bird. They call Tok Pisin the bird language." Got it, I thought. Pidgin English morphed into Tok Pisin; Tok = Language, Pisin = Bird. Garry Marchant, a Canadian who worked in remote parts of Papua New Guinea decades ago, had told me, "Their language was easy on the Anglophone tongue, though we needed to be mindful of cultural sensitivities when the words came out of our mouths." Garry spoke of a directive from his employer, PNG's Department of Health, to drop patronizing terms. The official memo began, he recalled, by saying, "Pidgin is a dynamic language." It explained to my friend the need to change the use of "words that are tending to be regarded as offensive by better-educated

Papuans and New Guineans." In the eyes of administrators, such changes in colonial expressions were necessary to show respect, and they gave clear instructions on how to achieve that.

For example, the memo asked that "man" be used instead of the deprecating "*kanaka*." Gone was "*meri*," in favor of "*gel*" or "woman." A house worker would no longer be referred to as "*manki masta*" but as "domestic." But, as Garry explained to me, "Existing phrases were so well established that use of the new ones took work no one bothered with. Lapses on either side of the cultural equation were explained away with '*Me losim tinktink*,' which means 'I forget.'" An example of this cultural insensitivity in reverse: miniskirts were popular among Westerners when Garry lived there, which Papuans termed "missis walkabout ass nothing." Tok Pisin ranks with English (and Hiri Motu, which I did not knowingly hear) as the nation's trilingual attempt to provide more widely-shared languages to ride alongside each person's village jargon. It was of passing humor when a porter tried to teach a trekker something of use. Bowrie had begun with my instruction, saying he would tell me "slowly by slowly." "*Buai pekpek*," a graceful Kipling taught Jim, as he pointed where he spit betel saliva. "*Hamamas*," said Jim hesitantly, feeling the word "happy" was a diplomatic response. Nothing quite matched the enjoyable lilt of Pidgin for "starting one's journey," which was "*throwim way leg*."

A guitar chord sounded ahead, coming from one of the porters. I'd not noticed the instrument at the beginning of the hike. Another chord. Strumming followed, and a tune came into being. A gentle chorus rose from the porters, establishing our mood and tempo. I trekked in the jungle with a choir. What I did not yet recognize was that the music was intentionally setting the rhythm of their walking. Perhaps to bridge linguistic differences for their guests, the song was sung in Tok Pisin, occasionally making words that sounded familiar but whose meaning was lost among us. Other racket competed with the singing, or underlined it. Birds sounded from wherever they were lurking. Water dropped from above, pooled on leaves from recent rain. And the shuffling of feet filled any break of music. But they were detected only because I listened for them. If I simply walked, they became a green noise that was comforting.

I stepped off the trail and used my walking sticks to prop me up so I could see who was playing the guitar. Bowrie stood off the path, too. A few walkers and porters rounded past us. In the distance and out of my line of sight, the guitarist shifted into high gear with a new tune that was exhilarating (or perhaps it was a new part of the song I did not know). To the porters, and unknowingly to us, it signaled a change in the trail's gradient. Of course, pride goes before the fall. I slipped, bounced backwards, and nearly fell over before I righted myself, losing any semblance of rhythm I'd been cultivating.

Bowrie was there to help me get up. "Someone had to be first. May as well be you," Simon said as he waltzed by. His foot got caught on a rock soon after and he tripped forward. Our smooth formation was disassembling. Tori stepped away to take photographs. New friends walked together.

We were soon alongside Goldie River. The current looked cantankerous. The trail settled even with the water. Brett corralled us near a swath of kunai grass (also known as Japanese blood grass) above the riverbank. After resting, we moved on. Soon we swapped our boots for water shoes. When we'd waded across the Goldie River, our first experience of being compromised by a cold creek, Brett said that in the coming days, we would cross "eleven rivers—well, creeks mostly—some a couple of times."

Across, the trail did not ease, though it wasn't difficult. "Uberi was here," said Brett, referring to a village that was nowhere to be seen in the overgrowth. "Once." By "once" he meant it was here during the war. It became a supply stop, and a place for the wounded Aussies moving through to be registered. It was deserted at war's end and there was no need to rebuild. Flowing grass has replaced the bustle.

Our walk was steady and enjoyable. When next I heard the guitar, it sounded closer. I came around a bend and saw those ahead had already taken off their packs for a rest. Trekkers scrounged in their daypacks for something to energize them or quench their thirst.

The guitar player was resting against a tree. He grinned as I walked up to him. "*Gude*," he greeted. "Hello," I responded.

"My name is Winterford," he said. He was one of the seasoned. He carried camp goods. His manner suggested seniority. He looked as at ease in his toque as any man I've met.

"It is nice to hear your music," I said.

He handed me the guitar. It was amber orange, polished. I declined, stepping back. "I do not have your talent." Then I asked, "What do the porters sing about?"

"We sing of family, of village. Of past, and of future." With that, Winterford strummed his way into lyrics of what I took to be a Papuan folksong.

Monk pulled a ziplock bag out of his pack. It held gummy worms in a variety of flavors. He passed them around as Winterford kept playing. Our porters stood away from us. Monk made his way toward them, holding out the goodies. It was a gesture of companionship long before we realized how much we needed them.

"Two minutes," shouted Woody, his red-bowed shovel held high.

We rushed to be ready.

I felt insignificant against the encroachment of fast-growing plants that strangled one another, blocked sun from lesser vegetation, and intertwined relentlessly. How long would it take to overgrow if the trail fell out of use?

We split away from the river and continued on good trail for half an hour, during which we made our way across Gasiri Creek. Monk came

Winterford was nicknamed "Guitar Man" and brought a pace to our trekking as well as peaceful late night strumming to the camps.

alongside me and said, "We're at the base of Imita Ridge, mate. That's tomorrow morning's trial. We'll want our rest tonight."

Soon we stepped out of the vegetation and into a stretch of short grass the size of a football field. A handful of one-room structures ran along the west side, each exposed to the elements. Their slat floors were raised a few feet in the air, supported on posts. Atop the floors were walls of cross-patterned thatch standing waist high, open above that for another five feet until being covered by a peaked wooden roof. There was a swing door to keep out vermin (or at least vermin that couldn't scale a three-foot thatched wall, i.e. roving dogs). A breeze blew through these homes, which were for our use that night. Two nearby places were boarded up.

"Camp Goodwater," said Brett. "Otherwise known as Dump 66, a code for the sixth dump, not the 66th. Some say the name Uberi could have moved here." No one was there to greet us.

"Toss your gear in one of those," said Yeoy, pointing to the see-through structures. "Set out your bags and flashlights now while it's light."

Bowrie followed me to one of the shelters and shunted my goods out of his sack and onto the porch. I hauled the bags inside, capturing an open spot near the door, figuring I would disturb fewer people if I had the exit nearby for middle-of-the-night bathroom calls (*nocturia* is the medical term).

"Imagine snakes could crawl up, over, and in," said Tori, as she and Rod took to their goods to a corner. I spread out my groundsheet. Rod hooked their mosquito net to an eyelet on the crossbeam, prompting me to do likewise. I looked to the field where porters pitched a few single-occupant tents. Yeoy claimed one of them and Kristy tossed her gear into another. Deirdre and Phil arrived off the trail as the final tents were set and they dropped packs beside them. Their respective porters unloaded there too. Robert and Michael S came in next and trailed by them to the shack next to mine where others were laying out sleeping pads.

The Melbourne group's gear sat mid-field and away from the huts, and down from the tenters. Two porters pulled four poles from under the structure where I was preparing to sleep. These were framed as two A's, lashed and propped up 20 feet apart. They strung a rope between them. "Help with this cross line," said Anthony to Martin, who positioned himself at one end. The porters pulled the rope taut and secured it with ground pegs. They tossed a tarp up and over the ridge rope. It unfolded in the air, flew open, and landed to form the shelter's roof. Anthony and Martin helped stretch its sides toward waiting tent pegs. All this in a ten minute burst of construction.

Monk and I walked by the Melbourne group's new shelter. We admired the shared solitude and camaraderie these six brought to the trek. "Nice digs," Monk said to no one in particular. Three porters lay large groundsheets against dampness. Darren and Mark unpacked camp chairs with backs; they'd come prepared for comfort. Whitey placed out four books in the look of a library. Anthony tossed pillows about. Michael sat in one chair reading a magazine while Martin lay on a sleeping pad. Monk said of their setting, "Looks like Kokoda's Club Med." By 4:30 p.m., camp was set.

When last I saw him, Yeoy was eating from a tin of tuna. Now he dozed in his tent, recharging while the rest of us fumbled about and spent energy we didn't know we didn't have. Simon and Kieran kicked a soccer ball, passing in and around Monk as he made his tent. It bounced off Simon's foot and high in the air. Monk headed it over Kieran's reach.

Porters strung a clothesline. The late afternoon was less hot, though not less humid. We hung our sweat-saturated shirts on the line. I strolled alone across the field and up a rise to where a blue church stood sentry overlooking the tiny community, its congregation nowhere to be seen. When I got there, Brett came around from the back of it. "Seventh-day Adventist," he said.

Beginning in these mountains where we camped, Seventh-day Adventists have played a prominent healthcare and education role in Papua

New Guinea for over a century. The church's influence with government is significant, as many people have a community or religious connection with the faith.[19]

Programs delivered by Adventist missionaries and church staffs in PNG involve schools for all ages, including an internationally respected college, and the training of individuals for trades and professional careers. The Adventist Development and Relief Agency has been a partner in addressing adult illiteracy. Adventists have constructed water systems in villages. They've addressed education about the contracting, and prevention, of HIV/AIDS.

Adventists began their earliest work in New Guinea in 1908. Missionaries arrived in Port Moresby to find that other religions had already each been assigned a portion of the town in which to serve, and there was no room or reason for them to stay. As soon as they had come, they left.

We were staying amongst the Koiari people, where those early missionaries sought "converts" along the relatively unknown Kokoda road. Early missionaries found the indigenous population practicing ancestor worship and animism, a belief that plants have souls and their world is orchestrated by universal powers. After a decade of frustration, Adventists along the Kokoda trail successfully established a mission school and a clinic in Efogi, a village our group would reach after three days' hike. In subsequent years, Adventist missionaries progressed along the entire path until they became the predominant religion along the Kokoda Trail by the mid-1930s, a standing that remains today.

As we walked away from the church, Brett told me that Europeans and Americans have called World War II in Papua the "war at the end of the

---

19 The PNG populace supports many faiths, almost entirely of a Protestant strain. Lutheran churches, for example, are a legacy of German colonial days. There are 500,000 participants in the Adventist religion in Papua New Guinea, compared with 1.2 million adults in all of North America. Witchcraft, a belief in sorcery called *sanguma*, is not uncommon today and can overlap with one's Christian faith.

world." Jim heard that comment and bridled at the viewpoint. "War at the end of the world? This was 'war on Australia's doorstep.'" But Brett laughed it off, reminding us that the context for most geography is local. Distance breeds disregard. He said, "Come on, Jim. Let's take our North American friend Rick here for a coffee at the end of the world." Bowrie was tending fire as we approached. A pail of water was boiling. When he saw us nearing, he scooped water into three cups and set them on a log near the powdered coffee and tea. "*Hamamas tru,*" he said. That is, *happiness.*

As he stirred his instant coffee into being, Jim continued to bridle. "Most Americans don't even know the Kokoda exists." Brett stirred a tea to life, giving a nod. I thought of my ignorance before Monk had first mentioned "the Kokoda." Yet there were Americans who'd lost parents, grandfathers, and granduncles in the Papuan Campaign of 1942. Do even they know what the Kokoda is? I wondered.

It was just before sunset. The porters' sleeping quarters were located across the field from ours. They went about making their own home for the night; jammed with flop mats thin as cardboard. A new fire sparked to life beside Bowrie's. Cooking utensils were hung on a wire. Next to it was a rock shelf sporting pots and frying pans. Holding mugs of warm encouragement, Monk and I walked to the field's southern hillside where the Kokoda Club Med guys stood, backed by a dusky blue on the horizon. Before dipping out of sight this first of many nights, the sun bowed our way in an uncompromised orange. Then it was gone.

"Dinner! Over here." It was Yeoy's announcement.

There was a long table with room enough for all of us. It had the atmosphere of a military canteen. Some took to the side benches in anticipation of being served, but soon realized this was to be our first of over three dozen self-serve buffets. We queued alongside the fire to get the main course: grilled chicken and carrots. There was plenty to go around. Janice had packed little canisters of tarragon and curry and dill into our packs; Monk and I also had pouches of garlic flakes and sesame sauce. We shared our spices too willingly that night, not realizing the value that the flashy seasonings would hold a dozen meals later, after such extravagances were long gone. There were berry muffins for dessert.

Yeoy told us to concentrate on the chicken and fresh veggies. "We can't rely on local supplies along the trail. Sometimes, we might get lucky. But livestock is rare and under watch. You won't have many Papuan delicacies."

Brett stood at a table corner, stirring hot chocolate in his cup and sipping. His posture was straight, his stance that of an instructor. He recapped the day's events matter-of-factly, starting with Bomana, saying, "You each likely began your emotional journey at the cemetery." In five minutes of trek-talk-mixed-with-history, he'd brought the day's deeds right up to our sitting together at the table. "Each night, one of you will be asked to recall the day for the gathering, and filter in your own observations. Tomorrow it'll be Whitey." Whitey was surprised, yet smiled in agreement.

With that, Brett turned to Yeoy, who swapped out the storytelling to ask a question. "What do you do when you're not out here lost in the jungle? Tell the rest of us why you're on Kokoda." He looked to his left for Michael S to begin. As each person spoke, it increased my respect for the hardiness of our unit. Not a superficial motive among them—each a variation of being worried, and each expecting to better their lives by trekking the Kokoda Trail.

When it was Kristy's turn, she said, "I'm here to get a better appreciation of what my Pop endured, and sacrificed for his country. I'm Australian, but my Pop was American and was in Papua during World War II. Pop was stationed at Sandy Creek in South Australia. In 1942 he was chosen as part of a group commissioned by the American Army to assist in building airfields at Milne Bay." She had the attention of the full group. "Pop met an Adelaide girl, Netta Mary Thomas. She was a volunteer at the Cheer-Up Hut."

"That was on King William Street," said Michael S.

"How 'bout this," said Kristy. "My Pop went AWOL at one point." There were snickers of enjoyment around the table. "He'd fallen in love and was desperate to track down Netta. When he found her, he proposed. She accepted. But before they could get married, the American Military Police hauled him back to his unit. He was questioned directly by General Douglas MacArthur."

None of us could see Kristy's story ending well, given MacArthur's legendary intolerance for misdemeanours. "Pop explained he wanted to spend the rest of his life with this Aussie girl. He asked General MacArthur for leave to marry her." Not one of us could conceive a response other than "No" from the gruff commander. A few heads were shaking. Kristy had a better ending for her story. "Today, there is a whole family who thanks General MacArthur for granting Pop's leave."

Kristy's story was a tough reminder that without the atrocities of war, many of our parents or grandparents would never have met. Like her grandparents, my mom and dad would not have; I'd not be alive. Kristy left it at that. We'd have to wait until near the end of the trek to learn more about her Pop and Papua.

When it came my turn to talk, it proved of momentary interest that I had stepped away from one career in order to write books full-time. Michael asked, "Books? What kind of books?" Simon offered to be featured if I wrote about this journey. Brett encouraged I spell his name with both *t*'s. I spoke to my honest motivation: "I'm here because Monk promised an amazing walk across the country."

"Walk?" laughed Phil.

"I might have lied a little," Monk confessed.

Bearing the brunt of my naiveté, I was happy when Deirdre offered a diversion, likely reflecting what the rest of us were feeling. "Adventure on its own is sufficient motivation for a trek like this," she said. Her phrasing caught my attention. Long ago, I'd borrowed a similar motif from something Amelia Earhart once said: "Adventure is worthwhile in itself." Deirdre's observation got me thinking about

Earhart and New Guinea, as well as a once-rumored, now disproven, twist in her story.

In 1937, in the run up to World War II, an American aircraft with Amelia Earhart in the cockpit left New Guinea, never to be found. Among the many explanations, it had been hypothesized the Japanese ended up with her airplane, retrieving engineering ideas to improve their Mitsubishi's A6M Zero fighter. However, it's now recognized that the Zero was superior to the American-built P-40 fighter plane (the Warhawk, or what Australians called the Kittyhawk). Among those who once believed the Japanese held Earhart, some implied similarities of the Zero to that of her Lockheed Model 10 Electra, suggesting components were reverse-engineered from Earhart's retrieved plane. But the Zero was already an advanced designed aircraft incorporating modern aeronautical developments (and, the Japanese had openly purchased US civilian aircraft well into the 1930s, meaning Earhart's plane would have likely been old news to them).

What technology could Amelia have had onboard that would have benefitted the Japanese? Sophisticated spying equipment is the only thing that would have been unique. Or, maybe the Japanese shot down the plane in retaliation for Earhart's alleged spying on behalf of the US government. For years, such myths had real currency. Indeed, while Australians were engaged along the Kokoda Track and Americans on the Northern Beaches, development was underway for the 1943 Hollywood movie *Flight for Freedom*, which used this aviatrix-as-spy narrative for a plotline.

The 40-year-old Earhart and navigator Fred Noonan had been delayed on their around-the-world quest by inclement weather in the Dutch East Indies. Earhart took ill with dysentery, recovering slowly. They next flew to Darwin in northern Australia, and from there landed on the grass runway at Lae Airfield on June 29. Their final leg would be crossing the Pacific Ocean. The first stretch was the 2,556-mile (4,113-kilometer) flight from Lae to Howland Island, slightly north of the equator in the middle of the Pacific Ocean. The last film images of Earhart and Noonan alive are from July 2 in New Guinea. It was 10 a.m. local time when the Electra lifted off at Lae, all devices and instruments reportedly working.

As they approached the vicinity of Howland Island, they could be heard by the radioman aboard the US Coast Guard's *Itasca*, responsible for guiding the aircraft to a safe landing. Contact was complicated by uncertain frequencies, static, and perhaps the pilot's inexperience with relatively new radio technology. Or was there another reason? The *Itasca* continued to receive information from Earhart, but could not communicate in return. Necessary guidance for landing, refueling, and relaunching toward the Hawaiian Islands did not happen.

Earhart's Electra disappeared.

Did swapping out more complete navigational equipment in exchange for greater fuel capacity contribute to a crash landing? Or—as recent analysis shows is the most likely scenario—did Earhart and Noonan overfly Howland Island, hours later landing on a reef of Gardner Island (Nikumaroro Atoll), dying as castaways often do—from starvation.

Two Japanese vessels participated with American ships in the initial search for the missing plane, particularly around those Mariana Islands. While Japan and the US were not enemies at the time, the powers were wary of one another. Disclosure of her discovery by the Japanese may not have been forthcoming. War in the Pacific started soon enough thereafter, with extensive conflicts near where Earhart reportedly disappeared.

Why, some ask, did Amelia call her plane the "Flying Laboratory"? What new American technology was being tested? Might the Japanese have blocked US Navy transmissions and radioed her landing instructions in flawless American English to divert her? Was the Zero's killing of Americans and Australians in the Papua Campaign enhanced by technology the Japanese found aboard Amelia's Electra? Given there is no proof the planes incorporated American spy technology, it is settled argument that the deadly Zero was Japanese technology throughout.

Across the field from our dwindling campfire flame and diminishing numbers, the Papuan porters were singing by their fire. The music sounded close to the earth, conveying day's end. Taking their hint, the remaining few of us dispersed to our shelters. Walking back from a side trip to the latrine, I saw Monk and Jim waving. At least that's what I thought. But no, they were catching fireflies. When I approached them, little insects flickered around me. They were almost uncatchable, yet Monk's quick hand managed to grab one. He opened his palm where the insect stayed briefly, having lost its glow. "They're beetles," Jim said. "Flying beetles."

"I've never held a firefly," I said as I caught one, careful not to squeeze. Quickly making amends, I let it go.

"That's enough," said Jim. "We need to be careful. They're dying off, like bees. We need them."

"What do you mean?" Monk asked.

"Maybe not here, but urban growth spoils the dead trees and watersides where they thrive. Light pollution kills them, too. Pesticides."

Jim knows a bit about everything, I thought.

"It's the tail that glows," he continued. "Two chemicals there make energy. Energy makes heat. Heat glows. Males light up until a female spots a guy she likes. Then she flashes from the bushes."

Even when the forest felt still, it wasn't. It was full of stories.

I left Jim and Monk with their fireflies and lingered alone in the middle of the grass field. I was sure I'd never seen a sky so full of stars. As I understand it, since the center of the galaxy is slightly below the earth's equator in the constellation of Sagittarius, there are usually more stars visible in the Southern Hemisphere night sky than in the north. The earth's tilt skews the numbers. While I knew there to be an octillion stars above me, the total number that can be seen by the unaided human eye is around 9,000.[20] And the earth is always in the way, blocking lots of stars from

---

20 There are 9,096 stars visible that are greater than magnitude 6.5, as catalogued by Dorit Hoffleit in the Yale Bright Star Catalogue.

one's viewing point, half the planet being in daylight. That night the waning moon further reduced the number of visible stars. What I saw was a couple thousand stars masquerading as a billion. Nevertheless humbled, I walked up the steps and into our night's shelter, where others were already asleep. My feet creaking on thatch-woven floorboards woke them.

I lay on my back surrounded by night, thinking about something Deirdre admitted by the campfire. "I have to do the Kokoda Trail now. For many of us, age is no longer our friend. We may not be able to do this in a few years." Her candor also identified a motive for my being here. We're tempted to think there'll be another day, another year, or another opportunity to do the things we want to do, once we find them. I've dead friends who thought that. I've watched infirmities rule out travel for others. Only a fool would awake each day and feel personally responsible for this life that cosmic circumstances had given them. Only a *damn* fool could go to sleep at night without wondering why the universe had delivered another day for them, much less feel themselves worthy of it.

Bomana Cemetery appeared in my rearview memory. Young lives full of tomorrows stolen by events beyond their control. I thought of my mom. After her years of military service were over and peacetime had arrived, our mother would say to us kids, "Every day on this side of the grass is a good one. But you must make it so. Never take for granted that you'll have a tomorrow."

Earlier around the campfire, Brett had warned about our immediate tomorrows. "For the next week you'll never really rest your body, or your mind. Or your conscience." Falling asleep, I felt anxiety for the coming week of blended days and blended nights.

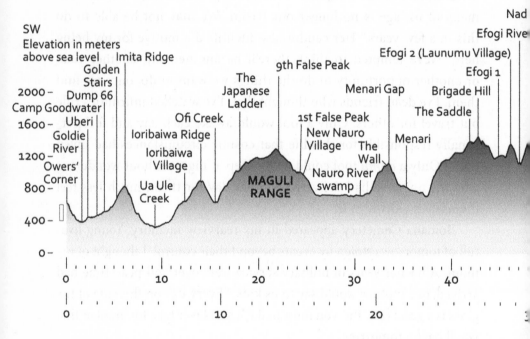

SW
Elevation in meters
above sea level   Imita Ridge

Golden
Stairs
2000 –   Dump 66
Camp Goodwater
1600 –   Uberi
Goldie
River
1200 –
Owers'
Corner
800 –

400 –

0 –

Ofi Creek
Ioribaiwa Ridge
Ioribaiwa
Village
Ua Ule
Creek

The
Japanese
Ladder

MAGULI
RANGE

9th False Peak

1st False Peak
New Nauro
Village   The
Wall
Nauro River
swamp

Menari Gap

The Saddle
Menari

Nad
Efogi Rive
Efogi 2 (Launumu Village)
Efogi 1
Brigade Hill

0   10   20   30   40

0   10   20

The author's week of "blended days and blended nights" on the Kokoda Trail is
the focus of this map. It includes most of the geographic indicators mentioned
in the text. As route diversions can be taken, distances may vary for other
trekkers, as could hiking times.

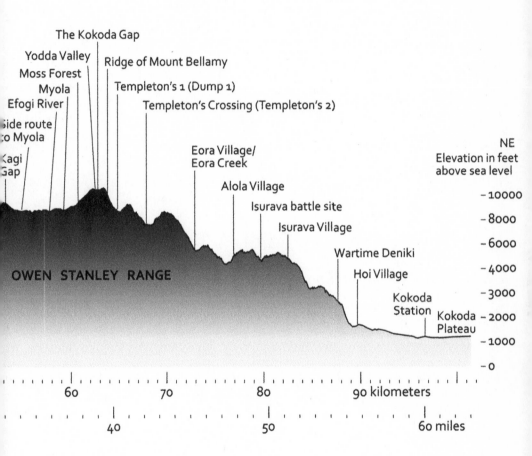

The Kokoda Gap

Yodda Valley   Ridge of Mount Bellamy

Moss Forest

Myola   Templeton's 1 (Dump 1)

Efogi River

Templeton's Crossing (Templeton's 2)

Side route
to Myola

Kagi   Eora Village/
Gap   Eora Creek

NE
Elevation in feet
above sea level

Alola Village

Isurava battle site   – 10000

Isurava Village   – 8000

– 6000

Wartime Deniki   – 4000

OWEN STANLEY RANGE   Hoi Village

Kokoda   – 3000
Station   Kokoda   – 2000
Plateau

– 1000

– 0

60   70   80   90 kilometers

40   50   60 miles

THREE

Beyond Forget

*"The people know the course of things, for the course of things may
be thousands of years old . . ."*
—Peter Matthiessen, *Under the Mountain Wall*

A t 5 a.m., Brett's alarm radio bounced to life with Abba's "Dancing Queen," loud and borderline obnoxious.

"Up!" he shouted, sporty but authoritative. "That's everyone."

I opened my eyes reluctantly. The porters had risen early and rekin-
dled last night's embers. Nothing smelled yet (except us), but I sensed
that there was water on the boil. Coffee. Sprinkle in apprehension and
excitement. Stir.

Pack-up routines varied this first morning on the trail. A few trekkers darted for the toilet before rolling up sleeping bags. Some stuffed
away their overnight materials with a disarming promptness, cleaning
where they'd slept so thoroughly it looked like no one had lain there.
There were mumbled reminders to take one's anti-malaria tablet.

Visions of fried eggs and crispy bacon drove me to the breakfast
nook, where all I saw was a display of unsalted crackers. Then the dis-
tinct aroma of fried Spam wafted through the air. The sight of cheese
melting atop a blob of formulated meat, with the yellow fringes crisping
to brown, made me hungry. The boiled yams were less appetizing, my

preference being for singed. Day-old bread was there to grab and tear. Containers of butter, jam, and peanut spread were open, knives waiting beside them. There was a jar of marmalade, too, and muesli, which is somewhat like granola. I looked for hidden bits of tasty raisins, and opted for the Weet-Bix cereal.

"Bacon, no. Eggs, no," someone grumbled beside me. I looked over to see Monk. Anthony was saying, "We're out of bacon?" Changing the conversation to his unfolded map, Michael said, "We're heading for Ioribaiwa Village for tonight."

Brett shouted, "Workout. Form a circle. You'll need to limber up, stretch carefully, and warm your body before stepping on today's climb. I'll lead this morning. Tomorrow it'll be Rod's turn. A different one of you will lead each morning. Pay attention."

Rod nodded acceptance of his assignment.

"Hup, hup." Brett's police lingo. We stretched, did running on the spot, rotated our hips and arched our backs. No muscle was left untended. It was the fun of grade-school calisthenics: jumping jacks and knee bends.

"Packs on," ordered Brett, closing us down. Michael yelled back a single line of the Aussie sports challenge: "Aussie, Aussie, Aussie." The rest of the Australians piled on with "Oi, Oi, Oi!" Woody finally sent us scrambling for hiking poles when he shouted, "Two minutes!"

We climbed the trail's rise through mist at 6 a.m. The trail led us beside the blue church and under the green canopy. Camp was left clean. Our footprints were everywhere, but the trash and signs of a sleepover were gone. The fires smoldered steam. I was impressed by the respect porters and leaders showed for their surroundings.

"Marley, off we go," Monk shouted. He had taken to calling his dreadlock-haired porter Bob Marley, a designation accented by the Papuan's rainbow toque atop his head. The smiling Kingsole was a strong-legged man with years of experience on the trail, and he was happy when Monk's hurrying put the two of them at the head of the pack on the morning climb, right behind Woody's shovel. Jim matched his steps with them, enabled by Kipling's stride. Soon we pulled up where forest now covered a once-cleared ground, site of Dump 44, a depot for the Aussie supply line during the campaign. It was no longer recognizable as such, but it smelled of hidden rust and unseen history.

Our short-term goal was Imita Ridge. The map indicated "up." We began with a sense of accomplishment. Then our map showed "steep" beside "The Golden Stairs." Here in 1942, engineers carved thousands of steps and inserted wood supports up the hillside. Soldiers had another name for what we were coming to: the Stairway to Hell. Anticipation of the endless staircase cowed most every trekker, certainly me. After we'd been hiking a while, pacing ourselves to our breathing and feeling good about it, Yeoy said, "The word grueling is about to enter your vocabulary." His breathing was even. I wished mine were. Brett told us, "The stairs have been rated seven out of ten for difficulty." He smiled in reference to another upcoming challenge we all dreaded. "The Wall is rated a ten."

Between spurts of huffing up the endless stairs, Whitey told us, "When I was last here, we had rain. After that it poured. Then the showers came." Pointing to where our feet met the mountainside, he said, "We had no traction. Mud gripped your boots and wouldn't let go. Every step, you sunk. Always, we slipped. Even with poles to prop us up."

"At least no one was shooting at you," said Kieran.

Michael was winded but Yeoy chided him. "Suck it in and toughen up."

Brett was near me, and said, "There are other places along the Kokoda also called Golden Stairs, but this set is the namesake." We proceeded hand-to-earth fashion, our backs bent into poles. The clay beneath our boots was prone to slide. We grabbed at trees for support. Frequently, we stopped to suck air into our gasping lungs. We took rests, wanting to collapse, then restarted our climb. The valley was lush, betraying beauty when we felt anything but, for this climb was hellish. Patience was an attribute, right behind persistence, we'd need to have if we were going to get to the top. At the crest, the mountain and trail flattened. By that time we had two-and-a-half hours of on and off hiking behind us and it wasn't even midmorning. We were in need of a longer break, so we rested on Imita Ridge. This was where the Aussie soldiers dug in September of '42, having suffered through a fighting withdrawal since late July, all the way from Isurava back to here.

Yeoy stood with a sheet of paper in his hand. He quoted Major General Tubby Allen about the circumstances the Aussies found themselves in. "'Further withdrawal is out of the question . . .'" Yeoy was unequivocal: "Imita Ridge formed the last defensible barrier. If the Japanese took control of Imita, they would have access to Owers' Corner. After that was an obstacle-free road to Moresby, twenty-five miles away." To the entrenched Aussies, losing this ridge would have ensured the fall of Moresby into Japanese hands, leaving little protection for loved ones back in Australia.

Across Ua-Ule Creek valley from here, and higher up, was Ioribaiwa Ridge. That was where, seven weeks after landing on the beaches, General Horii and his troops had halted, occupying the vantage point. Their intention was to use that position to secure the southern end of the Kokoda Trail, and bring in reinforcements. Yeoy said, "The Japanese soldiers on Ioribaiwa Ridge were motivated as much by their nearness to Moresby with its food provisions, shelters, and hospital as by its strategic benefits."

The loss by then of thousands of Japanese lives, the 3,000 comrades taken back to the beaches with untreated wounds or incapacitated by a nervous breakdown, naturally tempered the elation of the Nankai Shitai. Those losses left only 1,500 troops in suitable fighting condition at Ioribaiwa Ridge. They were living on a handful of rice a day, and low on ammunition. Getting to Ioribaiwa had lengthened an already dysfunctional supply line. The forced pullback of the Australians to Imita Ridge had ironically shortened their supply lines for ammunition, food, medical attention, and reinforcements.

Yeoy described the standoff. "Over the following days, skirmishes failed to change circumstances. Each side held their ground." Then the storyline was taken up by Brett, who explained that the Aussies, believing the Japanese had more soldiers and bigger guns, waited for the imminent and overwhelming Japanese assault that never came. "Instead of becoming the base for the Japanese attack on Moresby," he went on, "Ioribaiwa Ridge became the point of Japanese overreach. After all the mountainsides they'd conquered along the Kokoda Track, Ioribaiwa proved to be a ridge too far."

In war, as in life, context is important, and Brett provided it. "That August, US Marines had swept onto Guadalcanal in the nearby Solomon Islands to the east of Papua. There they took control of an airstrip the Japanese were building. Horii's superior, Lieutenant-General Hyakutake, oversaw both the Papuan Campaign and the Solomon Islands Campaign from his base in Rabaul. He now had to deal with faltering situations on both the Kokoda Track and Guadalcanal." Hyakutake rethought deployment of more resources to Papua to reinforce Horii at Ioribaiwa. Instead, he instructed Horii to stop any further attack toward Port Moresby and wait for further instructions at his present position. "He believed that Japan's retaking Guadalcanal after the US Marines' invasion would be swift. It wasn't." Brett left it at that for now, but not before saying, "Hyakutake's miscalculation cost the Japanese their position along the Kokoda Track." Brett promised more of the story when we neared Ioribaiwa Ridge ourselves. To get there we'd need to leave our rest spot, descend a precipitous path, cross a creek, and make our way up, up, then up some more. We retied our bootlaces, shouldered our daypacks, and made for the path.

Our hiking along the Kokoda Trail from Imita Ridge toward Ioribaiwa Ridge continued where only the Australian soldiers had traversed, since the Japanese never got that far. The Owen Stanley Range is made up of valleys and creeks as well as stiff mountains. The down side from Imita Ridge was on a steep path. At times water flowed down the hill on the trail, making mud. "God, I'd love a beer," I thought out loud, but only

Bowrie was close enough to hear me, or care. On one short piece of level ground, Marley sang "Ya, ya, ya to America . . ." and danced along. Two trekkers tried to imitate him, and slipped. The porters were in a lively mood. Neither the weight of their packs nor the steepness brought them worry. They sang for long spells and then stopped all together. Even their talking voices were happy. Why did none of us speak so happily in English? Was it possibly because sections of the path appeared to be vertical?

Nearly two hours in, we'd completed the harrowing descent and heard from Yeoy: "Three years ago, I did this with five climbers in pounding rain. It took us over six hours. We roped up at the top and stayed tethered throughout." We knew we were off that mountain side when Ua-Ule Creek broke open and flowed in a canyon.

"Boots off!" yelled Brett from behind, so the strung-out trekkers could all hear him. "Water shoes on." We sat along shore, packs off, swapping out our shoes.

"Twenty-two is the number you'll want to know," said Yeoy. I looked at him in puzzlement. "That's how many times you'll cross this one creek in the next hour or two." The creek bottom was covered with fairly small rocks that were harsh on the foot. Porters kept their flip-flops on, or if they wore boots that would chafe when wet, they went barefoot.

Most of us had hiking boots and a pair of sneakers for the trail. Trekkers also had a pair of sandals or water shoes to wear when crossing through water. I'd brought soft-soled water shoes that proved inadequate as they folded my feet over individual rocks in this stream.

Our first crossing was in water up to our calves. On the other side, we walked a short stretch on shore before going back into the stream again. Woody kept us moving, mostly in the water, alternating briefly with time on the land trail. I gave up counting how many water entries after ten, taking Yeoy's word that his count was accurate. In places the water was deep, and our stumbles and the cold slowed us. Yeoy called for a rest.

"Twenty-two?" asked Kristy, thinking we were at the end of our water crossings.

"Always good to have an accountant among us," said Yeoy. "There's no better place along Kokoda for lunch and a swim," he declared. With that, he was off to the stream's largest pool, curled into it with a splash rather than a dive, and submerged.

Rod was next. I watched him sink and then stand quickly with a look of cold pain on his face. Simon was in right after, and popped out with a comic, "It's fine. Water's fine." The water was *not* fine. The pool was fed by mountain streams from high up, flowing here through dark jungle, never slowing to lower its temperature. It was frighteningly cold, especially as my upper body sunk beneath the surface. There was neither depth nor length enough for warming strokes, but we rolled about and ducked our heads under.

The porters set lunch along shore. I looked at the pinkish pieces of Spam, wishing them fried. My appetite hesitated. I needed to switch up my thinking or I risked a certain dread at mealtimes. Then it struck me: Spam was our trek's delicacy. Set aside how Spam is created. Concentrate on mouth feel and taste. When I said all that to Monk, he suggested, "Think of Spam as *pâté*." It may well have been the first time I heard French spoken with an Aussie accent. We also had salted crackers, strawberry jam, and Aussie wafers called Tim Tams. Monk added chocolates and nuts to the table, letting them spill out as the centerpiece. They were gone in a whiff.

I refilled my hydration pack from the stream, dropping in a water purification tablet to keep me straight and an orange-flavored electrolyte tablet for replenishment. The effervescent concoction was nasty but refreshing, and absolutely necessary for our hydration. We wrung our shirts and squished our shorts free of water, swept water off our bodies, and changed out of water shoes. We put on dry socks and hiking boots and stepped back on the trail. We had a mountain to climb.

Now we encountered less in the way of tall trees and more jungle. Foliage intensified, broad leaves five feet in length were laced tightly together, camouflaging and concealing what lay ahead. Plants fought one another for sunlight. I smelled a damp aroma. En route, Brett pointed.

"Mahogany tree." Or, "That's nutmeg." The deepening jungle felt liberat-
ing, yet claustrophobic at the same time. There was a menacing thickness.

As we pushed on I thought of how New Guinea was for so long nega-
tively depicted in popular culture, thanks to Westerners who travelled to
this island in search of the unlikely and the lost. One example was the
book *Cannibal Quest* by Gordon Sinclair, a famous Canadian newspaper
reporter and broadcaster.

When the book was published in 1934, Fiji, the Solomon Islands,
and New Guinea were known as the Cannibal Isles. Sinclair travelled the
world for the Toronto *Star* during the Depression, seeking out exotica.
This particular book of his (he wrote many) may leave some miffed that
his storyline perpetuated Western prejudgments about New Guinea
instead of carving away at them. His story seems a missed opportunity
to understand the Papuans' richly different cultural practices. While
some behaviors were certainly strange to Western sensitivities, they were
worthy of respectful research. Westerners frequently choose to demean
places or conduct they don't understand. We ably do that by reinforcing
silly stereotypes, instead of trying to understand developed ways of life
that sustained curious cultures for centuries.

On reflection, Sinclair's observations defer to the context of their
time, and his home country, which is not to explain away opinions then
customary in many circles, judged a hundred years later and found
wanting. In those days Canada was treating its own indigenous peoples
poorly, a trend that began with European explorers and immigration
and continued for centuries. Sinclair was a man of his time. Fair enough.
But I have always felt that he carried with him a white man's sense of
superiority. Sinclair was possibly correct in calling 1930s New Guinea
"the only unexplored island outside the Arctic wastes." It being unexplored, he left it misunderstood.

We walked through the pretty camp of Ua-Ule, not quite a village but
a petite and unpretentious place that a local landowner and his family

maintain as a camp. Brett sang the name, making it *"Fa-Lay."* The cadence sounded reasonable to me. The residents had no expectations of gain from our passing through. There were eight or ten homes, and I concluded that's what the land could sustain.

"*Kakaruk*," said Bowrie. The term held no reference point for me in English. I interpreted it to be what he pointed at: a chicken, under the porch of a building. "*Gaden*," he went on, pointing behind a fence, thus continuing my instruction in a new language. I saw rows of cabbage or lettuce in a garden, and felt hope for my understanding of Pidgin's crossover meanings. We traipsed through the village and were soon hiking uphill, at a pace meant for conserving energy. The climb felt without end. This approach to Ioribaiwa Ridge did not disappoint its reputation as arduous. My boots took the hint and intuitively pointed upward. We trudged the mountainside toward Ioribaiwa Village.

"Bird-of-paradise," a porter whispered. He was ahead and out of my line of sight. Everyone stopped. Trekkers moved silently to where the porter stood, eyes searching. Bird-watching is a quiet man's game. "There!" Phil, who on the first evening had stated his wish to see one of the birds, swept his eyes around the jungle, moving stealthily closer to the pointing guide. He, too, whispered, "There."

The birds' faces are flattering. It is their feathers—blues, yellows, and reds—that give them commercial value. Indigenous peoples have long used headdresses for ceremonial purposes, which inspired an active trade and eventually endangered the species. Today they are protected, and exports of birds or souvenir feathers is banned. Decades of clearing the rainforest for logging or mining interests have also contributed to reducing populations for each of the 40 bird-of-paradise species found in Papua New Guinea. Whitey told us that Rugby is notionally PNG's national sport and Kumuls is the name of the national team, which in Tok Pisin means "bird-of-paradise." Today, some walk the Kokoda Trail solely in search of sighting the rare bird. It took the patience to stand still, and lucky timing, for two among us to see it. Lacking both, I wasn't one of them.

We arrived at beautiful Ioribaiwa Village around 4 p.m. We were healthy, had ample supplies, anticipated a nice meal, and were having good weather. Quite the opposite of when the Japanese occupied the area some 75 years earlier. I was mindful that soldiers on either side had arrived at this same spot almost too fatigued to continue walking, let alone fight, yet were forced to do so. The only thing we had in common with those men was that we were desperately hot, even though we hiked in one of the cooler tropical months. Each day's temperature reached the high 80s, but as we gained altitude it became cooler, especially at night. There's no real dry season (just a *drier* season, which was when we trekked). The threat of rain was uncertain until it happened, at which time it became predictable.

Yeoy's tent was up in a flash of energy that none of the rest of us felt. After enjoying a personal tin of salmon, he lay into his nap, oblivious to the construction around him. Porters set up tents and tarps with dispatch. Beds for those of us in shelters were ready within fifteen minutes. One porter lit a fire for cooking, and another lit one for company-of-the-non-talking sort. Roosters strutted away from us and under the raised hut floors. Even the village dogs looked tidy. But every clammy thing about *me* smelled. Humidity glued my body to my clothing. I saw Simon looking refreshed, and in a change of shirt and shorts. He'd found what I needed.

"Shower's a marvel, Rick. No lineup."

"I'm on it," I said.

"Water's warm," he called after me.

I went around a bend of bushes to see drain stones on the ground in a setting devoid of privacy. A two-foot plastic pipe was collared onto a six-foot high post coming out of the rocks. Gravity-fed creek water coursed through a sweep of hose and the shower became an avalanche. I stripped off my clothes and stood under the flow, head bowed. Ice-cold water pummeled my neck and splashed over my body. Near freezing water shockwaves hit my lower back. I felt alive, but I thought I'd die.

I'd forgotten my towel. I patted away the water with my shorts, wrung them out, and put them on again. Seconds later, returning to camp around the bush, I ran into Kristy heading this way. I repeated Simon's lie about the water. Memories aren't made from long, hot showers. They're made from quick, cold ones.

Only old people and trekkers talk about their bowel movements, and so it was inevitable that into our conversational circle came the unnecessary news that one of the group, let us call him Panther, was blocked up.

A porter advised, "Go before. If not, now is late. Your body stressed. Some take four days, more. Maybe six days. Then okay." The Papuan warned, "First one hurts."

"Dinner!" shouted Yeoy. Ioribaiwa dinner included *damper*, as Whitey called it, flour and water cooked in a rock cover built into the side of the fireplace (in effect, a local bread oven used by trekkers who could figure it out). With it we enjoyed (if that's the word) Monk's *pâté* of preservatives, chopped into chunks. Cheese slices could be added, if you were among the first at table and they'd not been already claimed. Someone had persuaded the cook to sprinkle on powdered chili. Soy sauce had been mixed in. The culinary concoction was runny enough to pour over your *damper* and tasty enough to make you forget hunger. There was fried rice and curry. Lifeless noodles waited limply for the attention of a sauce that would not appear. It wasn't a great buffet, but it was our buffet.

I sat with Yeoy while we ate and asked if he felt the day had been a good one. "Another day, another *kina*," he said with uncustomary flippancy. He tilted a bowl of broth to his lips and drank heartily. He told a story about the importance of *kina* earnings for the locals. Once, he was on the trail by himself with two others. "No satellite phone. No porters." They'd made swift time, he said, but "we were met by villagers who demanded to know where the paying guests were." I reckoned aloud that the trail runs the risk of becoming more about commerce in the eyes of locals, and less about the trekkers' experience. "You'll see that at Isurava in a few days," Yeoy said.

Other trekkers drew near us with their plates of noodles dusted with powdered Parmesan. I doused mine with ketchup. A few held steaming chocolate drinks, as though gathered for what we called "mug up" on camps when I was a kid. The other diners were drawn by the unwavering self-confidence of Yeoy's storytelling voice. "Ever have an emergency on a trek?" Robert asked.

"Thankfully, just once," said Yeoy. "Two years ago. A strong and capable hiker had heart palpitations. Situation turned critical. This man, he could have died here in the mountains. The satellite phone with us is for only such use. No, you cannot call your loved ones on it." He smiled as he said that. We all knew he carried it in his pack, testing it at night and in the morning to check the charge. He had one spare battery.

"We had to call in a helicopter to pick up the hiker," he said. "Many places here, you have seen for yourselves, you cannot land or even lower a rescue rope from a helicopter. This man, we carried him for many miles over rough territory. It was pitch dark." He lightened the drama, saying, "Of course, with headlamps, we could at least see the roots that tripped us." I could taste the dusk through my nose. The jungle around us that night was forbidding. It tugged us into his story. "It was the only way we could get the trekker to an open area where the helicopter could land at first light." He admonished us. "It is why I ask you to let me know anything irregular. Please, be honest with your heart." Monk leaned over to me. He'd not been paying attention and seemed remote in his own thoughts. That's when he asked me, "Wonder if my old man got this far?"

Before dinner broke up, Brett had more of the story he'd begun when we were at Imita Ridge regarding the dug-in Aussies waiting in fear for the inevitable onslaught of Japanese bearing down from Ioribaiwa Ridge. That story had unfolded near where we were camped, which is why he'd left telling it until now. Where we were, in today's Ioribaiwa Village, was not in the exact location as during the war, when the village of that name had been closer to the actual ridge. Brett began by saying,

"We'll attain Ioribaiwa Ridge proper on our morning's hike. That's where General Horii learned his highly anticipated reinforcements had instead been deployed to Guadalcanal. Within days news came that Horii's air support had also been reassigned to Guadalcanal."

We camped in the jungle near where the Papuan Campaign had formally reversed course, and the Aussie advance to victory had begun. In effect, this location marked the close of Act I in the Papua Theater of War.

We nibbled at chocolate chip cookies and sipped coffee. Monk asked me if I'd like a beer, laughing at how far away the nearest one might be.

The sun left our campsite in style, duplicating the previous evening's spectacular bow before disappearing, but we noticed it a little less this second time. Magic is like that; repetition reduces awe. The fire was ready for us. Flames galloped on dry wood. "Whitey?" said Brett. It wasn't a question; it was a nudge.

Whitey stood slowly, easing a cramp from his leg. "God bless muscle relaxants," he said.

"I recap today by saying I'm thankful it wasn't like my last trek here." We'd come to value Whitey's perspective. His comparisons of downpours versus our good weather differed from those of Brett or Yeoy, who seemed to relish the thought of rain. Whitey did not assume that our coming days would be precipitation free, as some of us had come to believe. We also became aware that 1942 had been a year of belligerent weather as well, turning the Kokoda pathway into a functionally useless stream. That September's torrential rains had swept away over two dozen Japanese bridges alone, further slowing food and ammunition supply efforts.

Whitey said, "When there's mud, you can multiply hiking time by three. Or four. Saying that, my highlight of the day—if you'll let me call it that—was those god-awful stairs that weren't stairs. I thought they'd never end. My legs cried. Thank God for the knotty parts to hold onto, or we could never have climbed."

Anthony observed, "There are more roots than ants in this country."

"On this trek, I feel more kinship with the Aussie soldiers—more, I mean, than when I was here before," Whitey said. "That trek was a hike. This trek is spiritual—if I'm saying it straight," he added. "Being here, and knowing why it matters. That's clearer to me this time." His words underlined the Kokoda Trail as one of the world's great pilgrimages. Knowing it was unlikely I'd be returning on a future trek, his thinking made me determined to assimilate all I could comprehend on this one. Unexpectedly, a Japanese phrase struck me. It is about knowing where you are when you are there, being in the moment instead of anticipating it or recollecting it later. *Ima sugu koi* is how I understood it. It translates as, "Be here now."

Whitey said that this time he was "here to understand. A few years ago I came here enamored by the adventure of it all, and now I realize that was a lesser motivation."

Our dinner and fireside chat—the entire evening so far at this campsite—felt a fulsome experience. I couldn't think of anything that would make it more complete. I didn't even wish away my sore muscles. Even the most fit among us could feel the early days of our trek in their calves and hips. Aches don't lie; it had been tough going. Yet we were hitting our stride in another way, too. We all got along well with one another. Any anxieties were personal, and largely left unsaid. I got up from the fireside, and walked—not so much walking to anywhere, rather walking away from the others. The others dispersed, too, headlamps aimed at the ground. All around was dark; the sky was starry. My chest bumped into the clothesline we'd strung. I sprung back from the rope and steadied myself.

Our camp glowed in pockets. A flashlight held for reading, a battery lamp near a trekker, a few candles by the table, and the fire. Winterford's guitar started a new song. For the first time, I recognized his tune. Then came English words from a group of our porters: "Let the sunshine in, face it with a grin. Smilers never lose, and frowners never win." It was Sunday evening and the Northern Beaches porters weren't obliged to

84

the Saturday Sabbath of Seventh-day Adventists; they were of Anglican influence and gathered in service to give thanks for the day.

Trekkers were readied for bed by 8 p.m. The day had done us in; our minds were as tired as our knees. Music continued to gloss over the field from the porters' part of camp. They busied with end-of-day chores, the result of their work for our benefit. They sang lightly, having first ensured each of us was set for sleep.

I couldn't be bothered to finish my field notes. Darkness took hold, and my mental lights went out.

"Big girls don't cry," Frankie Valli belted from Brett's loudspeaker at 5 a.m. My heart jumped. I'd been in a deep-dive sleep. Brett's music was right next to my ear. "I'm getting even for your snoring," said Brett. "I'm not sleeping beside you in Nauro tonight."

It mattered not that it was a Monday. Day three on the trail since Owers' Corner was what we tracked. We started our day at Ioribaiwa Village, somewhat confusingly heading on our morning quest to where a different place of the same name existed during the war, nearer to the actual Ioribaiwa Ridge. The morning drill was set: bolt awake to song; stuff packs; visit latrine; wash-up; biscuits, freshly toasted; and boot camp. None of us committed a clumsy move. I picked up a slice of fire-crisped *pâté*, pretended the Arnott's biscuit was a baguette, and enjoyed every mouthful. I went back for more. Then we assembled in an array of styles; varying shorts and jerseys, boots and gaiters—looking less coordinated than we were.

Rod led the warm-up with a big man's penchant for push-ups and long leg stretches. He rotated side to side with his hands on his hips. This time he led the extended sports chant, garnering our full rejoinder.

"Aussie, Aussie, Aussie."

"Oi, Oi, Oi!"

Rod was faster, louder: "Aussie! Aussie! Aussie!"

We were full of ourselves: "Oi! Oi! Oi!"

Clocks ticked to 5:58 a.m. Woody shouted that it was time to leave. *Steep* can become an overused word, but no other entered my mind. Pools of mud or dried earth had sifted between the roots to form natural stairs. The first hour was more about pulling oneself uphill than hiking. We made for the mountaintop. We were energized and rose with the mountain, meeting its demands. We just kept climbing. "If it gets more difficult than this, I may have problems," said one of the Kokoda Club Med.

"This part of the trail tests your heart, tests your legs, tests your mindset," Brett told him. "This is the stretch that trekkers are often thinking of when they say that they wondered why they came along."

We finally reached our morning goal, Ioribaiwa Ridge. "Let the war story become visible to each of you now," Brett began. "General Horii and his soldiers hunkered down here while awaiting orders to capture the port facilities. You can tell for yourselves, they were that close. One Japanese captain wrote, 'At night we are able to see the lights of Port Moresby, and the beam of the searchlight of Seven Mile Airfield on the outskirts.'"

Brett reminded us as we rested on the ridge, "Yesterday I mentioned that Hyakutake had deployed his resources at Guadalcanal while putting the attack on Moresby on hold." With that he glanced at Yeoy, who said, "The Japanese had not prepared a back map. Indeed, the Japanese language has no word for 'retreat.'[21] And so the officers at Ioribaiwa Ridge were commanded to turn around and 'advance to the rear.'"

During the days while Australians waited in foxholes at Imita Ridge, battle-hardened reinforcements from the European and African fronts had arrived to bolster their strength and their morale. Maroubra Force was now 3,000 strong. If the Australians had known how few Japanese were facing them, how hard up they'd become, they likely would have advanced earlier.

---

21 The travel gods allow guides and authors leeway when recounting well-turned phrases that leave the listener amused. The gods of history, however, require veracity. As a historian friend pointed out to me later, the Japanese actually did have a word for retreat, *taikyaku*.

We were ready to move off Ioribaiwa Ridge, following in the difficult steps of the Aussie Advance of 1942. "Take a moment to look at that plaque," said Brett before we left. He pointed to the ground. I was nearest, and peered at the name of Ian Bergman, a trekker like myself. He died here in June of 2006 from a heart attack brought on by the strenuous exertion climbing to the ridge. It had undoubtedly crossed the mind of each member of our party: Would one of us end up like Bergman?

Whether working your way up on a hill climb or creeping down a perilous slope, you cannot rush walking the Kokoda Trail. My muscles never wanted to, and my heart certainly didn't either. An experienced trekker friend figured his average rate of progress on the trail was less than a mile an hour. His total hiking was 65 miles over 70 hours. When I was on long hikes as a Boy Scout, oh-so-many years ago, we had what was called "Scout's pace," which meant, even on a bush trail, aiming for three miles an hour. That's also not uncommon city-walking for adults. Try walking up your street at a mile an hour. Snail slow. Yet it's considered a good pace on the Kokoda Trail.

Moving down off the ridge was tough. Heels slipped unless one propped a walking pole, found a branch to hold on to, or took sideways steps with extra care. Rating the angle of a hillside is guesswork rounded by experience. Yeoy tagged where we were descending as a 30- to 50-degree incline. We were on this steepness for the better part of an hour before arriving beside Ofi Creek. First onto the creek bank were Woody, Jim (with Kipling), and Monk (tailed by Kingsole).

We were in for a swim. It was only 9 a.m. but we were sticky with sweat. Streams cascaded together. Rod fell in with such force that anyone within a dozen feet was splashed. He dunked himself and rose out quickly, shaking and spraying like a dog. It was an enviable sight, and I tried to replicate it in a haphazard attempt to fully submerge. Five of us swirled to get underwater in one of the pools where it was a foot or two deep, and crowded one another out just in time for Tori and Kristy to shallow-sink. The creek was 30 feet wide. God, it was cold.

We were all parched, and the water was inviting to drink. Simon spurted a mouthful of it, high and off to shore. We'd not been given any reason for concern about water bugs or critters in such pools, though we were warned not to be swallowing untreated water. Parasites may be at play. And one does not know how the water has just been used by villagers upstream. In a creek such as this one, water was clean-looking and fresh, but any that we drank had to first be purified, however thirsty we were or however refreshing it looked. Even periodic gut revolt ruins a trip, particularly if it's one with intense walking. And that was avoidable if we followed prescribed practice and didn't gulp the creek water, despite the temptation.

We bounced out of the chill to be greeted with steaming Cup-a-Soups, which replenished our spirits. A trailside fire burned and, across it, a pot hung above the flames. We were refreshed to tackle the upcoming long and tough climb in the Maguli Range.

Within the hour we stopped where the Japanese once had a defense setup dug into the hillside, its purpose to slow the advancing Aussies while the bulk of Japanese troops retreated further toward the beaches. Their position would have given them a fair view of incoming Aussie soldiers. Today we witnessed the eroding network where the Japanese were able to move about in connecting trenches. But we didn't languish. Next was heart-pumping hours of merciless up, followed by a near equal slog down. Then, more up. My map designated the first section as "very steep," followed by merely "steep" for the following one. Such guidance was instructional, not inspirational, and also a bit illusional.

Every half hour or so, Woody held his shovel high and signaled a break. This gave more rest for the frontrunners, and less for the stragglers who caught up around the time the leaders were anxious to move on. Woody was generous to all. But soon enough came his familiar countdown to muscle pain: "Two minutes." By noon, everyone was exhausted from the constant climbing up or climbing down. We arrived at a clearing and were greeted by porters who'd moved on ahead and prepared lunch for us. They'd started a cooking fire and set up a wooden table decorated with newly picked flowers. A large bowl steamed with noodles swirling in a powder-to-tasty-sauce mix that pretended to be beef. We eagerly held our bowls out in front of the porter-cooks, and the meal was spooned out in friendly quantities. We grabbed biscuits by the handful, as there were plenty. There was a range of make-your-own soup packets: chicken noodle, beef in a broth, and tomato. This break came after having hiked five hours since breakfast. Kokoda Club Med slipped camp-stools from their packs, sprung them up, and sat eating, relaxed. Monk passed around snacks not so much as dessert, but as a sugar jump to the system. Deirdre summed up our benefit: "Good food, good mood." She liked the culinary sampling as well: "The Kokoda in six bites."

After lunch was cleared, we climbed one of the trail's epic sections, the so-called Japanese Ladder. We were mindful of the remains of Japanese trenches dug on either side of the trail and back into the hill-side. Their shallowness didn't offer much protection. Even the deeper ones were exposed to rushing soldiers and splattering shrapnel. We slowed long enough to look, contemplate, and shake our heads. We moved on and up with the hikers' mantra: "One foot ahead of the other. Keep going."

Trudging up, Darren asked, "Anyone else can't breathe?"

"You're breathing?" said Michael.

Within the hour, we got to Maguli's peak, at 4,281 feet. The view rolled away in a pleasing vista.

While we were resting ("recovering" is how Michael S put it), Tori brought her camera out to document our accomplishments. Seeing this, Brett remarked about contrasting images from contrasting times. "No one made more important pictures of the Kokoda drama than Damien Parer. But they were of war's mischance, not of today's beauty."

"Who?" Kieran asked, on behalf of us all. Well, Parer was an Australian cinematographer who won an American Academy Award for his movie *Kokoda Front Line!* The potential of such an award, how-ever, was never an inducement for him to make the film. His moti-vation was to jolt Australian citizens out of the complacency he saw when returning home from the jungle fighting in Papua. Parer, then the army's chief photographer, made the film in 1942. It was based around footage he'd taken along the Kokoda Track, showing live action of Australian soldiers under attack. It portrays the venerable Papuan carriers, christened Fuzzy Wuzzy Angels. Frame after frame, the film conveys the rigors of combat as well as honor and courage. Parer narrated the film, at one point saying to the theater audience, "I know what your husbands, brothers, and sweethearts are going through." A movie studio completed the film using additional footage unrelated to Kokoda but relevant to New Guinea campaigns, edited in for dramatic effect. The changes irritated Parer for their loss of authenticity in pursuit of emotional leverage over the home crowds, but his efforts to reverse their decisions were overruled. Audiences knew not of the fabrications. In the days before the advent of television, the film attracted line-ups at movie theaters and was screened in auditoriums overflowing with anxious viewers.

The film did achieve Parer's objective, though. It earned public respect for those fighting on the track, and banished public indifference. It brought home the threat of an imminent Japanese invasion of Australia. Unfortunately, Parer also dueled with bureaucratic pettiness. He wanted to return and photograph frontline soldiers to further convey their abominable surroundings, insurmountable odds, and heroism in battle. Job one, in Parer's view, was garnering ongoing public support for troops facing an overwhelming enemy with outdated equipment and a shortage of supplies. But his opinions were routinely belittled and censored by those in command. This grew worse with the film's popularity, as Parer became internationally recognized as a celebrity war correspondent.

The American producer David O. Selznick was president of the Academy of Motion Picture Arts and Sciences when Parer's work was brought to his attention. Moved by the film's depiction of war in a little-known land, Selznick urged that a new Academy Award be created in 1942–43, for Best Documentary. The winner was *Kokoda Front Line!* The recognition exacerbated Parer's fraying relationship with Australia's

Department of Information. His "star status" overshadowed the political profile of his superiors.

In November 1943, the United Service Organization (USO) brought the Hollywood actor Gary Cooper to New Guinea to headline an entertainment show for Allied forces. Parer and Cooper met, and Cooper told Parer: "We shall find most of our gold in the hidden details [. . .] by watching carefully, noting expression and gestures, and shooting circumspectly at the dead right moment."

The Australian military no longer granted Parer access to his own gritty images, curtailing his ability to tell the story as he saw it. Frustrated, and sensing more media openness, he instead teamed up with the Americans, which ended in his death. In September 1944, he was at Peleliu, a 5.5-mile stretch located in the Palau Archipelago to the north of New Guinea and the east of the Philippines. He was covering "a little island landing" of US Marines. The Battle of Peleliu[22] would become one of the costliest victories in the Pacific Theater of War. Parer spent the first night there in a hastily dug foxhole. By morning, the Japanese remained unmoved by air strikes and bombardments from US Navy ships. The Marines were ready to advance.

Two days after the landing, the deeply religious Parer said a quick personal mass on his last day alive. He boiled water for his "breakfast billy." With tea over, the 33-year-old entered the fray to photograph the fighting. An American tank was positioned to lead, crossing an isthmus 100 yards long and half that in width. The Japanese protected it from wooded areas on either side. Parer walked backwards while filming the American advance; the tank at his back was his only protection. His camera rolled during the assault, chronicling American faces of hope, fear, and inevitability.

---

22 In the Battle of Peleliu, 1,794 Americans were killed, while another 8,040 were wounded or reported missing. It was among the highest rate of casualties during an amphibious assault, comparable with Saipan, Iwo Jima, and Okinawa. And it was a costly victory in terms of other resources as well: each Japanese death resulted from over 1,500 rounds of US ammunition.

Suddenly, Japanese gunfire peppered Parer, the burst dislodging his cam-era.[23] The Marines advanced around his dead body, his camera stilled.

Our rest in the Maguli Range was nearing its end. I pulled out my map and waved over Brett. Woody came with him. We were preparing to descend again, heading to our planned camp at New Nauro Village.

"Let's talk about the 'false peaks,'" I said, pointing to where the map identified "nine false peaks" between here and the village.

"In a way, we have it a bit easier," Brett began. "We're heading north, so working our way down them. Well, up and down them. But psycho-logically, we're working down them. That's why the map shows us starting at number nine. If you were heading southward as the Japanese advance did, or as the Australian fighting withdrawal did, you'd approach the peak of the Maguli Range—here, where we sit—from wartime Nauro Village. It consistently looked to them as if they were about to crest the peak of the path, but every time a soldier stood on top, there was another peak ahead. They didn't see this peak of Maguli until they stood just below where we are, atop their ninth disappointment."

Woody, perhaps sensing we'd like to get on with it, shouted, "Two minutes."

We shuffled into the kunai grass toward the ninth false peak, and then tackled the rest in descending order. The eighth came into view. Each time the hill changed to up, we wished for the down. And when it changed to down, we wished for the up. No one seemed truly unhappy, though. This was what we came for.

---

23 In Neil Mcdonald's book *Kokoda Front Line*, he writes that, when Parer's body was found, after the isthmus was secured, "Souvenir-hunting marines had plundered the corpse'. The camera had been opened and around Damien's body were the reels of his unspooled film, and empty film cans." A reel of valuable film about the Peleliu assault was later found in Parer's bag. Reportedly, a chagrined soldier later returned the single reel that is now believed lost in archive storage in Washington, DC.

Fatigue is a dangerous companion for the hiker. There were slips. There were bumps. Shortly after 3 p.m., we were setting up camp at New Nauro Village. It had been nine difficult hours since leaving our camp at Ioribaiwa that morning. We were ready to lie back. First, though, we each had to sort shelter and lay out sleeping mats and provisions. Porters ensured each trekker had what they needed. Others started fires for preparing dinner.

There were villagers about but they were not entrepreneurial, and did not ask for money in exchange for local crafts or imported colas. The trail was here because they were here, and we were here because of the trail. They had not come *because* of the trail. A few kids looked on but did not kick their soccer ball our way, nor come closer to inspect the trekkers' skin color; our kind was no longer an oddity. I thought this behavior was more their expression of acceptance than indifference.

Like in other remote parts of the world, I'd found villagers to be generally welcoming. Most did not feel they had to display themselves to convey their friendliness. But there was also no sense in those places or here that the locals wished my vacation to be their responsibility. They treated us simply as people passing through one's home. The local culture is mostly unbothered by the chore of hosting strangers, without any thought we'd one day reciprocate for them in our homes. Here, though, on this night, I found myself wishing to enjoy the silliness of curious children, and wondered if they once were like that before being rebuked by tired trekkers, or if their parents kept them away from sometimes rude foreigners.

We stretched along the grass hillock overlooking our dirt site with the A-framed tarp covering Kokoda Club Med's site. Wet shirts and shorts draped over a clothesline hung off the side of our shelter and strung to a tree. Swum-in underwear and socks hung on sticks near the cooking fire, to the dismay of some. Five southbound trekkers and their porters trickled into our site. They mingled right away, one asking me, "What's tomorrow going to be like for us?"

"Well, I can tell you about the nine false peaks," I began.

"No thanks. I'd rather sleep tonight."

The afternoon wore into dinner. Before us was a big bowl of Kraft Dinner with its make-believe cheese. A separate dish contained elongated pasta with veggie sauce. There are many ways to camouflage noodles. We ate heartily, as there was lots. I sat to the left of Monk, who dabbed soy sauce on his food and passed along the container he'd brought. He gave it off to his right, and it was empty by the time it reached around to me. I took out a small container of tarragon flakes and sprinkled.

The table centerpiece had become a shared pile with sleeves of sugar, containers of instant coffee, packets of tea, boxes of powdered soups, and salt, pepper, and hot chocolate. I tossed the spice bottle and my remaining supply of dill in as well.

In early October of '42, MacArthur made a flying visit to Port Moresby. The general needed to get more troops into position if they were to be successful in pushing the Japanese back to the ocean. Allied intelligence learned of a route between Moresby and the Northern Beaches, one overlooked by the Japanese. It was to become known as the Kapa Kapa Trail.[24] MacArthur sent more than 900 Americans from the Red Arrow battalion over this poorly-charted territory. The Americans hiked 120 miles of incredible difficulty, its purpose and grueling circumstances seldom referenced by the American public today.

The trail abutted 10,000-foot-high Mount Obree. Natives feared the mountain because it glowed at night, a phosphorus reaction from moss in the forest. Natives called it "*Suwemalla*," and knew it to be frequented by *masalai*, or evil spirits. The Americans had their own name for it: Ghost Mountain.

---

24 This pathway to the east of the Kokoda Track had been called the Gaba Gaba Track after the village at the southern terminus, until that name was Americanized to Kapa Kapa Trail. Since it ends in the north at the village of Jaure, it has also been known as the Jaure Trail.

This American contingent was made up of young men never intended for such a hostile environment. Many came from the Wisconsin or Michigan National Guard. They were poorly equipped, and had received inadequate training—none of it related to jungle warfare. They plunged on without machetes or water boots. Blisters festered, mosquitoes pestered.

In mid-November, after a 42-day trek, they arrived two miles away from Japanese-held Buna. The troops were dehydrated and demoralized. Their reputation of valor was earned through wilderness survival rather than by skirmishes won, as there had been none of the latter. Still, they were sent immediately into the Battle of Buna-Gona.

When tales from their crossing of Kapa Kapa spread, they became known as The Ghost Mountain Boys.

Our Nauro Village camp that evening had an air of tiredness. Phil massaged his left leg's calf while smiling with satisfaction, saying, "I don't know much, but I know this hurts." Thankfully, there were no mozzies. We were at too high an altitude to be bothered by the pests. It made holding a mug of hot chocolate or lying on the grass propped up by one's elbow more enjoyable. I found it interesting to learn that butterflies handle higher altitudes better than mosquitos.

Later, around the fire, Jim was set to reminisce about the day. He stayed seated, though, explaining, "I'd stand if I could." Trekkers chuckled. "You all know what you did today, and I would not have changed a thing." He let the air hold his pause. Then, "Well, I would have taken two Advil before the day's hike and two midday, and two with dinner." We laughed. There could be a profitable trade here in muscle relaxants.

Jim settled, and found an important voice within him. "What you won't know is what's going through my mind. I'm so glad my two sons are here with me. But it's more than that. It's that my boys aren't off fighting a war they may never come home from. That's what I think about every step of the trek." The worth of his words settled on each of us and, as I have two sons, into the family corner of my heart. "Anyway, that's what I'm thinking about when I'm not thinking about plumbing," he added gruffly.

Kieran said, "And when you're not being headhunted by cannibals." Brett-the-arbiter broke off the talk effectively, if prematurely, by saying, "Cannibalism isn't always why people headhunted." Instantly, the night got darker. The wind stilted, and we fell silent. The fire crackled loudly, but couldn't brighten the mood. Then Kieran asked, "What's the difference?"

The practice of collecting heads of dead enemies is of a long tradition.[25] Where it occurred, including in Papua New Guinea, headhunting demonstrated having won a fight, with the victor showing off the victim. It was proof of death, or for a tally, as illustrated by the Native American practice of scalping. It was usually intentional rather than indiscriminate, such as seeking out adversaries in a war, or a person of interest because of their prestige. Headhunting was a symbol of manhood, and did not always involve consumption of the victim's flesh. That said, whole tribes often sat around celebratory fires after vanquishing neighbors on the local battlefield, and sometimes dined on the corpses after severing the souvenir parts. The head-as-trophy art was competitive within tribes, or between tribes. Often to better show them off, ornaments were attached to the cleaned skulls. Skulls might be displayed at birth, or at rite-of-passage ceremonies.

In comparison, cannibalism often demonstrates the dominance of one spirit over another. The academic designation is anthropophagy, "the eating of human flesh by human beings." The act of cannibalism provides muscle-building protein, and has the health advantages of a dietary supplement. Premeditated cannibalism as a rite seems quite

---

25 In fact, "trophy skulls" made a passing appearance among US soldiers during the Vietnam War.

separate from circumstantial cannibalism—an act arising in war or a remote airplane crash where one is forced between the appalling choice of surviving or starving. Anthropological studies tell us there's a difference between a society's willingness to practice necro-cannibalism, which is "eating of the already dead," as compared to the practice of stalking another human being with the intention of killing him or her for provision as food, either for the hunter or through a flesh market. Both premeditated cannibalism and circumstantial cannibalism have occurred in North America, Africa, Europe, Asia, and elsewhere, including the South Pacific. While no longer an active occurrence, the ritual of cannibalism was known to occur in Papua New Guinea as recent as 2012, referenced as an expression of culture.

Despite happening much less frequently than common stereotypes suggest, tales of indiscriminate anthropophagy in faraway regions of the world persist in Western culture, and when a Westerner goes missing in a remote jungle, it's often speculated they've been taken by headhunting cannibals.

I wondered: was it macabre fascination, rather than a search for knowledge, that drew Westerners like Kieran and myself to stories about cannibalism? The journalist Carl Hoffman compared the Asmat traditions in New Guinea with Christian and Islamic practices. "Headhunting and cannibalism were as right to them as taking communion or kneeling on a carpet facing Mecca."

It was well after midnight when I woke, and promptly forgot where the latrine was. Being a guy, it was handy—near the hillside jungle, but out of earshot. Walking back, I *felt* the sky—a sense the universe had singled me out for stalking. I stood alone in the dark, open to the heavens. I felt apprehensive. The jungle and fear merged. Little scare-things collected: fear of failing the trek, fear of getting ill, and the fear of being afraid of fear. Add the recent fireside talk's unnecessary fear of headhunters and cannibals.

I creaked my way along the shelter's wood floor to my bed. Alone and awake, the unnecessary fear pestered me. While not a common practice during World War II, headhunting also occurred in Asian battlefields, as did cannibalism along the Kokoda Track and the Northern Beaches. Some among the Allies were known to collect Japanese skulls as keepsakes, perhaps to show off once they returned home (demonstrating that so-called civilized societies wishing to demonstrate their prowess were not so unlike headhunters of the past). Apparently this did not happen during the German or Italian campaigns, but only in Asia. The practice was prevalent enough that in September 1942, Admiral Chester Nimitz, commander of the Allied Pacific Fleet, issued an edict forbidding troops to acquire enemy body parts as souvenirs.

The second before Brett's clock music was to wink us awake, Simon's blared a rap rendition of the Elvis hit, "A little less conversation, a little more action please." It set the tone for our day. Morning ceremonies were quickly completed, porridge downed, coffee taken.

"Where to?" asked Anthony, as we looked over the map sprawled across the breakfast table.

"If it's Tuesday, it's Menari," Yeoy said. It was our fourth day on the trail and most of us remained only casually familiar with upcoming place names. "It's a special place," said Brett. "Worth keeping that in mind as you struggle on the climb." I asked Bowrie for a refill of hot water from the big pail on the fire he tended. He scooped deep into the pot as though searching for the best part. He poured the water over my instant coffee flakes, all smiles. I smiled back my appreciation.

Simon led the pre-hike workout as a mock seniors' fitness session. The lack of push-ups suited me, as did the standing in position leaning, bending, and stretching.

"Two minutes," Simon shouted, his second preemption of the morning.

We took the path through and out of the village without having ever met our overnight guardians. They got a little cash from our leaders, as did each village that hosted us.

No level part of the Kokoda Trail lasts long, except near the Brown River where we were approaching (and much later, just before Kokoda Station). We walked by abandoned memories of wartime Nauro, another village resituated after its military purpose ended. Papuans along Kokoda Trail move their villages every twenty years or so, a habit that brings new garden lands and a renewed sense of purpose. Though it's overgrown, Nauro's airstrip was once an important supply drop for the Douglas C-47 transports, "Biscuit Bombers," that could deliver two tons of rations. Supplies included potatoes, sausages, and mutton, dehydrated in a way that unfortunately sucked out most of the vitamins as well. Tinned fruit didn't hold up much better. Butter and jam barely brought life to listless bread. This was, however, nourishment the troops needed, the standard ration. Japan's famished fighters sometimes found large caches of food left behind by retreating Australians. In some cases, the abandoned provisions had been intentionally contaminated.

We trekked the Nauro River swamp, in the Brown River catchment. When the trail was wider, I walked among the Kokoda Club Med guys. The forest was matted. By comparison with 1942, our trekking struggles were not worth mentioning, but they were ours. In the heavy rains, swamplands of the Nauro River Flats cover everywhere one needs to pass, and the clay track itself is dangerously slippery. Enjoying the brief respite of level ground, Anthony said, "We're getting off easy. Especially today. So far." About then, we reconnoitered the fast flow of the Brown River from a pebbly riverbank.

We'd already crossed many of the eleven creeks or rivers Brett had said we'd need to. This one was among the widest. A logjam of trees lay like pick-up sticks, straddling one bank to the other 60 feet away. Those trunks, trees, and branches had been uprooted in storms. Rushing waters carried them until they grounded. Wind and high water had made a walkway for us, fashioned by locals. Four porters made their sure-footed

After a rain, the path becomes a quagmire. Improvising is a constant companion along the trail, and not every water crossing was bridgeable; you walked, or waded, or balanced on logs.

way across the thicker pieces, crawling hand-over-foot in certain places where water had ripped bark from the trees. Bowrie and Kingsole strung a rope from a stump near where we stood. It passed across the logs at hand height for a walker, then was tied to sturdy branches to keep it taut. The porters took our daypacks so we could cross, unencumbered by anything that could shift weight and topple us into the river. Not one trekker took for granted their carefulness or thoughtfulness, as either could be lifesaving.

Kingsole stood in knee-high water, not far beyond the logjam. He held a coiled rope with a small piece of wood tied to it as a weight, in case he needed to toss a lifeline to one of the trekkers. He swung it nonchalantly. Like any canoeist, I am leery of logjams because of their powerful ability to suction the paddler into a trap. If one was to fall from the bridge, it was better to do so into the downstream rapids, away from the logs.

Robert crossed first. We watched worriedly. The log was glistening wet. Each step gained him only a foot of log, then he would shuffle his other foot closer and repeat the process, with only occasional bark for his boot tread to grab. Halfway across, his right foot failed to get purchase, and he slipped and almost teetered off the log. The guide rope took his weight as the porters at either end brought it tighter. Kingsole moved closer, his lifeline in tossing position. Robert stayed steady. Those of us on shore all exhaled audibly in unison.

Monk crossed early, too, and once off he went near Kingsole, camera at the ready. That someone would fall seemed inevitable. Later he looked disappointed not to have snapped a photo of someone splashing into the water, but he knew it was for the best; any fall was a potential catastrophe. I made my way across—at one point kneeling into the log for balance.

On the other side I saw porters drifting down the path out of sight. Some of them had taken to leaving us alone to rest while they sang to themselves. Sometimes a few of them would move on down the trail with their heavier packs of goods in order to ready a cooking fire or the night camp. Monk caught up to them as they were leaving, making sure no one missed out on the chocolates he was passing around. Then he walked back to where I sat on a log, picking its bark off in strips. "I'm tired," he said. "Downhill's rugged. Didn't sleep last night." That was as close as he would ever come to complaining.

I looked over to Yeoy trolling his bottle in the creek nearby, and saw him cap it. "You drop in a purifier?"

"Company policy is—"

I cut him short. "Yeoy, just the answer. Did you?"

To change the subject, he pointed at a prickly plant and called it "Wait-a-while," which I took to mean if you scrubbed against it the irritation would not be immediate. His foil worked. I was easily distracted.

We came upon a village that expected us, or expected someone, as there were crisps on offer, and Fanta soda cans in a bucket of cold water, for sale. Everything was displayed alongside flowers on an old shipping skid that must have arrived in a plane drop; it was that large and out of place, and would have been impossible to pack in unless dismantled. The dozen homes looked built to public park specifications of orderliness. Unlike the previous night, kids appeared, shyly at first. They were easily won over by the most gregarious parents within our group, Jim and Tori. Jim bought crisps and shared them with the kids. He pulled chocolate-covered breadsticks from his pack. Tori gravitated to kids the same ages of her own two children, and they came willingly and curiously to a foreign mom. Refreshed, we walked on with misplaced confidence in our stamina.

Later in the morning, Yeoy was with Woody, hiking in the lead, when the Papuan dug his shovel into the ground. Everyone came to a halt. Woody smiled, white teeth against the pinking stain of betel nuts. Slowly, Yeoy's head turned and looked past where we had stalled. His eyes looked up. Then he slowly moved his head around to make eye contact with each of us. He offered the same smile as Woody's, without the stain.

"The Wall," Yeoy announced. The mountainside ahead of us leaned at an unfavorable angle. "Rest," Woody said. Yeoy ignored him, as though he'd been given a cue instead of direction. "I've a challenge for those of you up to it." There was a stamping of feet behind me.

Simon was first to take the bait. "What challenge?"

"Anyone game for a race to the top?" Yeoy said.

"We're going up that?" asked Phil, looking as were the rest of us for a trail around it. Yeoy nodded, and made no move to get rid of his pack.

"Up The Wall?" asked Tori, possibly thinking as a nurse that she'd have a heart attack victim or two on her hands. Yeoy looked past her. His eyes settled on Michael, who smiled back. Two of the porters shrugged their packs as a racehorse would a saddle to make sure it's snug. They moved closer to Yeoy. My eyes darted to Kieran. He had the grin and stance of a competitor. Yeoy again: "You're all going to climb The Wall. Only difference is a matter of how long it takes you."

We'd been aware of this climb since we saw it on the breakfast-table map. It takes most hikers forty-five minutes to an hour to complete. Brett had warned, "If there are one or two of your muscles not yet aching, this is where you'll hear from them."

"I've done it in twenty minutes," Yeoy teased. "But that was keeping up to legs younger than any of yours."

Simon and Kieran and Martin started to put their packs on the ground. "I meant with packs on," Yeoy said. And with that—he ran. It was a dart so fast even the porters were surprised. Two porters chased him, as did Simon, Kieran, and Martin, adjusting their packs on the run. Kristy came out of nowhere, her strides long and quick. Michael took a deep breath and, before others were ten feet ahead, he too was off.

The burst of energy was palpable. They hit the cliffside, and it was knees up. You could see their strides shorten, but all of them kept running. Push. Push. Yelps turned to gulps. Woody pulled his gaze away from the disappearing trekkers, but kept his smile. "Two minutes." Gee, thanks for the rest, I thought. We retied boots as necessary, haltered up, and sucked on sugar snakes. We took swigs of water.

"Rule Number One ascending The Wall," Brett told us before starting, "is don't look up."

"Rule Number Two?" I asked.

"It's also 'don't look up.'"

"On trail," said Bowrie, who had chosen to hike behind me in case I fell. It was handholds and toeholds all the way. Everyone was in a constant state of grasping, hauling one's self up, and having your face in the heels of the person in front of you. If you stopped a moment, you'd be bumped from behind and knocked off to the side. If you stood straight to rest, it was so steep you could topple over.

We climbed hand over hand. It took a lot of ankle strength to force our bodies forward so we could reach branches to pull on. Switchbacks were brief. "There's a shortcut," said Brett, taking a rock climb to position above us. Several porters, including Winterford and his guitar, went with him. Twenty minutes into our climb, we heard a yelp from the top. "Race over," Tori yelled. Jim said, "That was Kieran's scream." Then another victory shout followed by a chorus of praise. The pounding of my heart doubled when I stopped to quaff air. Catch a breath, any breath. I could not imagine the full-throttle heartbeats of those at the top. The hurt of doing this, up or down, in 1942, Japanese or Australian or Papuan, enemy or friend—with a 50-pound pack, plus ammunition and a firearm—was unfathomable to me. Then I thought about a soldier doing it two or three times in a row to shunt gear. It seemed impossible, until you remembered that thousands of them did so. The wounded had to be carried over this precarious hillside as well.

Jim was perched to the side of the trail, bending forward. "I'd throw up if I could."

As we neared the crest, we heard first the guitar and then the singing. Porters climbing among us sang along. I had no lung for song. The Papuan singers congratulated us when we reached them. The racers were lined out, hands raised in slapping-palm greetings as each of us panted over the hilltop's lip. Winterford and his guitar sprang louder with each new arrival. Voices joined with him, none more so than when Deirdre, Phil, Robert, and Michael S arrived, inspiring us all with their guts and tenacity. Every one of us had made it. There had been no choice.

The hill's top had room to space out or keel over to savor the moment. We could see Mount Victoria, and better yet was the view of where we were headed. Race results were circulating. Michael's 22 minutes clipped right with Yeoy's. "I'm very happy with that," said Michael, with a gentleman's grace not to add that Yeoy had a head start.

"Beat that," said Simon.

"Beat you," said Kieran, having won the lot with a time of 18 minutes.

Yeoy said, "Nice work, everyone. All up here in an hour's time. Once, in the rain, it took our group over three hours. We roped together to make that happen. Count yourselves to be a weather-lucky bunch."

I followed Winterford into the woods where he'd led the porters so we trekkers could be alone in our self-congratulations. His music was alive, but no longer pumped up for our benefit. Out of politeness, I stopped out of sight of the porters. I listened from behind a tree. Porters sang, and I wished I had known their words. They were soothing. I looked around the tree and saw all the porters together, some fixing packs, others pushing gear into better balance. Every one of them made duty seem commonplace. They all sang the same song.

"Two minutes," Woody shouted from behind me. I returned to where my daypack lay on the ground.

Monk suddenly appeared. "Made it, mate," he said.

"Some *walk* across the country," I said.

We hiked on surefootedly, a confidence of accomplishment in our step. The ridgeline was steep. The air was cooler but constraining. When we reached the mountaintop, we stood in the Menari Gap. From this vantage, we looked out and down on a distant Menari Village where we hoped to make camp. As one might have expected, having clung our way up a steep mountainside, it was a likewise steep descent to the valley below. Almost from the start we saw another village that appeared close by, but that was an illusion. Even when we felt we must be getting nearer to it, there were switchbacks that made the journey longer than we'd thought. I found the false crests on the Kokoda Trail recurring in this deceptive way. We'd often feel good hiking with the crest of a ridge in sight, and then realize it was not to be—another waited for us beyond, and often another after that. This happened downhill too, but it was most off-putting when on steep climbs.

Walking to Menari, it dawned on me that I had no consistent place in the line of walkers. I'd done everything from straggling near the end to bolting to the front with Woody on some start-ups after a break. At other times—and by now there had been many segments of our journey—I found myself at varying positions, depending on a conversation underway or a pebble in my boot. Now there was no doubt to me that the sweet spot on the trek was somewhere ahead of Winterford, so his music motivated me, yet within sight of Woody's leadership shovel.

I heard a whipbird. This distinctive sound had been new to me a year ago when I first heard it in Australia. Its whip-snap sound is unmistakably that of a whip lashing in the air. It sounded to be in the near distance. Few birds have so appropriate a name. While I was watching for its appearance, Winterford and Bowrie stood near, curious at my awe over an everyday occurrence for them.

"Are you two snickering at me?" I said, lightly.

"What snickering mean, Rick?" It wasn't a question Bowrie wanted answered; it was a conversational enjoiner. Instead, they had something to share they thought I'd find interesting. They leaned against one another. Winterford said, pointing, "Bowrie's father is my father's son." I tripped on that wording, and asked Winterford, "You are his uncle?" "Yes, his father is my brother," said Winterford. "We all one village."

We arrived in Menari to a colorful greeting. It seemed all its 250 villagers were dressed in native fashions and Oxfam donations. What was more, there were tables of cut-up bananas and pineapples. Their crafts, such as clothing, souvenirs, or playthings, were on sale. Woven bags hung on pegs. Brett called, "Want to know it or not, you're halfway.

Being in Menari means you're twenty-five hours into a fifty-hour walk, or forty hours into an eighty-hour walk, weather adjusted. We're making good time, so closer to the former."

A few buildings were painted yellow, having an administrative appearance. An outhouse stood in a prominent position on the margin of a cliff, signed "Krappers 4 Kokoda." It had thatch-woven sides around a composting toilet. Three sides were walled in. A curtain hung over the doorway. Inside was a Western-style toilet base and seat complete with a lid, but no flushing mechanism. A large window formed the fourth side, boasting a full wall's open-air view to the jungle. Panther made his way to this facility. The field of his mates erupted with a cheer. When he reappeared minutes later, he announced "No luck," a disappointment shared by all who were monitoring his ordeal. Tori provided him with laxatives since the need could become dire, and we were in camp for the night, giving him a manageable response time.

One of the world's great swimming holes was down the embankment where the creek did not widen and boulders forced it to form pools. It was deep. Half-dressed or fully-clothed, we needed to wash off the perspiration that chafed our skin. Yeoy was first into the water; perhaps the rest of us second-guessed the shock of cold while he accepted it. Rod, Simon, Kieran, Brett, and myself were next, Kristy and Tori not far behind. We rotated through the plunge pool so everyone had a turn at full immersion, and then each settled into a smaller pool of his or her own to soak. I sat in the rapids enjoying the cold massage on sore muscles.

Cricket is a national pastime in Papua New Guinea, and who better to match up against than the Aussies? The grass opening was large enough for a makeshift cricket field. With camp set and gear stowed, this day finally found us in shape to play. A Porters versus Trekkers match took place off the side of our tent site and in front of the bunkhouse. I was new to the sport, but the others were proficient. The bowler set to bowl with the village's well-worn ball, the finest specimen on hand. The batsman used a piece of firewood. The rotation of players started. It was not long before I was goaded to bowl. I used an overhand pitch honed during years of playing baseball. That did nothing for the game. "Illegal throw," came a call out while I was in windup. Someone shouted, "Chucking." The batter swung anyway. With my sin exposed I was moved to batsman in hopes I'd be less embarrassing—or perhaps more entertaining, I was unsure which, but my combination of golf and baseball swings did little for my aim either. One harmless hit went astray. My next one connected. As the ball sailed high and away, Bowrie ran backwards in the field and made a nearly impossible one-handed catch. I took the cheers as my nudge to the sidelines.

Menari holds a special place in Kokoda lore. While it is easy to jumble designations for military troops deployed along the Kokoda Track, one stuck unconfused in my mind: Australia's Thirty-Ninth Infantry Battalion. "Formed in haste," it was made of men only eighteen or nineteen years old. These were the citizen soldiers assigned to garrison duty in Australian cities, never expecting frontline engagement, those referred to on our first evening as "Koalas." Their training was light and soon shown to be inadequate. Their uniforms were more appropriate for urban wear than in the humid jungle. Their weapons were from World War I and ill-suited to modern warfare. They were untried, untested, and unfit soldiers sent into battle against some of the Japanese army's best provisioned and most experienced soldiers. These Aussie troops were called "Chocos," insinuating that they were, in the name of a contemporary play, "chocolate soldiers"—ready to melt in Papua's tropical climate or wilt from the heat of battle. That was a fair assessment of their stature and the odds they faced, but it was to prove a misnomer when it came to their character, innovation, and tenacity. Within months, they had learned what Matthiessen called "the niceties of war and ambush." To the amazement of anyone who had ever mocked them, the Thirty-Ninth became known as "one of the greatest fighting forces Australia ever sent to war."

As the lyrics to Slim Dusty's "Kokoda Track" song put it for the folks back home, they "marched and fought and died." Early in the conflict, at Isurava, they held their ground for days and were mere hours from being overrun when fresh troops relieved them. Reinforced, they were able to mount a fighting withdrawal to Menari, which was where we camped in relaxed fashion that evening, aware of and moved by their bravery: 125 of their 433 mates had been killed or wounded. When the withdrawal found them in Menari, Colonel Ralph Honner asked the soldiers to assemble in the clearing where Monk, Tori, Robert, Phil, and I were now, each aware it was hallowed ground. Those diggers took parade formation in misfit boots and tattered uniforms. Some steadied themselves on walking sticks, having given their guns to men moving forward. Honner said, "As you stand here before me propped up by your mates, you are heroes, *ragged bloody heroes* standing tall."

Not many World War II Australian veterans were still alive as we trekked the Kokoda Trail, no longer around for us to thank for their heroism and sacrifice. But a Papuan was. "There are few living Fuzzy Wuzzy Angels," said Brett. One was from this village, another was in Kagi. We knew enough to be impressed, even before he said, "Claim is that he's over 90."

"Could we meet him?" asked Jim.

"If he's okay today, yes. If he's not feeling well, no. We'll ask." With that, Brett left our camp and went to a different part of the village, a few hundred yards from where we'd settled. When next we saw him, it was up a nearby slope. He waved us over. "This is the grandson of the Fuzzy Wuzzy," he said, introducing a man in his 40s who spoke on behalf of the family.

"It is my grandfather who lives last from the war," he told us. "His name is Faoli.[26] He helped Australian soldiers. He today will see you. It is

---

26 When Faoli passed away, he left only one of his peers. The last known Fuzzy Wuzzy Angel, Havala Laula, died on Christmas Eve 2017 in the village of Kagi. He was age 92, making him 15 when he was first pressed into service to help the Australians.

Faoli, one of the last two Fuzzy Wuzzy Angels (both of whom have since passed away), being thanked for his scarifies and courage by six Australians from Melbourne, those Monk tagged as "Kokoda Club Med."

five dollars." A wizened man came around the corner of a house and into the yard, aided by a youngster. Clearly, he'd made his way down whatever stairs lay between him and a room, as all the houses were on stilts. He was a Koiari tribesman. During the war, thousands of other stretcher-bearers and porters had been brought in from elsewhere in Papua. He, however, was one of the natives of the Kokoda Track. The old carrier moved toward a wooden chair and sat. His eyes shone in response to our good wishes. A beard bushed around and below his mouth, held up by serious sideburns. An Australian Army "slouch hat" shaded his large forehead. He wore shorts, and his bare feet rested in the dirt. Five medals with ribbons adorned his shirt, Australian and Papuan acknowledgements of the extraordinary sacrifices he represented. It was right and proper for each of us to approach him, to kneel and to say, "Thank you, sir, for what you did."

"Fuzzy Wuzzy" has been the name of soap bars, kids' games, poems, and war heroes. It originated as British slang to demean black indigenous peoples with sprung curls of hair.

As a child, I knew the term from an irreverent jingle about a bruin:

Fuzzy Wuzzy was a bear
Fuzzy Wuzzy had no hair
Fuzzy Wuzzy wasn't fuzzy . . . was he?

That the term began as a slur traces back to an English poet known for xenophobic tinges in his prose. A Rudyard Kipling ballad of 1918 adopted it as the title. Without being an apologist, nor wanting of revisionist history, I'll note that Kipling was a man of the nineteenth century and slights inexcusable today were condoned then, unless you were among the recipients of racial discrimination.[27] His poem's insinuation

---

27 Racialism was a term in use in the 1930s, though "racism," borne of the French term *racisme*, first came into common reference when describing Hitler's racial discrimination in the run-up to World War II.

gave way to an expression of respect from British soldiers to the fighters of East Africa:

> So 'er's to you, Fuzzy Wuzzy, at your 'ome in the Soudan
> You're a pore benighted 'eathen but a first-class fightin' man

The term entered the colonial glossary elsewhere the British reigned, notably in the South Pacific. It never gained verbal traction in North America, as there were already ample phrases to express white society's prejudices there.

Over the decades, use of the term "Fuzzy Wuzzy" went from derogatory to patronizing to admiration. It surfaced as a code for respect when the native peoples of Papua came to the rescue of Australian troops dying, out of food, low on ammunition, or distraught along the Kokoda Track in 1942. They were hard workers and mostly loyal to the Aussie defense of their island home, earning respectful recognition as "Fuzzy Wuzzy Angels."

All foreign forces initially treated Papuans poorly at the outset of war. Suddenly, they were needed. Their support as runners or supply packers or medical team members saved countless Australian and American lives. And Japanese as well.

On this, our fourth night, I'd taken a tent, swapping out with Phil who wanted to sleep on floorboards instead of the ground. I was getting used to the tent's confines when Yeoy's shout of "Dinner!" came. This many nights into our trek, I barely noticed the array of underwear and socks drying by the cooking fire. Spaghetti simmered in a large pot over the fire. When the water was poured off, the pasta tasted perfect. Chunky sauce bolognaise was poured from a smaller pot, the rehydrated, freeze-dried treat bringing smiles of culinary satisfaction to our faces.

Children came near our dinner table as we were finishing up chatting and chewing. Ten of them walked in a line right behind those of us on the left side. We got up and made room for them. They took our seats.

We stood across from them where the other trekkers remained seated. Start of day or end of day in a Papuan village is often "sing sing" for them, though the term is also used for special celebrations in the community. Tonight our presence merited a personalized "sing sing." They sang several songs in Tok Pisin. Their voices were young and inexperienced, not trained to curtail their own excitement when performing for strangers.

Then they sparked into, "*If you're happy and you know it clap your hands . . .*" This was the single offering of a folksong in English, followed by a seamless shift into their national anthem. Their voices carried pride and confidence in a country. The Aussies responded with their own anthem and, while heartfelt and meaningful, something in their voices was lacking by comparison.

A Papuan elder stood amongst them, acknowledged the youngsters, and turned to speak with us on their behalf. He began by asking their world's overseer for guidance. "Our prayer is 'Be with these trekkers, they have a long and difficult road.'" When the children left, we trekkers moved fireside, our "long and difficult road" very much in our aches and milder concerns. Earlier, Bowrie had told me "no rain" when I'd asked his forecast, but in the following twenty minutes around the fire, we noticed clouds gathering. Our speculation shifted from "It won't rain," to "It might rain," to "If it does, it won't rain hard . . ." I passed along Bowrie's prediction mindful I might not have gotten it right.

Misinterpretations of English and the Melanesian Pidgin can be confounding and comical. My friend Garry told me before I left that I needed to be patient and clear when talking with the locals. He recounted an occasion walking the Papua New Guinea trails with his translator. "The sky darkened over mountains to the south," Garry said, "so I asked the *turnimtok*, in English, if he thought it would rain."

"*Im e no rain*," the man replied in Pidgin.

Confident in this local authority's knowledge of the weather, Garry left his rain gear packed. The sky turned blacker, thunder rumbled down from the hills. Again, he enquired of about prospects for rain and was reassured, "*E no rain*." They kept hiking through jungle. Seconds later,

"Spontaneously the skies opened, rain pouring down as it can only in the tropics." Garry's bush hat was whirling a waterfall off its brim. His canvas boots squished the ground. The translator, rain bouncing from his bare chest, turned to report, *"Rain e come down, now."*

As the fire roared, Monk annotated our day for everyone, focusing first on our achievements, noting the cringing he saw on certain faces during certain stretches up, and equally, by name and pointing, having a go at those he saw wincing on the downslopes. To everyone's amusement, he passed me a packet of muscle relaxants, saying I had to be careful not to overdose on them. Then he turned to gift Panther Imodium and said, "You'll soon want these if the laxatives work. Say thank you." Looking at both of us, he said, "The word endurance comes to mind."

I'd never seen Monk go from chuckling to a solemn mood as quickly as he did that night, right in front of the fire and everyone. For Monk is not a philosophical man. Yet the blended days and blended nights on the Kokoda Trail were weighing on him. "I feel I'm walking with ghosts," is how he put it. "The jungle's full of 'em. Japs. Aussies. Papuans. American ghosts will be there when we get to the Northern Beaches." Right then, it started to rain. We all got up and moved alone to our beds. I suspected Monk was escorted by his demon. I knew his dad hadn't died on the Kokoda Track. Yet his old man having been hereabouts spooked Monk.

The rain stopped after midnight, but only once it had wet the grass, leaked into Monk's tent, and freshened the air for morning. The noise of the other trekkers packing was my wake-up call. Not that any of us needed an alarm; our internal clocks and our stomach growls woke us. A watch no longer had meaning, either.

The morning's banter between Anthony and Brett had become everyone's anticipated compass bearings.

"Day?" Anthony asked.

"Fifth," said Brett.

"Hours on the trail?"

"Six. Maybe more."

"Night's camp?"

"Naduri Village."

The trekkers we called The Four (Deirdre, Michael S, Phil, and Robert) had been moving slower than the pack over the past few days, arriving at each resting place after the main contingent, just when we were eager to resume hiking. So they approached Yeoy with a solution. They all agreed that the four trekkers and their porters would leave first this morning, almost an hour ahead of the rests of us. We would meet them down the trail later, then all of us would arrive at camp together.

Darren's workout pleased everyone. He was a big man and saw no need to overuse muscles until later in the day. His goal was to ensure that none of us strained ligaments or the like. Once warmed up and pliant, we were ready to go. Woody warned that the morning would be especially demanding. We were heading to Brigade Hill. This took us first to the valley floor. There, half a dozen logs lay across the river, strapped together with vines. To get to this improvised bridge we had to traverse a log ramp. Martin's announcer imitation advised, "Approach bridge with caution." Whitey told us that on his previous visit he had crawled across this bridge in pouring rain.

The balancing acts were fascinating to watch. The porters went first. Once on the other side, they strung handrail ropes for trekkers. We were eight feet above fierce rapids eroding large rocks. We crossed one at a time, gingerly stepping one foot ahead of the other, letting our boot treads find a grip. Midway, I stopped to take it all in: roaring water, tumbling rocks, and jungle—threats, fears, and consolation.

Away from the river, we started hours of constant up and up to Brigade Hill, still hours away.

Ahead of me, half a dozen trekkers stopped beside a gun pit with scraps of once lethal ordnance strewn about. As we looked over it, Simon tossed me a grenade that looked to be rotting. "That is a Japanese-made grenade, and it required a fuse to be sparked," said Brett. That seemed awkward to

Logs tossed together and propped in place meant a potential for danger and mishap every time we had to cross water, so porters deployed as safety markers, held the guidelines taut, walked close to the trekker, or prepped for rescue and first aid should that be necessary.

me. Brett told us, "The Aussies used British-made grenades, which were more easily thrown and were shellacked against the moist climate."

At a knoll called the Saddle, just below Brigade Hill itself, we paused for rest. Brett oriented us. "About a mile away is Mission Ridge, though the battle there is often merged in telling with that of Brigade Hill."

The Saddle was a memorial site, cared for by the Koiari people, to commemorate an Australian defeat. Brett thought it was okay to let our bodies relax, but not our consciences. He read the words of Private "Slim" Little about the prelude to the Japanese assault that drove the Aussies from Brigade Hill back to this knoll: "I'll never forget that night as long as I live! We dug in, in a bit of open Kunai grass and we dug a hole with a bayonet and a tin hat, and that's where we slept that night. And coming down the other hill towards the river were the Japs, hordes of Japs [. . .] We had to sit there watching them come up." The Japanese had been steadily advancing southward and the Aussies held them off for four days. They came under sustained fire from "the Jap's Juki," a machine-gun nicknamed "the woodpecker" for its constant patter of bullets. Determined to keep control of this strategic location, the Aussies thought they were prepared to defend the position. But at night the Japanese, led by local guides, sliced through the jungle. Australian lookouts neither saw nor heard any movement. They rested at the ready, unaware that they had been outflanked. Morning arrived. The Australians were attentive though unsuspecting, mugs of tea in hand.

"*Banzai!*" the Japanese cried as west-flank troops rushed forward in waves, trampling the jungle and firing rifles.

"*Banzai!*" screamed the Japanese frontal attack, swinging bayonets in search of Australian flesh.

The fighting was hand-to-hand, eye-to-eye, and bayonet blade-to-bayonet blade. Aussie soldiers plunged over the hillside into thick jungle, frantically forcing vines out of their way while bullets whizzed about them. Hundreds of the Australian infantry fought what Brett called "a withdrawing action, backing away from the Japanese onslaught, the odds seemingly two-to-one against them." The Japanese were well equipped, freshly fed, and strategically strong at this point of their campaign. They were the aggressor, winning battles and taking prisoners. As the Japanese captured enemy soldiers along the Kokoda Track, they used the prisoners for bayonet practice.

Our group was soon off the Saddle, moving downward for half an hour, where we found flat ground. It was a relief to ease off the push of our toes into the front of our boots. Then suddenly the trail went upward and sapped our muscles. "Am I going to make it?" someone behind me said. On the ridge, The Four who'd left camp early greeted us. It was good to be together again, though the occasion was made deeply sad by the whereabouts.

We found ourselves at Brigade Hill, with its unnerving other name: Butcher's Hill. There was space to spread out. I lay against my pack on the ground, exhausted. Yeoy walked over and spoke to Jim as a father, and to Simon and Kieran as sons. He bent on his haunches beside Michael to talk quietly, then he walked over to Monk. After that, he went to his packsack and pulled out a binder and a book. "We'd like everyone to join us here," he said. His voice had an emotional undertone, not the confident one we were used to hearing. I looked over the edge of the ridge and to the north. Below was a creek that once flowed with blood. Across from us was the mountainside where the Japanese had bivouacked. I tried to envision them charging up this hill. And then charging again and again and again and again the next day. The hill's positioning lent itself to a strong defense, unless one considered an enemy with sufficient men and enough time to encircle you and cut off the trail of retreat.

We stood among short posts that indicated where graves had been found after the war, soldiers often buried shallow where they fell. Others marked where bodies discovered later by the advancing Australians were buried; exhumed after the war and moved to Bomana Cemetery. The trekkers Yeoy had spoken with moved beside him, and he sorted them in the sequence he wanted, Brett among them. I felt too close and moved back. Yeoy and nine of our party faced us. Forty Papuan porters and packers stood on the slope behind us. The service began without formalities. Understandably, given the makeup of our party, we were saluting Australians and Papuans, not the Japanese, although a great many of them also perished during the battle of Brigade Hill.

I thought of the Papuan porters standing with us. Papuans are revered as guides and carriers during the war. Their small infantry also fought the Japanese. The Japanese called them "green shadows" out of respect. Brett presented a Papua New Guinea flag to two Papuans standing with him, and handed an Australian flag to two trekkers. He gave Monk a sheet of paper. Monk looked at it and let it fall by his side, his face taking on the look of having received something he knew by heart. It was clear from where he stood in the lineup that he would recite at the end.

Yeoy read notes cribbed from pages of books too heavy to bring. "In the still hours before the dawn of 8th September, the Japanese began their long-anticipated attacks. It is a day that will be long remembered as one of the most intense and costly actions ever undertaken by Australian troops."

Trekkers stood at an uneasy attention on the ground where young soldiers barely able to stand had raised their bayonets to defend against a charging enemy infantry. Soldiers riddled with dysentery had cut open the seat of their pants for the ease of a constant shit. Yeoy read about the company of soldiers "badly mauled after two weeks of savage fighting and three weeks of marching, exposure, and with a lack of supplies and sleep." He made us feel nearer to those Aussie soldiers. "They had endured a miserable night, the rain having filled hastily dug foxholes." With the scene set, others alongside Yeoy now took part in the tribute.

Jim-the-father had been asked to read from "A Soldier's Farewell to His Son," in which a father writes to his little boy before heading off to war.

I trust that you will never need
To go abroad to fight . . .
Or see your cobbers blown to scraps

A tear left my right eye, trailing down my cheek.

And that is why I leave you now
To hold your liberty,

My stare moved to the Australian flag unfurled between two trekkers. Beside them stood Brett, who drew a shuddering breath. Then he read the words of Medical Officer Captain Henry Steward, who was at the Battle of Brigade Hill: "My saddest sight at Butcher's Hill was that of a 23-year-old former golf professional. He had a ghastly, gaping wound of the throat, and although my eyes could see only darkness and death, his saw light and hope . . . Emotion clouds calm, clinical judgment, but the hardest thing is not to flinch from the gaze of the man you know is going to die."

I was the only one among us not connected to this drama by kin or country. A glance at the trekkers around me affirmed I was not the only one with watery eyes. Our porters were moved, too. Their grandfathers had carried the needy away from this spot—and did so at their own peril. Two Papuans at the front gripped the sides of their country's flag. My gaze settled on Jim's sons. Yeoy had placed another poem in their hands, which they now took turns reading out loud. It was about a little boy watching a parade of returning soldiers, his father not among them. That youngster's hands held medals of his fallen father, which he showed to an old soldier who stood beside him.

Simon began:

They belong to my Dad, but he didn't come back,
He died in New Guinea, up on the Kokoda Track.

Kieran continued in the voice of the Digger who explained:

For this great land we live in, there's a price we have to pay,
To keep Australia free, and fly our flag today,

Kieran's voice broke.

For you to go to school my Son, and worship God at will,
Somebody had to pay the price, so our Diggers paid the bill.

The space between Simon, Kieran, and Jim spanned a fresh understanding.

Monk breathed for us all, and said, "I've been asked to say The Ode."[28]

They shall grow not old, as we that are left grow old;
Age shall not weary them, nor the years condemn.
At the going down of the sun and in the morning
We will remember them.

The mountains went silent. Everything within earshot observed a minute of silence.

Then came a chorus from twenty Australians: "*We will remember them.*"

Monk said, "*Lest we forget.*"

Sixty voices responded, "*Lest we forget.*"

A murmur grew into the Australian national anthem, words too heavy to belt out.

Australians all let us rejoice,
For we are young and free;
We've golden soil and wealth for toil;
Our home is girt by sea.

Papuan males have beautiful voices, as I'd come to know from their evensong and morning camp singing. The national anthem of Papua

---

28 The fourth stanza from Englishman Laurence Binyon's "For the Fallen" is commonly known on its own as "The Ode."

New Guinea, while seldom recognized on the world's sport podiums or in events televised around the globe, must rank among the most stirring songs to celebrate a land. The porters sang its verses beautifully, and without hesitation.

> Shout our name from the mountains to seas
> Papua New Guinea;
> [. . .]
> We're independent and we're free,
> Papua New Guinea.

It was over. No one moved.

I'd never known silence to be so loud.

Then the small sounds of shuffling feet.

Brigade Hill has enough room to move about, but not to hide. There was space to lose oneself. I gazed out at the jungle. The soldiers, I winced, died so young. I thought how it is that, until we die, we happily remain a mystery of all that we might be. What, I wondered, might each of them have been? Yeoy must have seen my shoulders slumped at the hill's edge. He knelt beside me and spoke. "Every time I'm here it hurts for me, too. It stings the heart. And so it should."

I wanted solace for the Aussie fighting spirit that hung about here, neglecting to think of those hovering spirits that were Japanese.

It was fifteen minutes on when Woody walked around and solemnly said to each person individually, "Couple of minutes, mate."

Monk was standing near me, staring away. I wanted to say something about how well he'd spoken, but when I started, he interrupted. "Maybe my old man stood here."

Farther north on our trek was the Efogi valley, which the Japanese called the Valley of Death, designating the engagement as One Stroke Character, using the starkness of a single score in their writing to underline suffering.

Hereabouts Japanese fighters were decimated, even if they were able to continue inflicting severe casualties on the Australians in seesaw fighting in later battles during Japan's slow retreat along the Kokoda Track.

A root tripped my foot and I skipped along the trail, caught a tree branch and slowed my steps. "Steady, man," Darren said as he passed to my left and offered a steadying hand on my shoulder. I let porters and trekkers pass before I stepped back onto the trail, with Bowrie right beside me. Trekkers bowed their heads, watching carefully so as not to repeat my stub and stumble. Brett was further ahead, trailing close to Woody. He shouted, "Bone Man!" and stopped by a tree waiting for stragglers, which included me. "Take a look at that tree, the hollow-ish stump," he said. "Imagine yourself hiding there against the night."

As if on a theater cue, Simon collapsed to the ground, curled and crouched into the open tree. Martin pulled two branches over him and announced the news: "Never to be seen again . . ."

"Almost how it happened," said Brett. "A Japanese soldier got separated from his squad here when Australians ripped apart his platoon, killing most of his comrades and leaving the rest groaning for help until they died. The soldier crawled into the shelter of this very tree in an attempt to recover."

As I turned slowly, my mind created a diorama, taking in the jungle and trying to envisage the fierce fighting with seemingly weightless bodies tossed by bullets or flung by grenades. During open confrontations, the Australians, with their American-made Thompson submachine guns (which had earned a reputation during Chicago's prohibition years), held advantage over the Japanese infantry, who had no comparable weapon. When enemies closed with one another, struggling face to face, you could see in your enemy's eyes before one of you killed the other.

Brett kept the story tied to the tree. "After passing out, the wounded soldier woke to the stench of decomposing bodies. Cries were few. No one else would live."

A breeze coursed around the trekkers, and broad leaves swayed beside us, making it a spirit world.

"And then a ghost appeared," joked Kieran.

"Right you are," laughed Brett, but it was a dry laugh. "A wounded Australian limped down the track, coming from where Winterford is." Winterford stood on a rise of trail in line with the tree's hollow base, his guitar silent, having no suitable song.

"The two exasperated soldiers attacked one another," said Brett. "Only one lived."

The Japanese soldier was Kōkichi Nishimura, and this begins his story. It was evening when the Australians launched the day's fifth attack on the Japanese positions held by Private Nishimura and his company. Nishimura's personal account differs from those recorded in Japanese journals or Australian unit diaries, but they all concur with his view of the eventuality: "The Australians were very close to us, perhaps not more than thirty feet away, but we could not see them."

Next, they were on each other. The Japanese situation grew untenable under barrages of grenades and mortars and machine-gun sweeps. Nishimura took a bullet and collapsed into his trench, listening.

Dying Australian groans.

Dying Japanese groans.

Eventually, Nishimura pulled himself out of his trench and weakly rose in a landscape of the dead. From there he crawled to the hollow tree trunk and took shelter and passed out.

Startled by a noise, Nishimura watched helplessly as the Australian soldier staggered toward him.

The Aussie pressed his rifle to Nishimura's helmet. He fired. With the metal-to-metal pressure of the gun on the helmet, the bullet glanced off. The Aussie fired again. The gun shifted against the helmet. He fired a third time. All three shots ricocheted into Nishimura's shoulder.

The Australian ran into the jungle to reload his rifle. The Japanese soldier gave a hobbled chase. He drew a bayonet. Nishimura plunged the weapon into his enemy's chest. The Aussie kicked Nishimura in the gut as his bare hands pulled the blade out and away. Both soldiers collapsed in the jungle. Nishimura thought, "Why am I fighting this boy who I don't even know?"

Time pulsed. Wounds bled.

Darkness came. Exhaustion brought sleep.

Nishimura woke, thinking, "Where is the good sense in being involved in a war that metes out justice in this totally arbitrary way?"

Nishimura killed the Australian.

Nishimura listened to the morning moans of comrades and enemies desperately trying to die. Corpses propped against trees and across pathways.

A Japanese officer found Nishimura. He received medical attention and was patched up, though one wound lay open: he was disgraced for surviving. "Nishimura should have died if he wanted honor," went the thinking. Soldiers shunned him. "What brave man saves his own life when those around him die with dignity for the Emperor?"

Brett's depiction captivated us—it saddened us. It angered us.

Michael asked Brett, "Why'd you call him Bone Man?"

"I'll tell you that story around tonight's campfire."

Shortly afterwards we came atop a hillside, our hearts and feet aligned with our breathing, the walk having attained a certain "continuity of the old rhythm" for us individually and as a pack. Brett asked four trekkers to wait with him at the top. Before the rest of us began our climb down, Yeoy said, "Think of descending this with 50 pounds on your back and a rifle in your arms, and ammunition too."

"You'd tumble ass over billycan," Anthony said, as his foot slipped. He grasped to steady himself, without stopping his comment. "No free hands. No way to right yourself except to hurry your feet under your body." Beside him, Simon was sliding down in slalom, his feet slowing the descent in a semi-controlled fashion. Five leg-bracing minutes later and we were at the bottom where the trail flattened. We were ready for a rest, but saw Yeoy's stance, a kind of feigned nonchalance we'd come to know indicated we were about to be taught a lesson. "There, on the ground," he pointed. Something was partly covered with windfall.

"Simon, Michael, Rick, and Rod. Pick it up." Closer inspection revealed long branches lashed together with vines. We each took a post-end. We spotted wooden cross struts as we lifted the frame off the ground. It was a stretcher. "This is what they used to ferry wounded mates," Yeoy said.

I tried to brush away clumps of leaves with one hand, but the stretcher was heavy and tipsy; I had to use both hands to hold my corner. We put it down.

"Monk, lie on it," said Yeoy.

Monk winced with discomfort as he settled onto the stretcher. He tried to mold his body to the slat contours as Yeoy told the four of us to lift it. "Hard to imagine moving ten feet like this, let alone a mile," he said. Our lesson was clear. We bent to set Monk and the stretcher back on the ground.

"Carry him up the hill," Yeoy said. We all chuckled, but he was serious.

"This won't be easy," complained Simon.

Our descent down this very slope just minutes before had smoothed the path and made it slippery. There were no obvious footholds. We hoisted the stretcher with difficulty and stepped forward. Immediately it felt steeper going up than it had coming down. Simon and I lifted the back end higher to keep Monk level with the front, where Rod and Michael S lowered their holds, making them bend their backs.

During the war, the man aboard would have his gear carried by a Fuzzy Wuzzy Angel. Nonetheless, the weight of man and stretcher could be over 250 pounds. A day of transferring 40 wounded soldiers would require 300 carriers. Monk shifted away from a broken strut. "God. To think someone was like this for a four-day carry-out." "And being shot at," added Kieran, who had come alongside. "Don't drop me," Monk said, watching my face. There was no levity in his tone. If he fell from the stretcher he'd slide 30 feet downhill over mud. "Keep your eye on the trail." Jim, too, showed up to help keep the stretcher stable, taking a center spot across from Kieran.

There are times during strenuous hiking when your leg muscles yawn in a slow acknowledgment that they are tired and want to go to bed. My arms, shoulders, back, and legs yawned in unison. We were inept at the carrier task. Progress was slow. Midway up, we heard a shout: "Wait!" Yeoy sent Kokoda Club Med to relieve us. They took over with a hundred feet to go. Monk waved to Yeoy. "Thanks." He made to get off and go back down the trail, but Yeoy called out, "Stay on."

The stretcher bent to the side as the new carriers adjusted their grips. Monk grabbed for open wood to hang onto, lest he roll off. Six sturdy men, a cooperative "patient," and still it was a hell of a time completing the relay. At the top of the hill, Brett and the trekkers he'd kept back with him cheered on the stretcher-bearers.

"Well, that was easy," said Martin, coughing. Anthony called it brutal.

Brett replied: "Brutal was 1942. Think that September was the wettest month on record. This is just tough."

As Monk's carriers crested, the cheers muffled, all their eyes went on Brett.

"You four," he said, looking to those he had kept in reserve. He settled himself on the stretcher in Monk's place, and teased, "Carry me down."

Our drill over, the trail onward continued to be demanding. Even so, we took only short rests.

It is slightly confusing when seeing map designations Efogi 1 and Efogi 2. Efogi 1 was known as Efogi North years ago. Efogi 2 is known as Launumu Village today. Both have moved over time. Given their proximity, the general area is often simply called Efogi, after which a battle took its name.

"Efogi is midpoint between Owers' Corner and Kokoda Station," Brett said, standing beside a signpost claiming just that. "You're roughly halfway, geographically speaking."

"Ahhh, so being halfway time-wise isn't halfway distance-wise?" Simon said.

"Right," responded Brett. "Menari is designated midpoint of our trekking hours, Efogi is midway in terms of trekking miles." The postwar airstrip and First Aid building define Efogi's importance.

After Efogi, and before Templeton's, there is Myola, though getting there requires a side trek on the east side of the track that we did not take. If I were to return, I would want to see this wide, dried lake, as its openness is a unique terrain feature in the Owen Stanleys. During the war, both when they were in withdrawal and later on the advance, the Australians used it for airdropping supplies and ammo. Even with the openness, the airdropping was notoriously inaccurate. When the Japanese held Myola, commanders sent soldiers into the bush to forage for lost Australian food drops.

During the first week of September 1942, the Australians on their fighting withdrawal held at Efogi. They watched a peculiar nighttime occurrence. The advancing Japanese decided to move nearly 1,500 of their troops overnight along the ridge and through what is now Kagi Village toward Mission Ridge, bettering their position for the fuller battle at Brigade Hill. Emboldened by Australians pulling back, the Japanese decided to arch around them. The jungle going was tough. The Japanese accepted that the enemy had detected their move, so they went about it in an orderly way. The Japanese soldiers carried lanterns, knowing they were out of range of the Aussie weapons. Higher up and dug in on Mission Ridge, the Australians watched the enemy's movement, aghast. They nervously laughed when a Japanese soldier tripped, making his lantern tumble. The number of soldiers on the move frightened them. With no artillery, the Australians could do nothing but watch what they called the Japanese Lantern Parade.

We had hours of hiking left in our day. We took what nourishment was handy and moved on from Efogi 1's nice rest house and surroundings. Soon we crossed the Kavai River over fallen trees. They were debarked by weather and water, and reorganized by villagers. The narrow footbridge across the churning waters was made of five logs lashed together. Its uneven surface required slow steps and staying alert. As we climbed out of the valley, we looked back on Efogi 1, the only evidence of humans visible to us in the mountain panorama. Muscle tension in my calves reminded me how necessary it had been to sit there for a spell. I stretched out the tightness before continuing.

Often when we stopped along the trail there was a kind of group hush as we took in the magnificence of the setting or tried to absorb the hurt of what had happened there. Just as often someone—usually Brett—would pipe up with a pinch of history, as though a classroom had been set for us in the jungle. Most often such tales related to things going badly during the war. So it was that I was sitting on a log on the Kokoda Trail when Anthony started to talk. That's when I first heard of the *Montevideo Maru*. The way Anthony mentioned it was, "The deathblow of the *Montevideo Maru* was Australia's largest loss of life in a World War II event."

In June 1942, the township of Rabaul, on the island of New Britain, was home to the Japanese command, then planning their invasion of Papua and crossing along the Kokoda Track. Rabaul was also from where they oversaw activity on Guadalcanal. As part of preparations, the command wanted to remove prisoners of war they had taken in Rabaul. Many of the internees were young Australian soldiers of the Lark Force, held since Rabaul had fallen six months earlier. There were many of them and they were healthy. They would be transferred to Japan for use as forced labor. At Rabaul's port, they were force-marched up a gang-plank onto the Japanese transport ship, the *Montevideo Maru*.

For days the *Montevideo Maru* traveled across the South China Sea without escort. Unfortunately, nothing identified it as transferring POWs. The unmarked vessel had the appearance of a troop carrier. The ship's log of the US submarine *Sturgeon*, under the command of Lieutenant Commander William Wright, notes patrolling the waters nearby on June 30: "*Dove at dawn, surfaced at dusk. At 2216 sighted a darkened ship to southwest . . . evident he was on a westerly course, and going at high speed . . .*"

Once it spotted the enemy, *Sturgeon* tracked the enemy ship for hours, unable to attack because of its speed. Wright wrote: *"Determined to hang on in the hope he would slow or change course toward us..."* At about midnight, the *Montevideo Maru* slowed to await arrival of a destroyer escort that had been delayed. Wright noted: *"Sure enough, about mid night he slowed to about 12 knots... dove at 0146. When he got in periscope range, it could be seen that he was larger than first believed..."*

Before dawn on July 1, the USS *Sturgeon* sank the *Montevideo Maru*, unaware that it was carrying 845 Australians as prisoners of war, along with 209 civilians. Wright recorded the action: *"At 0225 fired four torpedo... range 4,000 yards... At 0229 heard and observed explosion... At 0240 observed ship sink stern first... his bow was well up in the air in six minutes."* The *Montevideo Maru* sank in eleven minutes.

Not knowing the name of the ship nor its cargo, Wright made that morning's final log entry related to the *Sturgeon's* engagement: *"Dove at dawn."*

A Japanese observer reported that after the explosions, a hundred or so Australians floated in the waves, clinging to wooden pieces of the splintered ship which they'd either been flung from by explosions or had abandoned. In the terror of the seas, the Aussies sang "Auld Lang Syne" to their mates aboard the *Montevideo Maru* as its bow tilted up and disappeared below the surface. All 1,054 prisoners, including civilians and 22 former Salvation Army bandsmen among the troops, died. It was Australia's worst-ever maritime disaster. Seventeen Japanese crewmembers survived. Japan lied about the incident, stating that only their countrymen were aboard. When Allied forces eventually retook Rabaul, many in Australia awaited word of their relatives and friends whom they believed were still being held there as POWs. They didn't learn the truth behind their loved ones' disappearance for years.

Hampered by an incomplete passenger manifest until Japanese authorities handed it over to Australian officials in recent years, there has been less than adequate respect shown to those individuals who perished. It was only in 2012 that a memorial was unveiled in Canberra, 70 years after the incident. To this day, the final resting place of the

Montevideo Maru is not charted, is not known. The US submarine's estimate of its position indicates the wreck would be around 18°37′ N, 119°29′ E. There is no commitment to confirm its whereabouts.

In a trekking day defined by inclines, it did not surprise us that nearby Efogi 2 (Launumu Village) was over the top of yet another hill. There was a spectacular horizon. Then we were among villagers, free to stroll or stretch. I felt antsy, bending knees and rubbing my lower back against a log, trying to ease out an anxiety that had appeared from nowhere, as though the war trauma was getting to my subconscious. Excising the apprehension was just starting to work when Brett brought up a story that troubled me anew.

"Nishimura returned here after the war to retrieve the remains of his fallen comrades. That's why he's called 'Bone Man.' He made his base here and built a stone cairn in Efogi 2. It's a tribute to all those who lost their lives on either side, not just the Japanese." Unexpectedly, I felt reverence for the Bone Man.

It had been Yeoy's plan that we stay the night near here in Launumu Village. Instead, ahead of schedule and with energy left over, we stopped at the village perimeter for lunch. Salami and crackers. Crackers and salami. There was also honey and a peanut spread; peanut butter is my favorite food, the one thing for which I have a gourmet palate, but at best I could only call this stuff "peanut paste." We left for the valley, climbing downward over rocks and dirt and dislodged wooden steps. Part of the jungle looked to have been rooted out. The ground was furrowed erratically. "Wild pigs," Brett explained.

Efogi River was 50 feet across where we greeted it, bridged by a mixture of trees that had drifted to this point in the river and bolstered with purpose-cut logs. This is a type of local architecture whose design is 1,000 years old. It was our first encounter with this river, which we would see again the next day as we climbed nearer to its source. When we were all safely on the other side of this particular crossing, there was again a collective sense of satisfaction that we had avoided anyone falling in. No one took it for granted, knowing we had been but one slip away from having to carry a companion or even helicopter out someone with a broken leg—or worse. Now we climbed. The trail away from Efogi River was switchback after switchback. The map of the day repeatedly stressed "Very Steep." There seemed no relief from the vertical. Having trained, and beginning to feel our strength with each day, we were not inclined to bicker.

We found a camp just before Naduri. Half a dozen trekkers and their carriers on a southbound journey occupied it. I wondered if the exhausted looks we saw on their faces mirrored what they saw in ours. The quietness of their campsite made me appreciate how different ours was, what with the singing of porters and the buzz of excitement each time we settled in. We moved on in search of Naduri Village. At first when we found it, I thought it so nicely arranged that maybe it was an aberration dreamed into being out of desperate want. Yet this was real. We set about to make camp in midafternoon.

A recent addition to the community was a full-fledged Medical Center paid for by the Kokoda Track Foundation—with funding principally driven by Australians. It was hard-roofed with firm wood walls and shuttered windows. The door locked, the floors were flat, the light switches worked. A verandah ran six feet deep across the front. Along the north side to the back of the building was a second set of stairs. Monk and I walked up the front stairs, but we were too late—Simon, Kieran, and Jim had a corner room staked out. Three guys from Kokoda Club Med had a second room.

"Here's the maternity room," Darren called out as he and Martin put down their mats.

We heard Yeoy laugh from a back room. "I've a single bunk. On twenty-five Kokoda treks, I've never had a night in a place with nailed floors and solar-powered light."

Monk tried a locked door. With no key in sight, he said, "Likely supplies of sorts, protected against intruders. Like me." Tori's foot pushed Rod's mat closer to her. "We can shift here for one of you."

"Monk, I've found a key," Yeoy called out, waving it in the air. He inserted it and the door's handle opened. We peeked in. The supply room had counters and a shelf. The floor was wide enough and long enough for Monk to roll out a mat and claim his territory. It was windowless. "I'll take it," he said quite happily, as though he'd scored the Gold floor in a Fairmont Hotel.

Bowrie was by my side, my gear in his arms. I asked if the verandah was taken and it wasn't. I followed him outside, placing my daypack half the verandah's length up from Brett, who was setting up near the back stairs.

Looking over the verandah railing, I watched the rest of our camp take shape. Kristy's tent was up, along with one each for Phil and Deirdre, and two spaces saved for Robert and Michael S. The Four, arriving shortly, continued to impress everyone with their tenacity, good humor, and camaraderie. The weather had turned cooler, but the campsite looked homey. The porters' compound was a shelter built off the ground and roofed with thatch. A fire burned near it already, water at the boil for tea.

There were reports of three decent latrines. Breaking news: Panther was finally a happy man.

Packers tinkered around the porters' fire, which was where they'd cook our dinner. Near them, a barefoot village child with a 12-inch machete ran over to help another little kid who carried an axe. This casualness would be unimaginable in America, where parents manage youngsters around such sharp instruments, or at least make sure they wear protection. Bowrie and Kipling kicked a second firepit into place on the ground in front of the Medical Center.

Monk was running from the shower. "It izz soo k-k-cold," he said. Simon was beside me, preparing to shower next, and he laughed at Monk, who scolded him. "It's so cold you'll have your nuts under your armpits," he warned. We'd hiked for seven hours. Tomorrow would be ten hours. I needed the shower to sooth muscles as much as to prepare my mind for the coming day. Once freshly washed, I toweled the ice crystals off my back, and dressed. Then I rushed from the cold to the fire that Bowrie had lit for us, and leaned into the flames for relief. By then, dinner was cooked. We rolled through the banters of dinner without rushing words, and eventually moved to the fireside.

Campfire smoke blew into my face. Tori and Rod got up and moved away to the other side of the firepit, rubbing their eyes. Panther glowed almost as much as the fire. Most everyone was now around the fire—the trekkers, that is. The porters were washing up after preparing the meal for us. Gentle humming without a guitar flowed toward us and softened the cool of the evening. The porters were always there for us when needed, and when they felt we should be alone, they left us. They opened their world to us, but would not intrude upon ours. I was struck by how willing they were to show us experiences they knew didn't exist in our worlds.

The fire crackled as if prodded by Michael rising. His style was slow and purposeful. "I ache in every one of my body's seven hundred muscles and two hundred bones." The raconteur bowed his head a moment in thought, and went solemn. "I shed tears today on Brigade Hill. To think of how they fought. How they died. Both sides." Staring into the fire, he said, "I came on this trek for the physical challenge. I never thought I'd feel so many emotions." He tapped into something we each struggled to articulate. "I sense Aussie soldiers everywhere. I could sense Japanese in those trenches. It's as if they're still headhunting each other as we walk by."

"Headhunting ghosts," said Simon.

"And then this Bone Man?" said Kieran. "What's that all about?

Brett tossed dry branches on the fire. It sparked right away, lit bright, and then settled back to low flames. We were tired, and open to a teacher's talk. With the fire sketching smoke into a scene, we heard the story of The Bone Man of Kokoda.

"Kōkichi Nishimura returned to Kokoda Track 40 years after he killed the Australian," Brett explained. "He came to find what was left of his fellow fighters. Mostly he found hands and feet, medals and boots. Wild pigs got the rest."

"A grave digger?" Simon asked.

"In a way," said Brett. "He wanted to repatriate the soldiers' remains to their families in Japan. And he sought honor for those he could not identify by cremating their remains in the Buddhist way. Nishimura wanted to put the ghosts to rest."

After military discharge in Japan, Kōkichi Nishimura became an engineer and businessman. He married, and he and his wife had a daughter and two sons. His marriage agreement with his bride and her parents stated his commitment to one day return for his slain comrades in Papua. Nishimura struggled in Japan's postwar society, his country occupied by foreigners. Their humbled emperor disappointed citizens. War veterans were not shown respect. Death in war esteemed a soldier's name, and those who lived were often suspected of dishonor. Nishimura was, however, successful in business. He founded the Nishimura Machinery Research Institute. Contracts came from Sony; Mazda reputedly mimicked his motor designs. Nishimura became a wealthy man.

Nearing the age of sixty in 1979, Nishimura convened a family meeting and explained his decision to return to Papua to find the fallen. It was thought uncustomary for a Japanese wife to debate her husband, or for children to oppose a patriarch's decision. Behind the closed doors of their home however, that acrimony is what happened. The discussion created an irreparable split in the family. Within hours, Nishimura left his home, his estate, and his company in the name of his wife and sons; his daughter sided with him. He never again saw the others in the family, nor enquired after his business affairs. Soon afterwards, Nishimura left Japan for the first of several extended stays in Papua, searching for bones. In a corollary to MacArthur's pledge, Nishimura stated, "I promised I would return. I never tell lies."

He pursued bone recovery for the next 25 years. Not only did he return to battlefields he knew, he also visited others that he learned of from the locals. Living in the jungle along the track, using tents or staying in villager huts, he often worked alone. He used a metal detector to find belt buckles and helmets buried in hastily constructed graves. He dug carefully, removing bones and artifacts and trying to determine a soldier's name wherever possible. When he was sure of a man's identity, he sought out the family in Japan (a task frequently as difficult as finding the soldier). He would present the family with his story and provide the remains. Often, he was thanked with weeping. Sometimes his gestures were rebuffed, as though the person in question was a failure: an embarrassment for losing the war. On several occasions, Nishimura was told to leave memories in the ground. "Who are you anyway, to do this?" some families demanded of him. "All I know is my own way," he would tell them. "I know nothing of the outside world."

Kōkichi Nishimura became so dedicated to his cause that he would later claim to have forgotten his own wife's name, but he never forgot the names of his comrades. When he died in 2015, he was among the last survivors of the Imperial Japanese Army's 144th Regiment.

"If an Australian had done what Nishimura did for the remains of his comrades, there'd be a statue somewhere, maybe in Melbourne," Rod said. And Mark said, "If an American had done that, his face would be on a postage stamp and his shovel displayed at the Smithsonian Institution in Washington."

Our tiredness transformed from talk near the campfire to dozing off on the verandah.

Near my sleeping bag, the porch bent around from the front of the building to the side. Two six-foot-long benches were built into that corner joint. Before dinner they'd served as unpacking platforms. Jerseys and underwear were washed and hung on the railings to dry. My valley vista became that of a laundromat.

Now, as day darkened, the benches were cleaned of shirts and gear, boots and poles. It was not a tidying-up. Instead it was making room for bums, legs dangling loose, and backs enjoying the support of railings. My bed area went from Laundry Room to Coffee House as wisecracking trekkers showed up with hot drinks. They languished, ready for chatter. Where'd that newfound energy come from? I wondered.

We had a porch-load of stories. Jim told us of raising two kids: "Can you imagine me coming home for dinner each day and talking about the toilets I'd fixed? And these two guys went into the same career!"

"Dad," said Kieran, "Do you remember the time the apartment building's sewer backed up and . . . ?"

"Maybe the three of us should come back to these villages and bring plumbing gear for them," Jim said. Kieran added, "We could get toilets donated and build wash basins next to them. More sanitary." Simon suggested that plastic pipes would not be heavy to carry in. "We could show them how to build septic fields and channel waste."

Five nights into the journey, we still filtered the Kokoda Trail's people through the lenses of our lives, but were learning to see it through theirs as well.

"We're not doing their teeth any favors by passing out candies," said Tori.

Monk was on it. "You are right. Probably don't have a dentist on the trail," he said. "But they sure love 'em."

"How'd you get dubbed 'Monk,' Monk?" Whitey asked.

"I love bananas. Eat 'em all the time. Friends noticed. Said I was part monkey. Nicknamed me The Monkey which became Monk."

Having thought "Monk" had a monastic origin, Martin's radio voice took up the low tone of an interviewer. "Then, you're not celibate?"

"Well, I was until fourteen," said Monk.

Everyone cleaned as they left. I scrawled notes. The lights went out, and the night turned black. The jungle was somewhere off in the dark, closing in. Even the porters' fire was almost out. Melodies wafted from their barracks. No solo voices. I went to sleep, until the scent of rain woke me around midnight. Or was it the wind-shifted sprinkle on my face? It was oh-so-dark. As my eyes adjusted, I saw fog. We were wrapped in a cloud. All evidence of people was covered. I heard not a snore, nor a creak of flooring. I could barely make out the lump that was Brett a dozen feet away. I thought. What must it have been like to lay here in the dark with fear of being hit by a bullet, or having an enemy jump from the jungle intent on killing you? In the minutes that followed, the fog lifted, letting out moisture to lighten its rise.

It rained.

The scene was eerie. I fell back to sleep.

I awoke to the sound of porters stirring. The retreating mist revealed Brett sleeping on the deck and the shape of a stilted house where porters were rising. The rain stopped. In its aftermath, what wasn't wet was damp. In this still hour, I sensed it would be a perfect day.

A rogue mozzie buzzed overhead. All combatants in 1942, regardless of race, faced diarrhea or dengue fever (the "bone-crusher disease"), but malaria took the most. The illness began in the lowlands, where mosquitos carried malaria, but never in the mountains. Those Aussie soldiers who suffered or died from malaria in the mountains would have contracted it in Port Moresby and its environs and carried it with them. Similarly, the Japanese who came down with malaria once above Kokoda Station had been bitten in Buna. The Australians experienced very little malaria on their march in the highlands, only to face an onslaught of the disease when they retook Kokoda Station and went to the Northern Beaches. Eventually the disease debilitated American troops on the beaches as well.[29]

The biology behind the mozzies' whine was worrying. If the buzz was from a female anopheline in the lowlands, her role was simple enough: pick up a blood parasite from an already-ill individual and carry it for later deposit to someone else. When the mosquito bites its prey, the

---

29 By one post-war study, the thousands of Japanese troops trapped at Buna near the end of the Papua Campaign suffered an 85% rate of infection with malaria. The Australian number for sickness, the vast majority of which were malaria-related, was 51%. Illness among Americans in Papua was 67%.

disease is transmitted to the victim. Night is their delivery time. During the Papuan Campaign, more soldiers were evacuated from the frontlines for malaria than for bullet wounds. If I needed a reminder to take my malaria tablets, it now lay dead beside me, slapped by my paranoia.

Song rose from the porters to wake everyone else. Trekkers disturbed one another as they stumbled into wakefulness inside an unfamiliar building. It was not yet 5 a.m. Brett clicked off his alarm music, and Simon's remained silent, too. On our sixth day along the trail, we were all up without morning reveille.

The dampness slowed us. Packing up inside or on the porch was moist but okay. Porters shook tents to get rid of the raindrops. People slipped on the wet grass. We moved about to get warm, then to stay warm. Breakfast was fun, because we had to think of it that way. Gourmet pancakes with Vegemite were swirled down with one's preferred libation. I took porridge from the pot at the fire and sprinkled on brown sugar I'd brought from home, and then passed the container around. Brett described our coming day as he ate. "Eight, maybe ten hours of hiking." He said our goal was Templeton's 2 for night's camp. (It was not until after the trip that I had advice from guide and author Peter Gamgee in sorting out the inconsistencies on various maps. He informed me about early names given to the locations by Captain Bert Kienzle, "The Architect of Kokoda." Bert named the stores supply sites as he built them, including Dump 66[30] and Dump 1, as well as the location "Templeton's Crossing." Bert's son Soc clarified the confusion around Templeton's 1 and 2. To ease an understanding for others, here's the explanation: Templeton's 1 is more correctly called Dump 1. Templeton's Crossing and Templeton's 2

---

30 Gamgee told me the numbering of the supply locations happened like this: Bert named them—"Dump 1" being the first. After "Dump 2" signallers told him that using only a single numeral made it hard for people to understand over the field telephone. From then on he started calling them "Dump 44" etcetera—and so we eventually had "Dump 66" rather than Dump 6. Soc informed us there is no "Dump 3" or 33 (though a third dump was at Alola), nor 55 (though a dump named "Ak Ak" was created at the top of Imita Ridge where "Dump 55" could have been).

are the same place. Where neither 1 nor 2 appear on maps or in conversation, Templeton's Crossing suffices.)

Our bodies fed and packs stuffed, we were ready for the trail once we limbered up. Kristy led a feisty and slippery workout in the mud with the full participation of all trekkers, ending with the splendid "Oi, Oi, Oi!"

Our morning's walk started flat, as that's what airstrips tend to be and the old airstrip of Naduri was beside us, replaced by neglect and encroaching jungle. Monk stopped ahead of me, pulling his stuck boot out of the mud with a sucking sound. "Can you imagine if it had poured last night instead of drizzled?" he asked, with the *thwuck* of another boot.

Whitey's experience from his last trek was helpful context. "Here, right here, it was inches deep of sloshing mud," he said. "We pulled calf muscles trying to yard our feet free of it." None of us envied his experience, but we were slightly envious of the hardship stories he carried with him after the journey was finished. "It was not about keeping up," he said. "It was about keeping up*right*." But now, the mountainside had mostly drained itself and our toeholds were visible. Darren remarked, "Papua New Guinea's flag should be a network of roots."

The climb felt endless. As we gained altitude, the reward was the shimmering green and glimpses of open sky.

We could see Kagi Village and all the way back to Efogi in the distance. We then faced north to an opening where the mountains became explicit on the unfolding horizon.

"Are we at Kokoda Gap already?" an elated Kieran asked. "I thought it would take till noon."

"It will," said Brett. "This is the Kagi Gap." The map confirmed the Kokoda Gap was still over three miles away. Where we walked at an easy pace ended with a stiff climb on Mount Bellamy and delivered us to one of our higher points on the trail.

Our difficulties were nothing. Near here, at Diggers Rest, the Aussies on withdrawal were worn down by the ceaseless battle, day after day without respite. No sleep. They were wet. They were sick. Fighting raged on. Even the wounded fought. Every time I thought of an ache, I told myself, "Shut up, Rick."

I walked between the guitar and the shovel. The pace kept us in proximity to one another. That differed from previous days when we occasionally spread out over a quarter mile. We hiked in short bursts of up, then down, then back up. Never, it seemed, were we long on any angle. The downs were often steeper than the ups, though no shorter. Each hour felt like two. Eventually we caught up with The Four, who had left camp before us.

"A level stretch starts here," Brett said. "Honest."

"About time," Anthony replied. "Where are we?"

Brett: "Moss Forest. It's peaceful."

"Looks sinister," said Phil.

Moss hung like mist, muting the branches. It clothed entire tree trunks. Stumps were moss-haired monsters. Moss looked to be crawling along the ground toward us. It was otherworldly.

"It used to be taboo to walk here," said Brett. "Before the war, I mean. Locals feared it."

"Feared what?" asked Deirdre.

Brett said we'd answer that on our walk-through. "If you don't get frightened, it'll surprise me."

Yeoy spoke: "Since the path won't stretch your muscles, let it stretch your minds. It may be your most relaxing walk of the trek."

"I'll bet it's only 50 feet," Tori said.

There was everything in this rainforest, from fungi the size of my two hands to pandanus trees. The pandanus looked like giants in the daylight; at night, they must have been alarming, especially when the wind was rough. I was taken with the structure of these trees. When short, they splay their roots above ground, tight together in a cone shape. When tall, as were the ones before us, the roots were high and splayed, as if framing a tepee.

Yeoy said, "This makes a great walk for reflection. The moss silences the forest. Gives solitude."

Simon said, "We're in the middle of Nowhere New Guinea and you want solitude?"

"For twenty minutes you'll be on your own. No guide. No porters. Make sure you've got safety gear. Compass. Pair up with another trekker. Or pick those you'd like a walkabout with. Leave five minutes between each departure." Brett was setting the tone. "Let yourselves be introspective. Talk about what the trek means to you so far. Share your innermost thoughts with a fellow trekker."

"We'll head off as one," said a Kokoda Club Med member.

"All six of you?" Brett wanted to know.

Nods all around. "Yup."

"Head off later, then," said Brett. "Let the smaller groups go first." He strode down the path ahead, pausing to call over his shoulder, "Give me five minutes head start." With that, he left on his own.

Five minutes later, Robert and Michael S walked into the moss forest and disappeared. A respectful time after that, Phil and Deirdre headed in and vanished. Monk and I sauntered onto the forest trail a good distance behind them.

Trees narrowed the trail, gloomily cutting us off from the trekkers we had left behind and those who had gone ahead. Moss flowed in every which way like wall-to-wall carpeting. It wrapped trees and hung from branches in streams and clumps. There was an orchid to our side. The forest was filled with ferns and plants that one presumed had names, though that didn't make them recognizable. We walked a land of inconsistent plurals: lichens, fungi, and mosses.

I fully intended to share a meaningful talk with Monk, but he didn't say a word for the longest time, so neither did I. And when I started to talk, he cut me off before two words left my mouth. "Can't shake my shithead father."

I was startled and could say only, "Huh?" It was the last word I uttered for the next fifteen minutes. Monk was on soliloquy. "My old man disappeared. From mom. From me. From my sister, from town.

One day he walked out to get milk and a newspaper. Never showed up again. For twenty years, the bugger disappeared."

I wondered how someone would cope with that.

"I was eleven years old." Monk told me this, as he did everything, in a matter-of-fact fashion, but as he talked his shoulders sunk. So did my heart. I couldn't comprehend being abandoned in that manner.

"We thought he'd died. Accident. A fall. Car crash." Monk growled. "At least, that's what we started to hope. We were deserted. There were rumors, of course. Debts. Petty larceny." Monk's outward mood was steady, but I felt he must have been caving inside as he divulged all this. "A little theft. Maybe a lot of theft. He had burgled a place, and the coppers were closing in on him. Moneylenders were pariahs. Bastard was mid-30s when he went. Left loans on the house. Not a coin in the bank account."

The moss muffled Monk's talk and matted my listening. The trail meandered. Any rise was gentle. The ground was mucky from the rain. Roots bungled the trail as before. Monk went on: "Everyone tried to find him. Except Mom. She let him go. Not a hint of heartbreak."

I had nothing to offer my friend, except to listen. Monk became disheartened in the telling, but not defensive. "When a man leaves a town, he gives up any chance of defending his name. Unsolved crimes surface in reference. 'Must have been that ol' disappeared man,' they'd say. An asterisk by his name. Guilty or not . . ." Then, as abruptly as he'd begun, Monk shut down.

The jungle's indifference could draw no more from him. Humidity upstaged humility. I tried to put myself in Monk's boots. What if my dad had cast me aside at a young age? Monk did not look for words from me nor offer any more himself. He was done.

The jungle had taken us into its soul. There was a silence you could hear. No birds sang. The farther we walked, the stiller it became. Then noise shot from the jungle. "*Aaaachch.*" Swung branches swiped an inch from our faces. My gut sank, taking my courage with it. Another raging *Aaaachch* pierced my ears.

Rage burst from the jungle. Menacing natives ran toward us. "Aaaachch . . . Aaaachch . . . Aaaachch . . ." One jumped from a tree, brandishing a knife at my eye.

"My God!" shrieked Monk, who hid against a tree. I cowered behind him. We had stepped into a trap. A spear flashed past my head. Six natives swarmed us. A camouflage of branches covered their heads. Their chests were bare and beating. Fear swelled our eyes. We were alone and under attack. A man swung his axe at Monk and missed. A machete waved by my neck and hacked into the bark. My heart plunged. It beat so fast I thought it would stop.

"We're done, mate," said Monk, looking stunned.

I'm going to die in the jungle, I realized, oddly detached. *I'm going to die right here, right now.*

"*Kingsole?*" said Monk. "*Kingsole?*" he said louder. "*Kingsole, you asshole.*" Mobbed, we fell to the ground, raised spears pointed at our heads. Our near naked porters collapsed in a roar of laughter atop us and on the ground beside, dropping their spears and camouflage. Their faces broke into lizard grins.

Before either Monk or I could take friendly revenge, the porters sneaked back into the jungle, guffawing, shaking their heads at our primal fear.

Brett came from behind the trees, a video camera in his hand. "Best yet," he exclaimed. Monk and I slunk out of sight, our faces burning with humiliation, tempered by anticipation: Kokoda Club Med was not far behind us.

Half an hour later along the trail, a few of the Kokoda Club Med guys, Jim, Simon, and I took to a wide stretch of trail after a breather. Jim said, "Nice to have time in the Moss Forest to think about being here with my sons. I have to say it made each of us more contemplative than I expected." One of the Kokoda Club Med guys said, "Not for us. We're six guys, mate. No need to be introspective." Another added, "Ya, we took the twenty minutes to come up with every name we could think of for a vagina."

"And?" asked Simon.

"Twenty-seven."

Seems that six Aussie men can solve any challenge, given time.

We were soon on the climb. Tension crept up our legs, then our backs. I could feel it in my neck. According to Brett, our approach took us along "the main spine of the Owen Stanley Range." The foothill portion had now given way to the mountain's steep side. Starting from the 6,600-foot level of the Moss Forest, we hiked hard to earn our way to 7,200 feet. Our trail edged around the peak of Mount Bellamy. While we missed the mountaintop, we were now at the highest altitude of our trek. Jungle pilots used this broad, 6,000-foot-wide pass to traverse the mountains, and had named it the Kokoda Gap. The Yodda Valley lay northward and distant, towards Kokoda Station. Our bodies begged for rest. We flumped on the ground.

Kokoda Gap (also known as Gap Lookout) holds a primer on leadership ineptness or, at the least, leadership misunderstanding. In question were the actions of MacArthur and his commander of the Allied Land Forces in New Guinea, the Australian Thomas Blamey, a career soldier whose World War I decisions and those unfolding during World War II would be the subjects of doubt about his judgment. This is the spot where Commanders Blamey and MacArthur planned to impede the Japanese southbound advance by blowing up the geography. It was a crock of an idea to those on site. Looking at topographical maps under dim lights in HQ had led Blamey and MacArthur to underestimate the complicated surroundings in which the troops fought, making for some poor decisions by the generals. They were about to make another one. They sent a directive to "Blow the Gap." It went unheeded by those who knew it would prove ineffective. Smartly, those on site also knew that blowing it up now would impede their anticipated counteroffensive at a later date.

Such unrealistic commands furthered rank and file dismay about those two generals. For his part, Blamey had already disparaged his own troops on more than one occasion (another reason he was not held in high regard by most of the diggers). The animosity toward Blamey is said to be a reason that the heroics of soldiers along the Kokoda Track were not widely spoken of for decades, as no one wanted to risk reflective glory for a man they disrespected.

Blamey's ignorance of the fighting conditions was notably revealed in an October speech to troops that had far-reaching effects on their morale. Already known as "that bastard Blamey," he uncorked in front of the Maroubra Force in his infamous Rabbit Speech. Having implied the soldiers standing before him had been defeated by an inferior army, he admonished them, saying, "Remember, it's the rabbit who runs who gets shot, not the man holding the gun." Correctly or not, his words were taken to mean that the soldiers "ran like rabbits," implying a lack of courage. At the end of the speech, those assembled declined to salute. When next they met Blamey, some of them nibbled lettuce in his presence.

MacArthur's dissatisfaction with the Australian fighting showed in different ways. He ignored what went right and dwelt on perceived wrongs. He is said to have filed reports he knew were misleading. Yes, the US Army Air Corps had been losing aircrew over New Guinea since March, and US engineers took casualties at Milne Bay in August, but MacArthur's reports often referenced "Allies" or "Americans" in action absent specific mention of Australians, highlighting his reticence to identify and credit substantial actions of the Aussies. He apparently reasoned that heralding their independent heroics might lessen his own leadership distinction. Such MacArthur communiqués did not go unnoticed.

The descent down the Kokoda Gap was *very* steep, requiring as much patience as muscle. None of us rushed; there was nothing left to prove to one another. Only the mountainside could be judgmental. A porter slipped, bashing his knee. Blood oozed around a tear in his pants. Simon shouted for Tori. She returned to where she was needed. She got the porter to raise his pant leg, and poured water from her bottle over the wound and stanched the bleeding. "Wipe this here," she instructed, providing the hurt porter with gauze and healing salve. After she'd directed him how to apply the medicine, she hovered a bandage above the sore and said, "Press." The porter applied the cover, thereby respecting Tori's uncovered hands. Swelling was a concern, and the knee area required support before the porter could continue the descent. Tori took an elastic bandage from her supplies and braced the leg one wrap at a time. We all knew it could have been any of us who slipped, and that the injury could have been much worse.

"It hurts great," was all the porter said, smiling.

A creek raged. We would cross it several times, but it never looked the same. Whatever its appearance, safety near it was always a concern. The water itself was not so wide here as it first looked in the ravine. Large boulders on either side anchored irregularly toppled trees, bridging 60 feet across. A porter stood on either side of the bridge as spotter, safety rope dangling. "You never get used to this," said Mark.

Once we made our way over the bridge, we filled our hydration packs and water bottles, added the off-tasting purification tablets and lemonade-flavored electrolytes. Then we ascended, again. It was a half-hour hike that felt much longer. Footholds were elusive and slopes were slippery. Kieran pointed out that, according to his map, leeches were plentiful in this area. Michael S, experienced in this country, had earlier reminded everyone to strap on their gaiters. But though we remained attentive to their potential, the relative dryness at this juncture kept the little devils away. The air was cool and thin. We made good time although the path was narrow and awkward. When we reached Templeton's 1 (Dump 1), we saw large gardens tucked behind six-foot fences.

"Why the fences?" I asked.

"They keep out wild pigs," said Brett. "They've moved into the hills for food. If they were around, locals would hunt them. We'd have ourselves a barbeque."

Hiking, I couldn't shake the feeling that bothered me earlier, when we stopped beside the depressions soldiers used as "stay behind" pits: you know what something is, but not what it really means. The pits were scattered along the track where selected Australian soldiers—and Japanese—were assigned to stay behind, to slow the advancing enemy while the rest of their battalion moved to safer ground. These pits could be where a single camouflaged soldier lay in wait, or they could hide a two-man machine-gun team beneath a blanket of broad-leaves, waiting to surprise the enemy when they got within ten feet. I shuddered for those surprised. The pits' very existence assumed their occupants would be overcome in the ensuing fights. I could not fathom their fear.

The next day would be the first one that we had been warned about. Brett said, "The battle sites will unsettle you." But at the time the sound of the creek dominated our mood. It rushed from tributaries in the mountains above, coming together in an ever stronger flow. Here it raged beneath logs bundled together to make a bridge platform. Railings were lashed together with vines to provide handholds. We walked in mud near the creek to approach the bridge, carefully crossed it, then made our way through more mud on the other side until the trail veered up and away from the splash zone.

When we reached camp, we watched in awe at Eora Creek's turbulence. Templeton's Crossing was a major site in separate battles. The Japanese won the first encounter during their September advance through here. The Aussies won the second engagement during their counteroffensive in October. That second clash lasted seventeen days and was, for both sides, the ugliest fight along the Kokoda Track. It was easy to understand how the creek's roar and boom provided cover for the Aussie diggers advancing in the dark. Unfortunately, during one October night the crossing winds had parted the clouds, giving Japanese snipers advance notice of the sneak attack. The Aussies continued their assault anyways. What came first in such fights, death or defeat?

*

How often on this trek had I rested exactly where Aussies had died? I tried to imagine stunned and weary men on this same slope, leaning against their rifles to keep upright and alert. With seven hours of hiking behind us that day, we happily fell without a care along the slope at Templeton's Crossing (Templeton's 2). We lay back on our packs as props to help us doze. A nagging thought kept recurring. Every good person I envisioned as having died here was Australian. The entire enemy was bad. Could that really be true?

Clouds and cold hinted at rain as we made camp. Porters constructed a tarp tent in an open field. It served as a long house to hold the fourteen of us not in one of the five individual tents. Yeoy was the first to be organized under the tarp with his gear. As others scrambled for locations, he napped. When he woke, he said to those nearby, "Good we walked the extra distance today. It means tomorrow's hike will take us all the way to Isurava. We can overnight there."

"That'll make for a nicer walk out the last day, heading to Kokoda Station," he added. He looked at us with respect. "You've done well."

Eora Creek was foaming *and* pooling, an invitation we could not ignore. Thirty feet away, a waterfall cascaded over rocks the size of houses. From there the creek rushed toward us over smaller boulders. The swirling water slowed to form a pond ten feet across and twice as long in front of where we stood. The rocky floor was slanted, getting ever deeper as we walked toward the center. The rocks were uneven and troublesome. Rod and Tori teetered on the gravel as they followed Robert and Phil in, then Rod stepped into the pool's depth and sunk. He surfaced and shivered. "That's refrigerator fresh." Brett shouted from on top of the big rocks. We'd not noticed him climbing there. He disappeared behind the waterfall. *Poof*—he popped out from a watery cave. He crab-walked through the rapids. "The inside waterfall's a real tumbler," he shouted.

I went into the cave, retracing the way he'd come out. There was another pool. The waterfall dropped right into it. I was chest-deep in the cave's water. My thoughts froze. Warmth never came, but the cold loosened its grip the longer I stayed. The waterfall plunged in three tiers. Rod and Simon called from above, ready to slide down the main water-fall and into the pool. I moved out of their way, to where a side water-fall tumbled from four feet up. I tucked my head under that shower. Instantly, my breath vanished. I gasped for air. My heart pounded. Water hit the stones and sprayed everywhere in ricochet pellets. Monk swam toward me, the look on his face in stark contrast to what it had been in the moss forest. Was it a newfound serenity? Or was he just freezing? Yeoy and Tori queued above to do the chute. Weirdly, I was reluctant to move out of the water's icy grip. Then I could stand it no longer. I swapped places with Monk, who yelped when the falling water hit him. Back on the pebbly shore, I scrunched water from my walking shorts without removing them. Simon seemed to be in three places at once: in the water ("Warmest water yet"), putting wood on the fire, and handing me a towel. Rod fanned the fire to life. Flames roared. Warmth came, banishing the cold to a memory.

We dined in a style befitting the setting: exotic. Spam may never have been appreciated anywhere in the world since its creation in America in 1937 as much as it was here. I could almost hear Martin's radio voice: "Tonight's feature, Kokoda pâté." What we had before us was diced, fried, and twirled into spaghetti with mushrooms, which moments before had been powder-dry. The meal was grand by our standards. My only food want of the trip was that local fare was not more readily available. We missed sampling the lumps of starchy sago palm pounded into culinary submission and served as *saksak*. Wild sugar, *pit-pit*, was never on the table. Also of insufficient supply for the villagers to share were potatoes, coconuts, bush cucumbers (though they appeared once), and breadfruit. Pawpaw and papayas and bananas made infrequent appearances. The setting, however, was beyond expectations. Whatever outdoor dramatics were festering among the critters in the jungle, they made little noise, no more than a background thrum. The sky had filtered to an ever darker blue.

There were a dozen or more types of grasses and flowers giving off fragrances that collided in mysterious ways. You only realized that soothing smell when you walked away from the fire or cooked food and concentrated on noticing it. So I did that. It was beautiful. Amid all this was the vista we sensed as much as saw, due to encroaching darkness. There was an unexplainable expanse around us, one made of jungle and sky and open grass and friendships. Michael called the setting peaceful. "If only that could be the whole country's reputation," Jim replied.

Dinner done, trekkers gathered at the campfire. Kieran was tending it when we walked over; he put the flames in Monk's care by passing him two logs, then left us in search of hot chocolate. The waterfall was background music. We were full and tired; out of energy and out of words.

Yeoy surprised me by saying that it was my turn to do the end-of-day talk.

Before I could collect my thoughts, I said, "I'm struggling."

The silence was broken with, "You're not alone."

"In a different way, I mean. I'm struggling with how much disgust I feel." The fire stopped crackling. The waterfall calmed. No one moved. "I struggle to cope with my contempt for the Japanese who fought on the Kokoda Track." Instantly, I wished I hadn't said that, but it was too late to do anything but forge ahead with my confused emotions. "I can't reconcile that revulsion with the Japanese friendships I have at home and in that country. I've walked the Hiroshima Peace Memorial Park with Japanese friends, and stood before the Atomic Bomb Dome with them, not knowing quite what to think. I've traveled in Japan a dozen times, being with Japanese colleagues. I love the wonder and amazement—the beauty of their culture, and the people. But . . ." I decided the only way forward was to be honest. "A kind of . . . aversion . . . hung over me on today's trail."

"It's not the people that disgust you," Yeoy said quietly. "It's what happened here."

I took that in. "I felt this . . . seeing Japanese relics . . . every Japanese foxhole," I said. There were nods, either of sympathy or empathy, from some of the group. Others were perhaps shocked, or embarrassed.

Yeoy saw where my comments could go, rightly interpreting that I—a non-racist guy—was making racist judgments. He added, "Everything we're taught during wartime ingrains the enemy as evil. Dehumanizing the enemy makes killing more palatable for young soldiers." Truth is the first casualty of war. Americans spread egregious falsehoods, such as the racist lie that, because of their eye formation, Japanese fighter pilots could not shoot straight.

It wasn't only the Japanese fighting in Papua that I abhorred. Most every description I heard of the war was horrible. War, face on, was unfathomable to me. Those of us who rely on books and movies to frame our interpretations pull up far short of war's inherent vulgarities.

Yeoy let it hang in a long silence, then said, "The Japanese we know today, the Japan we know today, are different than the Japan that went to war in 1942." I knew he was right. "Japan had a warrior culture then. It was the legacy of Samurai thinking. The Emperor was a deity. Maybe we call Japan's war behavior at the time that of a cult. I'm not really sure." Notwithstanding Yeoy's reconciling statement about a brotherhood I didn't recognize, and no longer existed, I was discomforted by my own shortcoming of prejudice.

"Once," I said, "a Japanese friend was getting married. His bride was new to our country. At the last minute, her parents couldn't make it over from Japan. The night before their ceremony, the groom and bride phoned to ask if I would walk her down the aisle on behalf of her father. On behalf of her family in Japan." There was a shuffling. Three people leaned in to stoke the fire. "I spent today recoiling from the Japanese," I said. "Tonight, I remember I love them."

Wilderness has a cathedral affect that makes me contemplative, reflective, open—and in the midst of the night's jungle, I told the other trekkers what I was thinking. "As I trekked today, I felt open to loathing. To pretend otherwise would be dishonest for me." Glossing over such emotions would negate the horrific nature of what happened here. My gut felt a terrible dilemma. Veteran groups that reached out to enemies after the war had taught us that time and distance might be the salve needed to heal. It seemed to have done that for Brett and Yeoy, who had dealt with the sites and sights on earlier treks but had not become numbed to the realities of war.

We were walking back from the campfire when we noticed half a dozen porters coming toward us. They were dressed for the cool night in jackets and long pants. They were side by side, moving methodically closer as we walked to our tarp tent. Then, suddenly, the porters broke to the side of the field. From behind them sprang seven bare-skinned natives. They wore grass around their waists. Their exposed chests were muscled and firm. Ferns sprung from their headdresses. They beat their drums in a tribal overture of fear, yet their smiles made them nonthreatening.

Our porter friends melded with the dancers as the entire group drummed their way up to within a foot of us. Bowrie was among them. We stared at one another. I blinked.

They were having fun with us again, playing against entrenched misunderstandings Westerners hold about this part of the world. They portrayed fighting as dance. They conveyed their music and traditional attire as if for our entertainment, but clearly also for our edification (and a lot of apparent fun on their part). They wished us to respect their festive approach. We had no way to respond except with our Western applause and shouts of appreciation. We mingled as one large group, some 50 or 60 of us in a close pack. We walked together toward the porters' accommodations, only drifting apart from their continued drumming when we reached the building, where we deferred to their privacy.

The ground where I attempted to sleep was marinated in battle history. I wanted to let the day's mental angst relax. I could not digest all that was going on. That night I searched for something to take my thoughts elsewhere. Falling asleep, I thought of being home, but didn't want to wish away my time in PNG, nor the conundrums the country was teaching me.

Breakfast and exercises the next morning shook off a coolish night, minimizing any distress about the day's walk. Our morning banter veered between setting trail expectations for Day Seven out of Owers' Corner and our hope to reach Isurava by day's end. Our group took Templeton's Crossing over Eora Creek to see firsthand the hellish conditions of a war engagement that helped change the course of world history. We worked our way through swampy areas, trying not to get bogged down by history or the hike. We clambered up a mountainside toward our first munitions dump of the day, one haunted by the soldiers who had died there.

In October 1942, the retreating Horii was ordered to hold this position, in hopes a Japanese victory in Guadalcanal would free up reinforcements and reverse the Aussie momentum on the Kokoda Track. Horii's tactics pinned down the Aussies at Templeton's Crossing for over two weeks. Soldiers on both sides hunched in water-filled trenches, soaked and shuddering. Often, they could not see three feet in front of them. Horii's admonition to his soldiers was, "Harass them by ceaseless activity. The enemy must never be allowed to escape."

The American tenacity in Guadalcanal helped the Aussies in Papua by keeping Japanese fighters busy in the Solomon Islands. Horii never got his backup. Eventually the Aussie push out of Templeton's Crossing, against the unassailable Japanese, broke through. The Nankai Shitai fled. It was the first time any of them had seen Japanese running from battle.

Having crossed the creek, we followed in the footfalls of that fighting climb. The Australians had taken a month to get from our camp, two nights ago, to where we now stood among the Japanese strongholds that forestalled them. Our comparable time had been measured in hours.

Looking at my surroundings, I, for the first time, realized that the jungle really hadn't changed in the last 70 years. The past lingered. The layout of foliage we were seeing was similar to 1942. That's unusual for war sites. Around the world, most battlefields no long resemble the landscape they were in war. But here, the terrain was almost identical now to then. It felt uncanny.

A spur of trail took us to a stash of rusted Japanese hand grenades,[31] small mortar bombs, and large artillery shells, artifacts assembled for display by the landowner who'd clearly felt a curator's concern to clean up the disarray. Dozens of unspent little bombs lay in rows. Piles of useless grenades rested in ready. Chipped helmets sat on the ground, showing where incoming bullets had shattered them. It was an outdoor "museum" of sorts, remindful of the beehive action as Japanese soldiers launched or threw whatever they could against the Australians, knowing that the jungle would deflect much of what they tossed. Regardless of jungle war's inefficiencies, over 400 Australians were killed or wounded during that entanglement. The Japanese suffered nearly 250 casualties.

Rod and Tori tried on the helmets, not at all wanting to smile with the gesture but to sense the vulnerability they conveyed. "This would not have been much protection," Rod announced to the rest of us. Tori allowed that, "I can't watch war movies, they make me sick, yet here we wallow in it, step after step." Simon coughed to draw our attention to where he'd tucked into a tunnel. "A lousy place to be if a grenade landed in here."[32]

These were not designer foxholes; they were functionary and rudimentary, some quite shallow. They'd have been difficult to make with the entangled roots. Stacking dirt as you dig helps build defense buffers, but bullets can easily go through two feet of loose soil. I reckoned that to hide my crouched six-foot frame for a few days, I'd need a hole three feet wide by three feet deep and three feet long. That's one cubic

---

31 Continuing into recent years, Australian Explosive Ordnance Disposal (EOD) experts, under Operation Render Safe, have cleared World War II sites in PNG of tons of unexploded hand grenades and mortars, some deemed potentially harmful.

32 Within a year of our visit, the locals who owned this land unilaterally filled in the tunnels and removed or covered the munitions display, without explanation.

yard of dry dirt, which weighs 2,000 pounds and could take a long time to dig, even in a flurry of activity—particularly if you didn't have a shovel. And, as Kieran was wont to remind us, if no one was shooting at you.

For a few hours we walked into and out of valley after valley, or at least ravine after ravine. We were either in one, overlooking one, or leaving one. Yet we were gaining altitude overall. I could not detect any elevation-influenced changes in the chant from the porters, though I assumed they knew well enough what was coming, and adjusted their music for resolve when facing a precipitous trail.

Our evolving fitness added to the walk's pleasure. No matter how fit one was at the start of the trek, one's endurance and muscle readiness increased each day. We'd all hit our stride, so to speak. Each person's gait was individual and never once questioned by Brett or Yeoy or fellow trekkers.

Our trail took an extended drop, which felt nearly vertical. My walking poles proved inconvenient for the halting steps I took. Some turned to climb down backwards.

Eora Creek Village, abandoned, appeared suitable for our camp, had we wanted it. But we walked through, and on, to find ourselves on a strapping bridge that arched over waters seething around rocks. Upright posts anchored each side of the bridge's platform, which was made of six or seven logs lain side-by-each. Vines tethered the tower posts to the ground. This construction may have been only a year old. Every rainy season, many bridges are swept away and have to be rebuilt. Simon went first, prancing across the structure. Then Tori and Rod crossed together, a change since most bridges supported only a single trekker at a time. I stopped midway to take in the waters splashing against, around, or over boulders before regaining an angry rush downstream. It felt hazardous, and to me was the most difficult we'd made our way across.

Mindful we'd just had yet another experience for the ages, we shucked our packs and flopped on the bank on the other side. It was time to replenish our drinking water, as what flowed around us looked deliciously refreshing—which of course was a misshaped idea, as it could be laced with diarrhea enhancers. We took the necessary precautions. I had moved on to pellets that attempted the taste of wild berries.

We wandered along the trail with the creek flow never out of earshot, a reminder that we were not yet finished with it. Nor were we anxious to be. Every crossing was different, every bridge its own structural achievement. We felt increasingly nimble whenever we crossed, but it was a deception brought by overconfidence. Some among us foundered, but no one fell off a bridge.

Later after more up, down, up, down, and very little level land beneath our feet, we sloped toward Alola Village, our troupe trailing out along the mountainside. Our view was of roofs and open field coming ever closer until we were finally there. Greetings of *tok gude* went between villagers and the front walkers. Here, I could be a *welman* or *dripman*, both explained to me as Pidgin for "wanderer" (which I later learned were also terms for vagrants). As we walked in, we saw a tub of water-cooled colas and orange sodas. A display of chips sat beside it. We celebrated as though we'd found gold in the creek. Monk and I took a bag of crisps and two sodas, and sat on a hillside overlooking the valley. We pushed off our boots and massaged our feet (yes, using the same hands with which we ate the crisps; one's standards slip . . .). We took off our shirts in the misguided thought that the sweat would dry. It was a tidy, dry village with thatched rooftops and clear sight lines throughout. There were drowsy houses, all on stilts. Every home had swept earth near the stairways and under the raised floor. Recently washed clothing hung from floorboards. Flowers defined some yards. I asked Yeoy about the fresh vegetables. "If trekkers buy the vegetables, it pushes up prices for locals," he explained. "No good in that. We carry what we need and sometimes get a nice surprise." With that, he passed us a platter of cut pineapples, whose supply was plentiful. The fruit stung our taste buds with its sweetness.

Our original trip plan had us overnighting at Alola Village, but we were in the mood to keep going, as we'd made extra progress yesterday. The result was our arrival a little later at Isurava where we camped instead.

That afternoon, when we arrived at Isurava battlegrounds, kids played soccer in the field where we pitched our camp. It was the most welcoming Kokoda vibe of the journey so far. Tori always took to the children and them to her, a willingness brokered by smiles all around. They eagerly let us take part in their football game. I kicked a strong shot on goal and a youngster swatted it away. It bounced back in front of me, only to have a five-year-old's foot tip it out of my reach. He passed the ball around me and back to himself. With the ball under his control, he bolted downfield. The little kid's next kick landed the ball right on his teammate Simon's foot. From there it plowed right by Kieran, our goalie.

I looked over at Yeoy enjoying his afternoon tin of fish. This time it was salmon. When he finished, he strolled down the hillside toward a memorial site. He had asked us to hold off going to see it, as there was something he needed to sort out. I met him where he was talking with a member of the village. There was a gate in front of them that looked of recent vintage, though not made of new parts.

"Man won't open the gateway," Yeoy said, turning to me. Others were there too. Our gang was not intended to reinforce Yeoy, but it had the effect of making the man stubborn. He shook his head. Yeoy explained to us, "There is a feeling the village does not benefit enough from trekkers going through. We pay a fee here like to other villages, but because they have this tribute they want more."

"But the Australian government built the monument," Jim argued.

"True," said Yeoy. "But it's on this man's land."

"Then we pay? Each of us pays." This, from Jim, seemed the simple answer.

"Point is," said Yeoy, "up until a month ago this fencing wasn't here and no one paid. So it's a standoff. If we pay now, we'll always have to pay."

"We can't not go in," said Monk.

Wordlessly, Yeoy took an Australian 50-dollar bill and gave it to the man. The gate opened.[33] We followed Yeoy and Brett down the hill and onto a concrete pathway.

All of the trekkers moved toward four black granite pillars, each about six feet tall and set in a half-arc. The memorial stones each had one chiseled word:

COURAGE

ENDURANCE

MATESHIP

SACRIFICE

Below the pillars was a viewing area with interpretive postings. Each was roughly two feet square, though wider than they were in height. An image and text were carved onto metal facings, angled toward us. They either told of the fighting that took place here, explained the engagement's geography, or shared a human story.

Monk and Kristy walked from the first one, following the narrative rim. Monk suddenly shouted, "God! That's . . . my dad." His words spit like a burst of machine-gun fire. "Right. There. Spitting. Image. Him."

Monk took a step back. It drew everyone nearer. Monk was dumbfounded and swallowed uncomfortably. A photograph screened into the metal showed men, heads down, hauling loads across a stream. One man looked ahead, giving a momentary smile to the camera as the shutter made peace with the setting.

No one spoke. Then, "Which one?" I asked. Monk pointed. He moved closer and slammed his fist next to the plaque. "Bastard."

Monk looked as if he had been punched in the gut. In the quiet that ensued, we walked down the hillside away from the tribute pillars and nearer the jungle. Others had started to gather there around Brett.

---

33 After our trip, Australia's Department of Foreign Affairs and Trade (DFAT) negotiated a longer-term resolution and removal of the fence.

Isurava looks unfavorable for battle. The Australians experienced a frontal attack here in August after withdrawing from the Japanese below on the Kokoda Plateau. The Japanese soldiers screaming *"Banzai!"* as they charged had belittled Aussie confidence. Brett said, not pretentiously but ominously, "The actions of many brave men slowed but did not turn the tide of this conflict. One individual in particular is recognized for his boldness, though they all faced an unforgiving enemy. It happened right where you stand. Man's name was Bruce Kingsbury."

I remembered that when Monk saw Kingsbury's grave back at Bomana Cemetery our first day, he'd told me, "The man was only twenty-four years old," which made him just a little older than Monk's father.

"The job of Private Kingsbury and his mates," Brett continued, "was to relieve Australian troops you've heard called Ragged Bloody Heroes." Brett's posture was almost that of a soldier at attention. He stood firm but talked casually, just a few feet away from us. "The ground game of the Japanese relied on relentless waves of screaming, shooting." We shifted, nervous. "General Horii sent a flow of infantry to follow the mountain gun bombardments he rained down on the Aussies. The Japanese had fixed bayonets, anticipating hand-to-hand combat."

Kingsbury's platoon came into a small clearing to find the Japanese had broken through. That put the Australian foot soldiers in death's path and threatened the headquarters behind them. A line of Aussies went forward, firing their guns. "Kingsbury fired his Bren from his hip. His short bursts sent the Japanese heading for the treeline." Brett brought our surroundings alive from over 70 years ago. "The Aussies advanced over open ground." I sensed Brett would have acted this out if it were not already so vivid. "Kingsbury kept moving toward the enemy with sweeps of his gun. The Japanese moved into the trees."

"Run, you buggers," muttered Simon.

Brett pointed to the big rock which he said was on the perimeter of the action that day. As Kingsbury and his mates moved further in the open, two Aussies sat atop the rock where they'd held a position when cut off by the Japanese attack. Kingsbury and a fellow soldier were on the lower side of the rock. In his authoritative *Field Guide to the Kokoda Track*, Bill James quotes veteran Bob Thompson on what happened next: "Foolishly, Bruce and I stopped to speak to the men when a shout and a burst from Jim's (Truscott) Tommy gun coincided with a loud explosion. Bruce was killed instantly."

After the Japanese sniper's shot felled their mate, the others recovered position, stabilized their situation, and awaited orders to advance or withdraw. The war went quiet for a spell.

Brett said, "It's called Kingsbury's Rock."

Solemnly, we strolled the slope back up to camp. Words hung in the air, but there was nothing to say. As we walked by the four pillars, I set my eyes on the one reading SACRIFICE.[34]

There was no rush to dinner. When it happened, the pasta had fresh-tasting meat tucked in it. I thought it might have been a stray chicken or something freeze-dried and suddenly brought to life by water in time to be fried or boiled. Although I'd had quite enough of the ubiquitous noodles, hunger is hunger, and we ate what we needed to. My first bite was delicious, but I couldn't help thinking that a nice Australian Shiraz would have enhanced the meal.

As we chewed on dessert cookies, Yeoy told us that if we wanted a Papua New Guinea carving, our porter would make one for us. "It's a lot of work for the carver, so you need to order tonight," he explained. The next night, near Popondetta, would be our last with everyone together. Jim, Simon, and Kieran, along with Kristy, Robert, Michael S, Phil, and

---

34 The first Battle of Isurava claimed 100 Australians dead and 111 wounded. The Japanese lost 131 men and 226 were wounded. The second Battle at Eora-Templeton's resulted in 400 Australian casualties, about half of them deaths, and 250 Japanese casualties, again half of them deaths. All in, the battles along the Kokoda Track killed or wounded 1,760 Australians and 2,050 Japanese. In the broader context of the Papua Campaign (Kokoda Track, Milne Bay, and Buna-Gona), there were 3,000 Allied deaths (and 7,000 wounded) and 13,000 Japanese deaths (with 4,000 wounded).

Deirdre, were set to fly out of Popondetta the following morning. The rest of us would head to the Northern Beaches. Before that, a closing banquet of sorts was planned. Part of that evening would be a presentation of the carvings.

Bowrie walked over to me while I scavenged among the dwindling pile of sweets at the table. When you've been with someone for several days and usually see him weighted down by a pack (a pack of your own heavy goods at that), the person appears lighter than air when they're freed of the load. Bowrie was shoeless, coming over the grass and onto the dirt floor of the cook shed. He walked gracefully, as though the pack still swung behind him. This unintended swagger made him look more confident than he actually was, but true to the respect he earned. Seventy-five years ago, Bowrie may have been drawn for porter duty during the war. Among the Fuzzy Wuzzy Angels, Bowrie would have been strong and steady, Winterford a luminary, Woody a legend.

Bowrie asked, "Rick, you want carved stick?"

"Please, Bowrie. A carving. Not the trek name."

"You want long stick? Short stick?"

A foot-long stick carved with art I would never see elsewhere would be a treasure. Bowrie would have carved it, and that meant even more to me.

"Rick. Long." To Bowrie, this was commerce. A long stick was worth more.

"Short, Bowrie. Short stick. No words. Your design."

As he walked away, Yeoy had come alongside. He pointed to the lower valley, and a glimpse of our objective: Kokoda Station. It looked inevitable. In the morning we would walk out of the jungle and off the Kokoda Trail.

I walked over to join the others and drained my cup of hot chocolate into the firepit, the taste of it no longer a treat. The fire was down to flickers. It was after hours with the Aussies. Rod recapped the day in mock breathlessness and brevity. He re-descended only one hillside, and made jittery steps while talking about that difficult downhill.

Porter and mentor, Bowrie became a conversational friend, though not a confidant. He taught the pace of living as well as the pace of walking. He was first to wake and last to sleep, just in case his support was needed.

"Gone fast, seems now," said Robert, who was followed on by others tossing out synopses.

"Won't miss the word 'steep,'" said Deirdre.

"*Bloody steep*, you mean," Michael S retorted.

Darren said, as much into the fire as into the group, "Before I came here I didn't know what I didn't know about Kokoda. I've learned so much my head hurts. I just thought I'd have a backache, not a headache." Chuckles filtered in with the smoldering smoke. The group enjoyed the knowledge that tomorrow's walk would not be hard. We'd approach the village below coherent in our fatigue and individual in our accomplishments. I drifted away from the fire and the others, leaned against a tree trunk, and took in my surroundings. I'd come to know two things about my fellow trekkers on the Kokoda Trail: each had taken the risk that they might not make it, and each of their lives was now more than it had been.

I looked around our camp. Porters carved. Each piece of art was being tailored. Most trekkers asked for their name on the memory stick. A common request was for a walking stick, four feet long, which required hours of work. Porters created their own designs from childhood influences, or by interpreting the work of a craftsman. Bowrie squatted on the ground by the porters' fire, a foot-long stick wedged by his left foot against his right knee. With his knife, he made art for me. He forced the blade away from his chest, carving into the bark. Fire glinted off his knife's blade.

"Seven days over," I thought. "And most of the hurt's over, too." That last bit I realized was selfish, as this was a country of hurt and mine bore no mention now that I knew what went on here—long before the war, during the war, and since the war.

Before he passed away in late 2017, my Canadian friend Garry Marchant, who was then living in France, sent me his patrol notes from the 1970s when he worked in Papua New Guinea. He'd arrived in Port Moresby nearly broke and with "no profession or trade in a country with lots of unskilled labor." A few weeks later, he hitchhiked a ride from a public health official who asked, "Why don't you become a malaria control officer?" Shortly thereafter, he took up home in West Sepik, on New Guinea's north coast.

It was a time of cultural confusion, with concocted "club settings" (boating, drinking, dancing) where "the European community can close in on itself," as Marchant put it. "The natives used to go out fishing, catch this incredible fresh fish, sell it in the market, and buy tinned fish in the store," he noted.

Marchant soon found himself tagged with the honorific "American boy" after he explained in Pidgin that Canada and the United States were "*wantoks*" ("one-talks") or "friends." He spent months "landing on jungle airstrips too rough to be government approved, usually sitting on a box of vegetables or beer in the back of a small Cessna, with no safety belt; patrolling the coast in huge outrigger war canoes; visiting leprosariums and camps of political refugees from the Indonesian regime; walking through the sacred burial grounds of natives, eaves piled high with skulls and bones." He added that he had grown used to "having children screaming in terror as I entered their village, too petrified even to turn and run because they had never seen a white face before."

While he encountered leprosy and yaws (a bacterial skin disease), TB and elephantiasis, and the bloated stomachs of little children, it was "the yellowish skin and eyes of malaria" that underwrote his role as a malaria control officer for the Papua New Guinea Public Health Department. He said that although malaria was not well understood by Westerners at the time, it was "the most widespread damaging disease known." He called it "history's deadliest killer." To disrupt the spread of the disease, the PNG patrol officer and his spraymen carted an arsenal of DDT to carry out a program specified by the World Health Organization. While this tactic was used in Papua New Guinea, the situation was much different in the US, Europe, and Canada, where authorities were lining up to ban DDT's unfettered use. Wildlife habitats had been poisoned by it. Alarms had sounded when human birth defects had been linked to DDT in mothers' milk. All this was traceable to crops deluged with the insecticide, where groundwater seeped into streams and oceans, waterfowl and fishes became infected, and the predator-to-market source of contamination was proven. Marchant learned of these dangers through the long-delayed delivery of North American newspapers and magazines. He concluded in distress: "While people elsewhere were waking to the dangers [of DDT], I was passing it off in primitive villages as another benefit brought by the white man."

Marchant writes candidly about the irresponsible antidote. Known more formally as dichloro-diphenyl-trichloroethane, the insecticide DDT was successful in pest control for several decades before its disastrous side effects became public knowledge—if only in some parts of the world. He conceded that at that time, DDT was saving lives. When he visited Bewani Mountain villages, he arrived abreast of seven native spraymen and their pumps, prepared for misting houses with the product. They gathered together each tribe to inform them of the process and benefits, provide basic health education, and identify protocols for their visit. Their corresponding distribution of anti-malaria pills and routine taking of blood samples to determine and monitor the disease was all to the good.

One village had a handful of homes that each slept a dozen people. "Palm leaves are folded to make up the roof, and the bark of the tree cut in long strips is used for the walls. Doors are about four feet high and without windows. Cooking was done by women hovering over a fire on a pile of sand in the middle of the room. There was no chimney so the ceiling was black and greasy; the house reeked of wood smoke." Not surprisingly, many of the inhabitants coped with eye problems.

"Sickness is more the rule than the exception. Hot countries are not healthy. Every scratch festers up and takes weeks to heal. Grille, too, is common. It's a horrible, dirty-looking skin disease that makes the skin to peel off in giant ugly chunks, making a whorly pattern over large areas of the body and sometimes all of it. It is caused mainly by unclean living conditions. Skinny mongrels and little pigs run around the compounds and at night sleep in the houses with the people. The women even suckle these pigs, sometimes giving them preference over their children. In tribes where this is common practice some of the women have one breast dangling lower than the other."

Marchant was taken by their status symbols. "Some of the older women wear leather armlets, as many as ten or twenty. One has her arm from elbow up covered with them. They are made from stretched pig rectums. When a hunter shoots a boar, he makes an armlet for his wife. The more armlets a woman has, the better hunter her husband must be."

Their completion of the anti-malarial tasks set in motion repercussions. "DDT on walls, cockroach poisoned, chicken eats cockroach, dead chicken," wrote Marchant. Then, "The angry housewife brings me the chicken. I explain that these things happen occasionally, but what did she want, dead chickens or dead children? 'Chickens cost money; children can be made for nothing,' she replied."

And in a final observation of the you-win-but-you-lose battle with nature, Garry said: "While our spraying reduced malaria in people, it did the same for village rats."

After Garry dug out those early journals for me, he asked, "Are any of us better today at educating ourselves about local traditions and expectations before we try to educate other people whom we think need our help?"

My sense of smell was the first thing to awake in the morning. It told me the air was wet. Next came a whiff of smoke from the porters' fire. Memory awoke after that, moving from a dream: I had been at Isurava, seen the dying Japanese and Australians, and watched Papuans lug away wounded bodies in an effort to keep them from slipping into the afterworld.

The rustling of the fellow trekkers served as a signal for the rest of us to rise in silence. We dressed in slow motion, leaving the packing of the gear until later. There was no music, no alarm, nothing in Brett's voice until he said into the dark, "Down the hill, please." We moved in ragtag formation. I was with Monk, who had come toward my shack from his tent. We didn't speak.

Yeoy and Brett led, but we all knew where to go. Day had yet to dawn. "Circle round," Yeoy said.

Our rounding came to a three-quarter circle, the curve of the memorial tablets completing it. Each weighed three and a half tons, placed in support of a single word. Yeoy called them sentinels.

COURAGE

ENDURANCE

MATESHIP

SACRIFICE

Brett motioned that I should follow him. We went to where Kristy was looking at a note, flashlight in hand. "You okay to speak this morning?" he asked Kristy.

She whispered yes.

"Rick?"

I was lost in thought, watching others fan out so they were physically together but alone in thought. "I'm okay," I told him.

The sky bridged dark toward light. Penumbra.

Into the still walked our Papuan partners. They formed a single-file crescent. They were part of us, but separate. Yeoy spoke as though giving stage directions. "We are here because *they* were here." It was how he began, and it said everything. We knew where "here" was. We knew who "they" were.

"Last evening, we asked two of you to share a personal story as part of this service at dawn. To reflect on what being in Papua New Guinea has meant as we near the end of our trek." Everyone was aware of this, but he was giving Kristy and me time to catch our breath.

"Kristy," he said.

I felt a calm tremble beside me, then a draw of air. I sensed, but did not see, a welling of emotion.

"I'm part American," began Kristy. She hadn't mentioned her nation-hood since our first camp. "Australian on my dad's side. American on my mum's side. Mum's dad, my Pop, was an American soldier." This reminded us of the context to her grandparents' meeting in Adelaide in 1942. "My Pop is why I'm on the Kokoda Trail," said Kristy. "Papua New Guinea was his war."

The morning air went taut. "When I say Pop, I'm meaning a man named Harol Nathan Brown." She pronounced it clearly, no *d* at the end of his first name. "He fought alongside Australians. He talked fondly of Aussie mateship, and proudly about the endurance of the Fuzzy Wuzzy Angels." I sensed she looked to the Papuan porters when she said that, a glance of appreciation. "Pop was among twenty-one American soldiers selected as a group to go to New Guinea to build an airstrip at Milne Bay. In Pop's telling, after the Battle of Milne Bay, they eventually made their way to the Battle of Buna. Of the twenty-one men that started out together only seven made it back." It settled on all of us that those odds were heavily against Kristy's Pop being a war survivor.

"He was a quiet achiever, and modest," she said. "He rarely spoke about the war. When he did, he told us he was a chef for the boys, down-playing any significant involvement in battles. The family accepted that. Years later I learned that in fact he was a sharpshooter, a sniper. The truth was that my Pop had saved the life of many American and Australian soldiers, but was never inclined to say so himself. Heroes don't brag. It was one of his fellow soldiers who became a lifelong friend who finally told our family about Pop's courage and sacrifice. He said Pop was the joker of the group, always lifting the spirits of the men." All of us standing there with Kristy felt admiration for this man we never knew.

"The United States awarded my Pop two Bronze Stars. One was for the Battle of Milne Bay and one was for the Papua New Guinea campaign. He was also awarded the American Defense Medal, the Good Conduct Medal, and the Asiatic-Pacific Theater Campaign Ribbon. Pop was a sig-nificant influence in my life and taught me to never give up. Happily, Pop and Grandma were married for sixty-two years, until Pop died at age ninety-one in 2006. He showed me what family should be and what true love looked like. Pop had a passion for life and never ever took anything for granted. He became an Aussie but was always an American."

I tried not to move a muscle, not to let the swell in my throat get in the way of swallowing the dryness. Reverence pulsed in everyone present. Kristy's words attracted a brightening sky. We'd have welcomed the absent wind. The rising sun cast shadows in the etched letters on the pillars, accenting their depth. Her story made me consider her grandfather's love and understand her motivation for trekking. She made us all admire why she stood before us that morning. In my heart and gut, I realized my task was to do likewise. I knew I should begin . . .

"I stand with you at Isurava, humbled," I started. "Though an enemy also suffered on this ground, that's not why we pause this morning. We bow to Australia. We honor Papuan friends and their country's sacrifices. And we salute Kristy's American Pop. Last evening around the fire, I was asked if Canada had its Kokoda equivalent. Or, as put by one of you, does Canada have a Gallipoli? Said another way, your questions asked if my country endured defining events when our young men laid down their lives to take control of a chunk of someone else's geography in a fight for freedom. The answer is yes. However, unlike Papua and Australia, those tragedies were nowhere near our country. Canada's battles were far from home." The quiver was on my tongue more than in my throat. "Canada lost over 60,000 soldiers in World War I. Where Australians speak of Gallipoli, giving your nation pause and pride, my country's comparison comes with names like Vimy and Passchendaele. Horrifically, another name, Ypres,[35] is where German forces first used chlorine gas in World War I. In the face of that horror, Canadians stood their ground on behalf of the Allies. In the aftermath, my country decided that never again would the British Empire declare Canada's entry into war. On those

---

35 The Second Battle of Ypres, Canada's first battle in WWI, took place three days before Australia's Gallipoli landing in April 1915. People refer to Vimy, in 1917, as Canada's Gallipoli, though the Second Ypres in 1915 is appropriate as well.

battlefields we became a self-determined nation. In that way, Vimy was Canada's Gallipoli. World War II brought honor and horror with names like Dieppe in Europe, and Juno Beach in Normandy on D-Day. Those were Canada's Kokoda."

I felt the comparisons necessary only in as much as I'd been asked to provide them. This moment was about four pillars that stood in the morning's ever-lightening hue. We were family.

"My uncle Alf has carried shrapnel in his body from 1944 to this day. At the age of 94, he can rub at a splinter of metal in his chin. My father Al never went overseas, but he taught young men how to shoot rifles, how to kill people they'd never met but arrived in Europe or the Pacific hating. He was on a train heading to Vancouver to board a ship set to take him across the Pacific to fight when they got news the war had ended. I'm embarrassed to say I've never thanked either my uncle or my dad for what they did during the war. I promise this morning that because of what you've shared with me on the Kokoda Trail, I will return home and express my respect for their duty met.

"You have made me part of your Kokoda." I felt my heart thump. I motioned my right hand toward the monuments. "I cannot stand with you at the pillar for Courage. Nor can I walk with you near the pillar of Sacrifice. It's not my place next to the word Endurance. Yet, that fourth pillar . . . For me, that word will always define you, my fellow trekkers and Papuan friends. And for that . . ." I choked. I tried very hard not to blurt my next words, but to say them solidly. ". . . thanks for letting me stand with you and Mateship."[36] It ended that way.

Sunrise was complete. Those that knew the words sang the Australian anthem, many with a Papuan accent. It sounded more robust this time. Then came those beautiful voices with their chest-raising words of the Papuan national song.

---

36 In 2017, as a sop to international usages, the Australian government used the word "Friendship" instead of "Mateship" when panels were erected at the track's southern entrance. Veterans were upset, one 92-year-old claiming, "If you didn't have a mate on the frontline you were dead." The wording reverted to "Mateship."

Winterford, the guitar man who'd brought joy along the difficult path, spoke on behalf of the Papuans. Even without accompaniment his voice conveyed song, though he didn't sing. "We remember those Papuans who helped those Australians—" he paused with a look toward Kristy, "—and Americans, who had come to help us." Monk stood at attention, eyes glistening. He began with an earlier verse this time:

> They went with songs to the battle, they were young,
> Straight of limb, true of eyes, steady and aglow.
> They were staunch to the end against odds uncounted,
> They fell with their faces to the foe.

The valley showed through the fog.

Monk let the book fall to his side.

Eventually our voices rose in response: "*We will remember them.*"

Monk: "*Lest we forget.*"

Echo: "*Lest we forget.*"

Dawn brightened, and the sky turned blue.

Freedom.

We'd spent a week walking with ghosts over our shoulders. Here, they'd become personal. Personal yes, but indistinct. There was no apparent difference in Papuan ghosts from Japanese ghosts, nor those of Americans or the Aussies. They gave a transformative feeling, in their way. They deepened one's appreciation of the dismay their earthly beings must have felt in all of this. Heading back toward camp from the valley side, I held off until I was alone making my way up the hill, not wanting to lose the sense of place and purpose that enveloped me.

We observed our procedures for the last time. Wash-up. Pack-up. Breakfast featuring Kokoda pâté fritters, and cornflakes with powdered milk. Workout. Day eight on the trail defined more endings than beginnings. Brett promised, "You'll enjoy tonight near Kokoda Station. Real food. Maybe a beer." Anticipation was high. First, a walk on gentle hills, mostly downward with long stretches of enjoyable movement. From Isurava that morning, we looked on the Eora Valley and the village of Hoi, where smoke plumed as if in welcome. The plantations—rubber trees, food crops, and palm oil—appeared prosperous. We headed off in the direction of Hoi without hardships.

We trekked an hour or more, crossed two creeks (or was it one creek two times? I'd stopped noting), slowing at one point for a final top up of water. Several of us ignored purification tablets to risk sampling the fresh mountain water. We were not far from the Yodda Valley, where the Mambare River runs, and where a gold rush in 1900 brought an early infiltration (some may say infestation) of white men to the Kokoda region. The old Kokoda Station began in those years, as upwards of a ton of gold was taken out annually. The commerce and growing population resulted in government administration of the area.

Along the ridge near abandoned wartime Deniki, we could see all the way to Kokoda Station on the plateau, with its once-fought-over air-field nearby. In the first two weeks of August during the war, such a view by the Aussies would have looked upon Japanese troop movements, supply shipments, and airfield activity, making the defense of Deniki crucial for the Australians. The Japanese and Australians also fought over Hoi, where we approached. Brett filled us in as we walked. "Imagine foggy days instead of the clear weather we enjoy. Think of the jungle indecipherable from the trail. Think of walking where we walk, not knowing where to put your foot for fear you'd step on the toe of an enemy. You'd smell his breath. Then he'd bayonet you."

It's hard to imagine a more self-aware moment than being bayonetted.

I would face that unbounded horror when I came across an interview[37] by Dr. Peter Williams with the veteran Athol Geare, a private who fought somewhere between Deniki and Brigade Hill, possibly right where we strolled. I could see through his eyes; they were mine—if life

---

37 Dr. Peter Williams, private interview collection, Queensland, 2011.

had delivered up different circumstances. He told about the "kill or be killed" mentality on the Kokoda Track: "One of them, a Japanese, just came straight at us you see, and I got him with my bayonet, got him in the groin. I didn't have time to fire my rifle but we had our bayonets fixed and we had been told of the three vital places, the throat, the groin, and the stomach. We were trained not to stick the bayonet too far in or you wouldn't get it out. And this bloke was coming right at me and I just put my rifle and bayonet straight down automatically, that was to do with our training. I killed that bloke."

Brett continued to jolt us out of comfort, out of the present. He told us how a handful of Australian soldiers had gotten lost in the fog of that same battle. When it lifted, they realized they were behind enemy lines. Japanese troops had bypassed them while advancing. Undetected, both sides had avoided ambush. Now, "The Aussies saw well-armed Japanese ahead of them and behind. Then a heavy fog wrapped them again. They snuck wide around an enemy eager to kill them. Relieved to be reunited with their mates, they turned and faced the enemy head-on."

The villagers of Hoi had watched our campfires go out far above and gauged that we would arrive by noon. The entrance to their village was stonework. A path wound through with the intention of slowing us down, so they could engage us in commerce. There was no mistaking the display of vegetables and passion fruit on sale. The village was clean. A skirted woman wearing a South Pacific beer T-shirt swept dirt beneath her home, the branch-broom searching for litter, smoothing the soil. Butterflies escorted us—if one did not see their unique blue color with clear eyes, you'd think a touch-up artist had fabricated them. Locals prepared lunch. Chicken was on the boil. Cans of Fanta and Coca-Cola sat in a bucket. Monk placed kina in a waiting palm, and picked out two. He pull-tabbed both cans open as I walked by, handing me one with, "Let's toast our arrival, mate." I walked over the submerged boulders that took the trail through Faiwana Creek. Brett said, "That's number eleven. This pleasant crossing marks the last creek." The water moved over the rocks. It was slippery where I splashed. The paste of humidity made clothing uncomfortable. It was windless.

Yeoy, Simon, and Martin were already stripped down where the water pooled in bathtubs of stone. Yeoy claimed one and sank out of view. He popped back up with a nonchalance that belied his shivering. Martin was more truthful. He stepped gingerly on the floor of a pool. He grimaced. He submerged. Then with a splash and a yelp, he bolted upright.

Hoi (or its former name, Palm Camp) was flourishing. Undoubtedly, this was the prettiest village we visited during the whole trip. Kids played everywhere. We left them to take our final steps on the Kokoda Trail, following a tractor road toward Kokoda Station. The porters anointed us with headdresses made from long grass, with flowers pinched into place for color and pomp. They laughed as they placed these tiaras on our heads.

Our strides on this stretch were longer than usual. It was a pleasant pace and we were used to exerting a spring in our step. We were on rhythm as a pack of hikers, cohesive in our sauntering style though differing in our internal emotions. The anxiety of a nearly-completed task hung about us. For some, the horizon was closure. For others, it signaled a return to norms. Still others felt it unwanted, preferring another day in motion. These I know because people hinted at them with their smirks, smiles, or faces of relief. Monk was kibitzing, and there was the inevitable merriment that swarmed near him whenever two or more of the others gathered. He scampered to where I walked alone, my mind not yet calling the trek a success, while acknowledging how far we had come with everyone in good health. The trail was sided by low choko creepers, with room for us to walk beside one another instead of trudging single file and talking over one's shoulder. Monk's laughter evaporated as soon as his step matched mine.

"Been thinking about my old man," he began.

"Think that's really him in the engraving?" I asked.

"I hated that smile," he said. "Always thought it a quirk. Mean."

"But it looks like him?"

"Never actually saw the asshole much," he admitted. "But if eyes and smirks can carry a man's story, I see him in that picture."

"You sure?"

"It's him."

There were twenty feet between where we walked and where Kristy moved alone in front. I felt Monk might want to walk on, leaving with me what he'd just said and finding a new topic with her. I slowed so he could exit without a second thought. He slowed, too. In the next minutes, I learned what Monk needed to share. Thirty years after the man went missing, Monk's mom heard that her husband had been found. Monk's dad was alive. He was rooming in a home for war vets. There he was provided reliable meals and safe surroundings: the basics he had denied his own family. Going against the grain of his soul, Monk made the effort to see his father.

"When I contacted the nursing home, they didn't believe me," Monk said. "He had told them he didn't have any family. To prove I knew what they knew, I asked, 'Got a gunshot scar in his left shoulder?' Woman on other end of the phone confirmed the man had an odd-looking scar on his left shoulder.

"'That's him,' I told her. He came home from Kokoda with that. Or so we were told. Never explained it."

Other trekkers kept their distance from us on that stretch. With my head hanging in sympathy for Monk, the two of us undoubtedly looked to be in serious conversation.

"I connived with the head nurse," he said. "She approached him to say I'd be coming by for a visit. He told the nurse, 'I don't have a son.'" Monk shook his head with incomprehension. "When I finally saw him, my old man looked like Colonel Sanders."

I thought that image a welcomed one. Warmth. Wisdom. Reconciliation. I was about to say so when Monk blurted, "The bastard looked away. He wouldn't match eyes with me."

He left that sad recollection in the foothills of the Owen Stanley Range, and walked ahead.

It is, I suppose, impossible to make a collective experience become singular. There was nothing overly individual about traipsing across a mountain range with mates except one's own pains and perceptions. We were walking like a group picture. Ahead of us was an arch, initially small in its distance until it loomed large and readable: KOKODA TRAIL. It covered most of the path. To avoid walking under it would have meant an intentional diversion. Why did I want to avoid it? Kitsch? I thought so. Like the arch at the beginning of the trail, this hallmark in the wilderness indicated tourism, and I didn't want that. It mocked the emotional completion unresolved in my mind.

Our porters lined up on the other side of the arch. They felt we should walk the last stretch and cross the finish line unaided. Trekkers were scattered along the trail, subconsciously in the groupings evident over dinner that first evening on the trail. At the lead were The Four, deservingly being the first of us to complete the trek as a woman and three men who had made good on their tenacity, and they walked beneath the arch. The One was not far behind, having always been the most likely to complete, followed by The Two, a tranquil husband and wife, not far ahead of The Three, who remained the most boisterous. The Six walked abreast one another right ahead of me, as the roadway was wide. There no longer seemed too many of us.

My legs felt a sense of accomplishment, but did my heart? I'd anticipated a satisfaction of sorts at this stage of the trek, a mental and physical conclusion, but it evaded me. I was weary of all things war, in the way one is overly full after an intense meal. That feeling was complicated by an eagerness for the new setting on the Northern Beaches. Then Monk was beside me again, on my right. His arm slid on the inside of my elbow. He gave a laughing jar. He removed his arm and slung it over my pack, and wrenched my neck in a left arm hug. He moved it back so we were arm-in-arm. And that's how we walked through the arch.

"Made it, mate," smiled Monk.

My smile's strength matched his. "Made it, mate."

A large field lay open before us on the Kokoda Plateau. To one side was the Kokoda Station War Museum. We flopped to the ground, following our packs where they dropped. We were at the end of the walking part of what would eventually be our 120-mile journey from Port Moresby to the Northern Beaches. A few guys lay on their backs, accepting sunrays of benediction.

When the Australian advance arrived at Kokoda Station, they found the Japanese had left. Today the most celebrated Australian and Papuan acknowledgement of the Papuan Campaign is on Kokoda Day, November 3,[38] the day the Aussies retook Kokoda Plateau, its village, and its airfield, and raised their flag. Securing Kokoda Station was the close of Act II in the Papua Theater of War, completing the Kokoda Track phase of the battles. The Australians prepared to advance from there along the Sanananda Track, and to Buna, Sanananda, and Gona—as quickly as possible, in case the Japanese won at Guadalcanal and redeployed those resources to Papua. So it was that the Australians advanced beyond Kokoda Station, the American Ghost Mountain Boys arrived over Kapa Kapa Trail, and the American/Australian alliance marshaled at Milne Bay. In coordinated movements, these Allied forces targeted Japanese strongholds on the Northern Beaches.

Across the onetime parade ground sat a tall cairn to the fallen and to the victors, alongside a memorial recognizing the native carriers. Nearby was a tablet contributed by the Japan-Papua New Guinea Goodwill Society, inscribed: "To all the war dead, Japanese, Papua New Guinean, and Australian in appreciation of their greatest courage." Stone facings

---

38 As they were not involved when Kokoda Station was retaken, the "Bloody Ragged Heroes" of the Thirty-Ninth Battalion separately commemorate Kokoda Day on August 8, in recognition of their first taking of the Kokoda airstrip, which was then lost only days later when the soldiers ran out of ammunition, withdrawing to Isurava.

on the tributes had fallen away. Tiles on the war memorial's base were damaged. I wasn't certain what this lack of care indicated. Was it that the Kokoda Trail's current function as a source of trekker tourism trumped the story behind it in the eyes of today's Papuans?

We boarded a public motor vehicle, known as a PMV. There is still no road through the Owen Stanley Range and none is contemplated. But, from Kokoda Station to the Northern Beaches the land is flat and serviced. There's a decent road by PNG standards.

"Bet there are no maintenance records for the PMV," said Monk as we tossed our bags aside. We soon retrieved them as buffers to lean against or sit on to lessen the board seats bashing into our butts. The truck's nuts and bolts held the frame stiff and uncomfortable all the way to Kokoda Camp, known on more amiable terms as Kouelo Village. We pulled into a fantasy. Buildings were arranged away from the parking spot. There were plenty of sleeping platforms. What's more, there was a kitchen, and dinner was being prepared over flame: chicken crisped, beef blackened, and corncobs rolled as the cook sprinkled salt. "All we need now is beer," joked Anthony.

Monk has a sixth sense when brew is involved. He whistled from further down the building's side, and his hand waved a come-on. Anthony and I followed as sheep. "Lookee here," Monk grinned, holding the lid off a plastic cooler. "Put your hand in there, will ya." He'd already done so, and held a beer bottle sweating ice. He handed it to Anthony. "But still, put your hand in . . ." I did.

"To Kokoda," Monk toasted.

"To mates," added Anthony.

The readiness of dinner meant a quick sorting of our lodgings. Porters jettisoned packs. They had carvings to finish.

We entered the dining area. The table was wide and long, with room for all of the trekkers. There was agreeable space nearby for the porters, creating the ability for us to filter in with one another, as there were plenty of crossover friendships bred from days of crossover reliance.

A counter ran the length of the open-air room, on the top of which was a feast. Grilled everything: potatoes, carrots, peas in pods, steaks, chicken parts, sausages rolled from God-knows-what animal's innards, and salad. Everything we had hungered for the past week, except bacon and eggs, was on offer. Monk arrived with an armful of beers, dispensing them as presents to Kristy, Deirdre, and Tori. He set others down in front of the Kokoda Club Med men.

I walked with him to fetch more. We were each on our fourth, but there was plenty to go around. We continued as gregarious waiters, whether or not the others wanted us to. Time lapsed. The main meal was over and our stomachs groaned with pleasure. Incongruously, strudel appeared for dessert, the pastry fresh. The fruit in them was delicious, if unidentified. Ice cream, too, got passed around.

Brett took the floor, a piece of paper his only prop. "Attention, you riffraff."

"You'll see the last of us tomorrow," Simon shouted. "You'll miss me then."

"Ah, he's got Northern Beaches with us for another four days. Who's to miss?" said Whitey.

Martin rose from the bench, a split-second ahead of Brett's attempt to gain control of the formerly beer-deprived, and now rehydrated, trekkers. "I have a toast," he said formally.

"Toasts are later," Brett said.

In his commanding voice, Martin took control: "There'll now be a toast." He raised a beer and studied the faces of his audience. "Where to begin?" Suddenly, he looked befuddled. "The porters?" It was a question, but taken by all to be his proposal. We chimed: "Cheers to the porters."

"The cooks tonight?"

"Cheers to the cooks tonight," we hollered. Martin sat down. Itemized toasting could take half an hour, given all to whom we were indebted for our pleasures, safety, and accomplishments. This day needed no recaps; it needed nightcaps. Monk returned to the table with more beers.

Brett took back control. "Most of you ordered art carvings," he said, handholding an imaginary microphone. "I'm going to read off your name and that of your porter, and what you asked to be carved. Come forward to receive your stick. Say a few words when you're up here. Most of the porters, but not all of them, will head back to their villages before you're up in the morning. Tonight is thank-you night."

Brett and Yeoy had primed us that if we felt a tip was in order, tonight would be the time to pass that over. "We'll do a group contribution, but if it's personal, hold it in your hand and palm it to the Papuan you wish to thank." US dollars are the accepted currency, as a black market exists for exchange.

A porter may earn 70 kina a day, so 500 or more for the completed trek (perhaps 150 to 160 US dollars). (For comparison, security guards in PNG earn 5 kina an hour.) That covers from where they meet trekkers and load packs on their backs to the end of the journey. The payment includes eight days of hiking, with nothing for the extra work that comes with hunch-weather, delays, or distractions. Tips are welcomed.

Brett worked through his list. Tori and Rod, with their shared porter, received a long, beautifully decorated stick. Robert's porter passed over a full-length walking stick intricately carved from top to bottom, and with a gnarly top. And so it went. At each call, a trekker swayed to the front and met their porter. Gracious words were said. "Couldn't have done it without you." Humor was attempted. "Next time, I'll carry your pack." Jim went on at some length about, "One day I'll return and teach plumbing to your villagers."

"Monk. Kingsole," said Brett.

Much laughter as Monk stood, the neck of a beer bottle in his grip, and wrapped his left arm around Kingsole's neck. Then he patted the multicolored Bob Marley toque. "Sometimes my life depended on you, mate," said Monk. "Other times I know you just liked hiking with me." When Kingsole gave Monk a carved walking stick, it conveyed the respect of one man to another.

"Bowrie. Rick."

Bowrie approached, beamy-eyed under shy lids, head stooped, though I was the one needing to show deference. He held a short stick.

As with each carving, Brett read out what was ordered, "Short stick. Art, no words." Bowrie handed it to me. The curled design was deep-cut and floral. He'd rubbed carbon from a dead fire to highlight the art in white relief. Bowrie held it up in display before letting go so I could see the work in more detail. Nicely done, I thought. I took it in my hands and rolled it. The other side, in inch-high letters, read: KOKODA TREK.

All present belted out the two national anthems, unhindered by certainty of words. They rang with a vigor usually shown at sporting events when your team wins. In this case, both teams had.

There was a slow cavalcade to the toilets. Digestive systems that had adjusted to tasteless noodles, Spam, and an absence of liquor rebelled. Unaccustomed to overeating and bubbles of brew, to say nothing of barbeque meats and gravy, trekker bowels could not hold. There were two outhouses, one of them broken.

FOUR

Nearest Faraway Place

"The only thing new in the world is the history you don't know."
—Harry S. Truman, President of the United States

W e had a breakfast of leftovers and hangovers. Sunday was our last day together. The group was splintering. Some had arranged flights to Moresby. Others were headed overland to the Northern Beaches for a few days. The remaining porters were going home as well. A flatbed truck with a canvas top arrived in the yard and went into reverse so we could board with our packs.

"You like carving?" Bowrie asked.

"It's beautiful. Thank you." The piece came from his heart as much as his hand.

Off we went toward Popondetta, on dirt roads with more potholes than smooth patches. We bounced, not unhappily but uncomfortably. Alongside our road, homes were sporadic, side roads irregular, and cooking fires plentiful.

We left the rugged Owen Stanley Range headed for more hospitable contours. En route, the truck rocked where the Japanese had retreated to the beaches with the Australians in hot pursuit. Part of me wanted to be finished with learning about battles, and have time to dwell on the satisfaction of our Kokoda Trail accomplishment. That was not to be.

We had entered the setting for Act III in the Papua Theater of War. We drove near Oivi and Gorari,[39] nine miles east of Kokoda Station. Japan's South Seas Force was defeated there in the campaign's second largest battle. Nankai Shitai's Horii and others ended up on the bank of the Kumusi River, having rafted and hiked toward the river's mouth. The small group took their chances in a borrowed canoe and set to sea with plans to head along the coast. Tropical storms, however, have their way with small boats and inexperienced sailors. A thunderstorm capsized the craft six miles out to sea. Horii and his orderly swam for shore. Horii announced he could swim no further, and told his aid to report, "Horii died here." The old soldier raised his arms above the sea and shouted, "*Tennōheika Banzai!*" And with his last words pledging, "Long live his majesty the Emperor," Tomitarō Horii sank below the surface.

Our PMV passed through a corridor of history, with those of us on board anticipating a paradise and welcoming Papuans when we arrived at the beaches. It would not always have been the case. Over 70 years ago, these communities of Buna, Sanananda, and Gona were forced to host both the opening act and the closing act on the Papua Theater of War's main stage (off this main stage, action in New Guinea continued into '43 and '44). The Japanese retreating off the Kokoda Track were both trapped by the ocean barrier and saved by that same sea that allowed marine deliveries and evacuations. Villages of the Northern Beaches spread along the shoreline with Buna southeast, Sanananda central, and Gona northwest. In all, the stretch of swamp and open land in front of Buna-Sanananda-Gona is ten to twelve miles across, though it would be much longer if measured in coastline.

To the end, the Japanese never gave up on their belief they could salvage a stalemate in the war. They were confident they would win

---

39 The Japanese lost 840 killed and wounded here, the Australians 340. Twenty Japanese surrendered after the battle, an up-to-then unheard of event in the Papua Campaign.

in Guadalcanal, then mount a counter-counteroffensive in Papua with renewed troops and air and naval support. But the Aussies and Americans would not let that happen. The Allies launched a concentrated advance on all three Japanese strongholds, each a defensive array of pillboxes, bunkers, and trenches.

Before we got to the beaches, we dropped by Popondetta. It was unwelcoming. What we saw was contemporary PNG at its worst, unreflective of the hospitality found elsewhere. Those *raskols* staring at us when we arrived clearly viewed trekkers as a commodity. Our PMV pulled up to a large grocery store, and the parking lot's gate swung open barely wide enough for the truck to drive through. We entered a compound surrounded by barbed wire that separated us from the *raskols*.

It is of course a more complex situation than that. For us, any perceived threat to our safety was passing. For the local population, it had become everyday life. Most families are affected by the *raskols* factor. For some, it is the loss of a child into the fold of crime. For others, it is being a personal victim, or seeing their community as victim. Others wrestle with the lure (aggrandized or forced) to participate as a member of crime organizations. The ubiquitous presence of *raskols* affects the pulse of work and idle time. And it can not but exacerbate the disparities when they are made to hover outside a fence separating them from batches of Caucasian trekkers who enter a grocery store only to reappear laden with grocery treats, which are not shared.

Like discredited relatives who are not talked about over family dinners, I realized we'd not discussed the *raskols* with our porters. Nor had they been a point of conversation among the trekkers, given their absence along the trail. Yet their stories came up. Being in Popondetta reminded one that when Kōkichi Nishimura returned to Papua in the 1980s to retrieve the bones of his comrades, he made his home here. Popondetta is where he stored artifacts, including disabled Arisaka rifles once used by the Japanese. *Raskols* stole them while he was out on the trail seeking solace for the men who had once fired them.

We were soon at the airport, which was not much more than flat land where an airplane could come to a stop. There was a building with garbage around it; inside was broken seating, and possibly the world's most revolting washroom. We were there for goodbyes. People said, "Hope to see you again," which meant, "I've no other words right now."

Kristy, Jim, Kieran, and Simon made ready for the plane. They were leaving along with Robert, Phil, Deirdre, and Michael S. Yeoy was off as well. That left Brett as our custodian, more friend than leader at this point.

"Hugs," said those of us staying, our arms open. Those departing sheltered into the fold and we wrapped in short embraces that implied, "We'll miss what we've had together. Think of me sometime." Their plane took off and banked into the clouds, taking their depiction of this tale with them.

We were a happy lot left behind: Tori and Rod, the Kokoda Club Med six, Monk and myself. The sea was only a dozen miles away. We anticipated beauty and relaxation, and walking without a jungle canopy. Our truck was crowded, as we'd invited some of the remaining porters to join us. One of them was Winterford with his guitar. He and the rest lived in the villages we were going to visit. They were smart enough to move forward over the main wheels, where the ride was more stable. Bowrie and Kingsole hung from the back of the deck, holding on to roof iron. They seemed to enjoy the bounce-a-minute potholes. They were almost home to family and time off the trail, not to mention home-cooked food prepared by wives and mothers and neighbors.

"We arrange a bank account for each porter," said Brett, dispelling my impression that they had "money in their jeans." He explained that they were one of the companies doing so, in part because it reduced the need for trek leaders to carry cash. It also provided porters with what he called "a start at the mechanics of managing money."

I thought the older porters would have sorted that out already. Brett corrected me. "Their earnings go to their family," he said. "Sometimes they don't see much of the money themselves. Theirs is a sharing economy, known as the *wantok* system." In brief, the *wantoks* are your extended family, as in ones who speak a common language, a morphed Tok Pisin word for the English "one-talk." It is centuries old. It is the basis of tribal welfare, given how numerous and diverse the tribes are. *Wantoks* are definitive in the social structure of Papua New Guinea. *Wantoks* are those who care for you—and for whom you care, particularly if you're a source of income. Thus the establishment of the referenced bank account for a porter makes them more central to their community, and helps prevent money slipping through their fingers. Brett put it this way: "It gives them an ongoing role instead of simply handing over little wads of paper money at trek's end."

This approach reflected the trekking company's values. The firm also flew porters from Popondetta to Moresby when they were starting a trek. Some organizers require porters to show up at Owers' Corner on a certain date. They hike without packs from north-to-south in a few days in order to turn around and make the start of the northbound hike with a trekker's goods on their back.

The ten trekkers leaned into their arms or put chins on packs as we bounced to Buna, through Oro Province. Buna's vicinity was our destination, as it had been in 1942 for advancing Allied troops with killing on their minds, and the retreating Japanese with evacuation on their minds. As Japanese soldiers phrased it, "Heaven is Java; hell is Burma; but no one returns alive from New Guinea."

As we neared Buna, the porters made their way onto the truck's roof or hung forward to see their village come into view. They were boisterous, being out of the territory of other tribes and into that of their own. The porters had been described to us as putting "village first, tribe second, and PNG last." All the while, they sang a song we hadn't heard on our journey with them. It was uplifting, even though we didn't understand a word. The music was as wonderful as the physical surroundings. It was their homecoming song. "Cocky's Sorrow song," said Winterford. "It is a courtship song about the bird, the Bush Cock, a rooster crow. Now, we sing as a lullaby." We were among the Orokaiva peoples. This song of theirs celebrated reunion. Martin tried recording it, but the song was over before he got organized. A short while later, our jostling was over too, as the PMV rolled to a stop on the beach.

Anthony hopped off the truck and made for the water. He dropped his pants and shed his shirt. He dove in, waves cresting over his back. Out he swam.

"Any crocodiles?" yelled Darren.

"None would want him," said Michael.

"This. This. This is what I've wanted!" Anthony shouted. With water up to his chest, he raised his arms high above his head and looked to the world above for the attention we withheld.

We ambled behind Brett. "A handful of rooms opened here last year," he said. "Your visit makes you a novelty." The village was out in full, their population numbering in the hundreds. Bare-chested men and bare-breasted women greeted us with song. They danced around us, then in front of us. Their traditional attire, which turned out to be everyday wear, impressed me; it was not costuming for our entertainment. "Maybe two or three hundred outsiders came here last year," said Brett.

We bowed toward their happy faces and accepted the blessing of floral necklaces. Our gear disappeared in a final gesture by the porters, who were about to disappear themselves. Villagers narrowed our pathway, ensuring we walked on course to our overnight lodging. A tall man with the bearing of authority waited before us. He spoke in Tok Pisin. His hands pointed in different directions, indicating we had permission to walk anywhere and speak with anyone. We learned that a religious jamboree of sorts was happening this day and the next. His smile concluded with words I took to mean, "Make yourselves at home."

Our shelter was open and airy. There was enough room for all of us. The wood frames and woven roof were not yet faded by sun or rough weather. Our packs were on the porch. Trekkers tossed them into rooms with space for two travelers apiece. Monk picked up both our bags and walked to the last doorway. Our new home was lovely.

"I liked the look on Anthony's face when he was in the water," said Monk. "I'm going." We hitched on our swim trunks and made for the beach. We would explore the village later. First, though, we'd take a swim in the Solomon Sea.

Walking alone along the beach later, I was struck that while we had left the jungle and were off the Kokoda Trail, we were no less bothered by the war. American, Australian, and Japanese soldiers fighting here faced dismal situations. The slush of swamps and the disorientation of flat lands, the bullets and bombardments that came from so many directions, took hundreds of lives. Later, when I was back home, I would be forced to reflect on this beach moment when Dr. Williams showed me a photograph of three war casualties beached on the sand as waves washed toward them. It caused a sensation when published in America's *Life* magazine in September 1943 with the caption, "Dead Americans on the Beach at Buna." It was taken right where I strolled, oblivious to their sacrifice.

Given the tropical paradise, the war contrasted starkly to our sunny days with peace on shore. I felt I knew the Kokoda *Trail* as a walk; I could understand that experience in my muscles. Knowing the Kokoda *Track's* military history, however, tested my understanding. How could one reconcile nicknames like Bloody Buna and Maggot Beach with the paradise we experienced? Said another way, we were making camp exactly where the Allies mounted a cumbersome but capable obliteration of the Japanese defense, taking Gona, then Buna, and finally Sanananda. One newsreel documentary of the time portrayed the victory as having "hurled the enemy back into the sea."

Maroubra Force drove the Nankai Shitai from Kokoda Trail to Oivi-Gorari and back to the Northern Beaches. The American infantry arrived by air and water from Milne Bay, undetected by Japanese intelligence until it was well advanced, at which point over a dozen Zero fighters targeted American transport barges, sinking several. The Ghost Mountain Boys, having clawed over aptly named places such as Fever Ridge, and suffering an assortment of illnesses from pneumonia to rashes, jungle rot, night blindness, and beriberi, arrived here on November 14. Every one of them feared the elite Japanese troops they were about to face. Eventually, the Allies were able to land tanks, the first appearance of such weaponry in the Papuan Campaign, as the Japanese did not have them. Allies added howitzers and the formidable 25-pounders, but no heavy artillery. It became as ugly as war can be.

An Australian correspondent, George Johnston, who also filed with *Life* and *Time* magazines, was with the Allies on these beaches in 1942, and recounted this story from an American private: "We'd been advancing for hours through stinking swamps up to our knees when we reached better country in the coconut groves, but when we pushed through the plantation to the beach we met heavy machine-gun fire . . . We attacked in a broad, sweeping line, charging across the sand with fixed bayonets and grenades, and stormed our way right into the position. It was the wildest, maddest, bloodiest fighting I have ever seen." A late December issue of *Time* magazine informed the US public about the situation near Buna, saying, "Nowhere in the world today are American soldiers engaged in fighting so desperate, so merciless, so bitter, or so bloody."

It was a contemplative afternoon for us on the Northern Beaches, not pressed by chores, hiking, or responsibilities. We read and relaxed. We talked about how seldom New Guinea attracted the world's attention. Into our conversation came the name Michael Rockefeller, and his disappearance in New Guinea during the 1960s.

First the facts: 23-year-old Michael Rockefeller traveled to New Guinea in 1961 searching for Asmat artifacts to be displayed in New York's Metropolitan Museum of Art, founded by his grandparents, John D. Rockefeller and Abby Aldrich Rockefeller of the Standard Oil fortune. Rockefeller's interest was sparked by his father's collection, assembled through brokers and displayed in the Museum of Primitive Art, adjunct to the Met. Nelson Rockefeller wrote about the Asmat's "staggering abundance of artistic ideas and the vitality which marks the execution of every piece."

Michael Rockefeller's fateful journey began as a provisioned trip to procure drums, wood-carved masks, shields, and *bisj* poles. Michael and 34-year-old Dutch anthropologist René Wassing embarked in a 40-foot dugout canoe with pontoons. Their two teenage rowers could not navigate toward safety when the weather turned in the Arafura Sea. Waves flipped the catamaran, loosing its provisions. Frightened, the two boys swam to land three miles away. Rockefeller and Wassing hung onto the overturned boat throughout the night.

Wassing was adamant they await rescue. In fact, the first rescue boat languished out of gas, ten miles away. Impatient, Rockefeller strapped two empty fuel containers to his belt for flotation. As he swam away, the former wrestler said to Wassing, "I think I can make it."

That Rockefeller was missing created an international news furor, given he was the son of New York's governor. Nelson Rockefeller left New York with Michael's twin Mary. They flew to Hawaii, then to Hollandia (today Jayapura) in New Guinea, which put them and their 100-strong press corps near the search area.

Within two days of their mishap, the Dutch Royal Air Force rescued Wassing from where he floated with the overturned boat, but Michael was never to be seen again. At the time, searchers remained optimistic, and a favored outcome many hoped was true was of Michael making shore, being rescued by natives, and slowly regaining his stamina in one of their villages. As more and more time elapsed, that idea morphed into stories of Michael refusing opportunities to reconnect with the civilized world, remaining as a full member of the tribe. That scenario was revived in 2008, when documentarian Fraser Heston found forgotten reels of 16mm film. In 1969, a cameraman had spent time among the Asmat people. The resulting film was developed and shelved in England until discovered by Heston during his making of *The Search for Michael Rockefeller.* Footage shows a white tribesman of Michael's physique and time-hampered appearance paddling with nine Asmat men. The photograph's tantalizing inference has not been corroborated.

More recently, journalist Carl Hoffman visited the Asmat. It culminated in his book *Savage Harvest.* He drew confessions that their elders killed Michael Rockefeller. With that oral history, Hoffman fashioned a storyline of Michael being speared as the waves lapped shore around his body. Hoffman closes the account with speculation that the Asmats' secrecy over the years reflected their expectation that if the truth were known, the Rockefellers would be honor bound to seek physical retribution.

In Hoffman's telling of the speculative drama, Rockefeller swam into capture by cannibals. I'll work with the inferences: They plunged a fishing spear into his ribs, piercing him to the beach. The blow of a stone ax to the neck likely followed, after which the practice would be to pry his head apart from his body with their knives. In this scenario, they could have lit a cooking fire on the beach, carted Rockefeller's dismembered body atop it, and celebrated the day with a hearty meal, eating the anthropologist and thereby absorbing all that was good with his spirit.

In the custom, as I understand it from Hoffman's book and other readings about headhunting and cannibalism, the head was prized for the brains, which would have been roasted and eaten, after which the skull would have been displayed. Eventually, the cooled bones could be fashioned for knives, drumsticks, or trinkets. After the hair was singed over the fire, it could be mixed with charcoal and blood and a little sand for texture, and then used to paint the victors' bodies.

What struck me when I later went to recount the story here was how easily I slipped into a sensationalism for which I chastised earlier writers and current bloggers in their perpetuation of stereotypes such as "cannibal savages." Yes, cannibalism and headhunting were practiced, under specific circumstances in that general area at the time, so it's not a complete stretch to consider that Rockefeller might very well have met this fate. However, there are other completely plausible ways in which Rockefeller could have disappeared. On a subconscious level, people may want to believe Rockefeller was killed and eaten because it's the most outrageous outcome.

With the mystery unsolved to this day, the Rockefeller family maintains drowning as the cause of death. To be sure, it makes for a more comfortable storyline around which to grieve.

Brett called our attention from atop the stairs of an open building. Dinner came our way off a wood-fired grill. If there were a posted menu, it could have stated: "Fresh corn cooked in husks, butter melted within. Chicken grilled in a sauce you'll never identify. Our pasta has a seasoning we won't admit to you. And there'll be a fruit you don't recognize. You'll never taste anything this delicious again in your life." Platters were brought to our rectangular table. I wondered if local families were going without their portion so the display for guests would be impressive. No, we were told. There were sufficient resources to share, and share they did.

Strains of the hymn "Blest Be the Tie That Binds" reached our table. I recognized it immediately as a nightly staple from summer boys' camp. Evensong.

"Seventh-day?" I asked Brett.

"Not here. It's Episcopalian, a bend of Anglicanism. Inroads in a competition for the faithful," he said. "The German part of the big island is Lutheran." One God. Many ways. There were only so many souls. There was only so much money.

I walked toward the music. A hundred or more people sat on the ground or in foldout chairs. Kids ran about, quietly though. They were all in song. I sat behind the congregation. A man and woman with two children motioned me forward to sit with their family. A guitarist, a trombone player, and a drummer riffed on stage. The drum was a *kundu*, found throughout Papua New Guinea. "Snake skin," the man told me, indicating the material used in this instrument. I've since learned that many believe playing such a drum summons voices of the village's ancestors. That evening, though, the drummer and his trio were sharing one theme: salvation. "On a hill far away, stood an old rugged cross . . ." everyone sang. Even with all my years' absence from church, the lyrics came back. "The emblem of suffering and shame."

"How long will the band play?" I asked.

"An hour and some minutes," the man said.

I stayed for most of that. There was nothing pretentious in the band's appearance or in the assembly. Their devotions were comforting, though they are no longer mine. I didn't sing aloud, though the words of the old time religious hits ran through my mind, brought to life by those around me.

I returned to my friends. We wanted beer. The previous night had whetted our tongues and we'd returned to basic longings. It was growing dark and the consensus among us was that the wide open sky would soon fill with stars in an exhibition we'd never before experienced. Even Aussies, with their enchanting Outback, nod respect to Papua New Guinea's equatorial proximity and brilliant night sky. "If the sky's going to be lit, then why not us?" Monk said.

Anthony asked, "Where can we buy some beer?"

"Ask Woody or Winterford," Brett said.

"Where's Woody?"

"With Winterford."

"And Winterford is . . . ?"

"With Woody."

Martin intervened, pointing. "That them over there?"

I tagged along with Mark, Anthony, and Monk.

"Where might we find beer?" Anthony asked the two men.

Woody and Winterford looked at one another as though they knew something they shouldn't tell. "Well," the ever-affable Winterford[40] smiled, "There's the store over there. It has beer."

"Or had," snickered Woody.

Anthony, Mark, Monk (with a dog's nose for beer), and I set off across the field to the kiosk. The shutters were open, hinged at the top. Chips and soda sat on the counter.

"He-l-lo," said Anthony, looking for the clerk.

There was no answer.

"He-l-lo!" he trilled again.

A woman came from behind the small building and smiled hesitantly over the counter.

"Is there any beer?" asked Anthony.

"Beer?"

"Beer!"

"Two bottles," she said. With that, she looked behind her. Seeing something move, she said, "One bottle."

"One bottle?" said Anthony.

"Yes," she said, once more looking behind her. Something moved again.

She said, "We're out of beer."

Monk leaned his upper body all the way across the counter to look in, then stood back in place. He laughed to the three of us. "Follow me."

Monk led us around back of the kiosk. There stood Bowrie, Kingsole,

---

40 In September 2017, dispiriting news came from our trek organizers. "One of our local Kokoda Trail team members, carrying equipment on behalf of a Getaway Trekking client, suffered a cardiac arrest." Monk and I were saddened by what we learned. "Despite the best efforts of our Wilderness First Aid trained staff member and qualified medical personnel, Winterford Tauno was unable to be revived." Guitar Man had been on the approach to Ioribaiwa, where now a memorial garden blooms in his name.

and two locals we hadn't met. On the ground in front of them were empty beer bottles. In their hands were two newly opened ones, the last of local inventory.

"Is there any more beer?" Monk asked Kingsole.

"Yes, more beer," was the reply.

"Where?" asked Monk.

"Next village."

"Can we walk there?"

"Take too long," said Kingsole.

"Then we'll run." Monk does not let go easily, especially of beer.

"It's dark," said Kingsole.

Monk had a desperate want. It came from being denied.

Kingsole offered, "He will run." He pointed at Bowrie's mate.

"But it's dark," said Monk.

"He always runs in the dark," said Kingsole.

We pooled cash and gave it all to a kid we would not recognize in the light of day. Kingsole said something in Tok Pisin. The boy ran from us. Kingsole sipped the last cold beer in the village. To us he said, "Later."

Two hours after our challenge had been identified as a lack of beer, the lad sent to fetch it walked into the circle of trekkers lying on our backs on the grass gazing up at the stars. He came upon us so quietly we were startled.

"Who are you?" asked Tori.

"Beer man," said Monk.

The boy had a case of beer under each arm. Twenty-four. Heavy loads. Kingsole and Bowrie walked up beside him. "The next village was out of beer," said Kingsole. "So he ran to the next one. It was out, too. So he ran on." We broke into hoots of respect.

"More money?" asked Rod.

"No. You are guests." After Kingsole's statement, the three of them left.

"Beer's warm," said Martin as he opened a case.

"Let's find a refrigerator," said Whitey. "Save them for tomorrow afternoon."

Instead of drinking warm beer, we lay on the grass in the dark and told star stories. No longer did anyone feel inclined to reminisce about our day's hardships, or share self-knowledge. One by one our circle grew smaller as a trekker rose, made for the shelter, and succumbed to sleep.

We awoke to our day of least expectations. Buna proved the perfect setting for that. Kokoda Club Med was the first up. They skipped breakfast and headed to the black sand beach with a sense of purpose. Monk and I followed, taking our time. Morning music flowed from the day's first religious gathering. Villagers were still returning from wherever they'd gone in last night's dark. They were greeted with reminders of their chosen course for salvation in tunes both joyous and infectious. The entire village was in song. Voices drifted over cooking fires, coming from women raking the ground's little rocks, or filtering out of male coffee klatches not yet ready to join the throng in person but game to participate in the singing.

Brett jogged to catch up to us. When he neared, he stated a plan for a day without plans. "Going to see crashed World War II planes in an hour. Japanese Zeros. American P-39s. Rod and Tori are going. You wanna come?"

"Sure," said Monk.

I once saw a downed American warplane in a museum in North Korea, where it was propped in a celebratory pose chosen for propaganda purposes. Here, I anticipated it would be displayed more respectfully, and wanted to see it.

When Monk and I got to the beach, our trekker friends were either neck-deep in the ocean or knee-high kicking waves. The Solomon Sea rolled in.

"Honest, the water's finally warm," Anthony said.

Wanting time alone, I kept walking past their splashing and down the long beach. These villages, this beach, once crawled with Japanese who were hell-bent on ravaging Papua. In fact, when landing, they anticipated their Papuan Campaign as "quick work." It was hard for me to envision the surviving Japanese soldiers who retreated here. They would have been bedraggled, crawling more than walking, insect- and malaria-ridden, and too tired for an ocean bath to shed the lice. The salt would have stung their wounds.

I roamed off the beach along a pathway, toward homes built back from the winds, and where high tide would not surge. It was a neighborhood of sorts, off from the main village. It was their normal morning, and my odd appearance was smiled upon. Kids cackled. I felt I was able to stay so long as I didn't disturb.

Three of our camp gear porters were there. Not ones I knew well, even though we'd shared a trail for nine days. They recognized me—white and six feet tall among a village of brown-skinned people—before I noticed them. I waved. They tilted their faces in sync and smiled. We had nothing to discuss, really. It was nice to see familiar faces of another origin, a curiosity for each of us. I let my head follow their lean as a returned salute.

They walked with me in silence. Used to caring and escorting, they fell in as unobtrusively as the air, and hung near me without a word until I was out of the village.

It might have been half an hour later when I returned to the beach. Monk was pushing off a boat. Fishing poles stuck up from the gunwales. Michael flashed a net in the air as though to catch butterflies, but it was meant for fish. There looked to be ample room aboard for the six trekkers and three locals. When their skiff was out of the sand's hold and the water deepened, the Papuan mariner dropped oars. With hard pulls, he set the boat toward the horizon, not a cloud, not an island, not an obstacle in sight.

"They'll be back in a few hours," said Monk when I neared him. "With tonight's dinner." More promising was an old man and young boy in a boat 100 feet from shore. They dropped nets and sat back in the boat, eyes away from the sun.

Tori and Rod were waiting when we got back to the barracks, an unhurried air about them. We'd fallen into friendship that didn't need a lot of words. We headed away in single file, picking up Brett as we walked. There was a road out of town, and we took it. We trailed Brett off of it and onto a hard-to-see path in tall grass. Fifteen minutes later I'd have said he was lost, but he kept going and we kept following. Abruptly, we came onto an airplane wing overgrown with tree vines, sticking out from the ground in the jungle.

"American," said Brett.

Rod stomped on reluctant branches and pushed others out of the way to reveal more of the jagged form. Japanese on the ground would have huddled in fear of its destructive power. A well-placed, or lucky, antiaircraft gunner changed all that. Confident pilot, payload of bombs, insignia of American might—all tumbled to the ground right here. The plane plummeting to this very spot must have brought cheers from the Japanese, if they had had the energy at that point for such false joy.

Close by was the fuselage of a Japanese plane. Its engine no longer glistened. The Mitsubishi-built plane was for long range and had likely come out from Rabaul on its last day. Brett told us that the Japanese had taken off armor and fuel safety features to enhance distance flying. "Japanese called it a flying cigar, or *hamaki*. Our pilots nicknamed it 'the flying Zippo.'" Brett (who I suspected of making up the name, but maybe he didn't) said that by the middle of 1942 the Allies had begun giving Japanese planes spotter names for reporting; bombers got girls' names—this one was "Betty"—and fighter aircraft were granted boys' names. *Betty*'s wing had separated and was punched into the ground.

However good the pilots were, whatever code of honor they served, the dying of these American, Japanese, and Australian crew lacked individual relevance in the moment we stood there. That felt uncomfortable to me. Battles often leave the dead of one side indistinguishable from the dead of the other. People "back home" in Australia or Japan or America would have felt despair for loved ones who never returned. And over the ensuing decades, people talked of the dead in phrases that amalgamated individuals, first into "our boys," and then "everyone who died." We were looking at two items on that tally.

"I have a tough time keeping my head up," said Monk. His depression was contagious.

"It's beyond sad," said Tori.

I offered, "They'd have had but seconds to curse or pray forgiveness."

As testament to the victorious march forward, we touched an American mortar weapon tucked in the ever-growing camouflage of the jungle, obviously mounted here when the ground position was gained after the air crew's sacrifice. The gun's powerful presence was accented rather than diminished by corrosion.

MacArthur was frustrated when Buna and Gona did not collapse as quickly as he wished. His orders were sometimes erratic, and disobeyed. Among them, "Remove all officers who won't fight," and directives to advance "regardless of costs." There were counter insults from experienced Australians who felt their troops were better fighters than the newly-arrived Americans encountering the Japanese for the first time. All this took place as an influx of Allied troops outmatched the Japanese two-to-one by the end of 1942.

MacArthur had earlier reasoned that the Australians were driven back along the Kokoda Track because of their inability to match the Japanese fighting force. This seems a fair assessment in that the initial deployment of militia did not include soldiers toughened in previous battles. They clearly didn't have the same experience as the highly-trained Japanese troops who had been tested against the Chinese.

MacArthur's insult (as it was taken by the Australians) came back on him when some of the American troops on the Buna-Gona front were reported as "listless and tired and not hardened for jungle operations" and refused to fight. Commander Blamey told MacArthur he'd rather deploy Australian troops on the Northern Beaches, "because he knew they would fight," as one historian put it. The view was that the available US troops were not as good as the available Australians. In Blamey's words to Australia's Prime Minister Curtin in early December 1942, "My faith in the [Australian] militia is growing, but my faith in the Americans has sunk to zero."[41]

MacArthur knew that if victory eluded him in PNG, it would elude the Allies in the South Pacific as well, and his own reputation was riding on the outcome. He had fought successfully so far "on a logistical shoestring." Now he wanted to take the lead position on behalf of all Allied forces as they moved toward Tokyo. To demonstrate his capabilities and secure that role for himself, he needed to win in Papua before the US Navy's pending success in Guadalcanal. He ordered American General Eichelberger to take Buna "or don't come back alive."[42]

As Tori, Rod, Monk, Brett, and I returned from the plane crashes, I wondered about the different Aussie and American fighting styles during the most prominent battles in the vicinity, the Kokoda Track and Guadalcanal. I said to Brett that I thought the difference between the two battles must have been significant: "Kokoda a constantly moving confrontation with very little but the wiles of either side in play, Guadalcanal a conventional military action with a traditional face-off and the effective use of every tool available, ships, large ordnance, and planes."

Monk interrupted. "The Aussies became very good at guerrilla tactics, whereas the Americans were good at scorched earth and preferred

---

41 Peter Williams, whose forthcoming book is about the Northern Beaches battles, offered this comment: "The essential problem was the Americans would not actually attack the Japanese trenches. They'd plan an attack, and do a lot of shooting, but then the infantry would just advance 50 yards and go to ground again. The term soldiers use about attacking is to 'close with the enemy,' which means get right up to him, kill him, and occupy his positions. The US infantry at Buna would not 'close with the enemy.'"

42 A reported variation of this statement is: "If you don't take Buna, I want to hear that you are buried there!"

to blast away from a comfortable position." Brett, always the clarifier, put it another way: "The American approach may not have succeeded on the Kokoda Track. The Aussie tactics may not have worked on Guadalcanal." And before I could articulate my thinking, Rod said it for us. "When the two armies joined in the final battles, the combination of skills and styles meant the Japanese had no chance."

We slowed our walk in front of a dusty schoolyard. A shell crater from World War II was part of the playground. Tori set up a photograph, and then didn't take it when the kids moved out of frame, losing the contrast of subjects. Kids kicked a soccer ball toward goal posts in what is the world's best hope for diplomacy: an affordable sport played with passion and little regard for a competitor's looks, financial acumen, or skin color; instead, each player bends in deep respect for others' deft moves and tenacity. A soccer field's goal posts may be the world's most ubiquitous peace symbol. Play ended, and the open-air classroom reloaded with chattering kids, some leaning out the window to gawk at us as we stood gawking at them. They, and we, envied the others' apparent happiness. A boy student waved, his smile as broad as his learning.

"No fish," said Mark. He was the first of the returning boaters we saw back in the village. "Skunked," he offered.

"What, no dinner?" exclaimed Monk.

"They'll have something," said Anthony, trailing behind. "Someone has to know where the fish swim."

After four hours in the boat, they had been beaten by the sun, washed over by salt air, and defeated by the fish. "Beer would be nice," said Michael.

The previous evening, Monk and Anthony made a half-hearted attempt to find a refrigerator when the warm beer arrived. They'd returned to announce: "Found a fridge. Found a plug. No place to plug it in. No ice. No cold." Cooling the beer had been left as a morning chore, assigned to Whitey and Darren. Thirsty Australians will do anything for a cold beer, but Aussie ingenuity had lapsed on the grass; no one thought to put the beer in the cold stream out back. "We fixed their fridge," Whitey told us now. "Well, fixed the generator for the fridge."

"It's been broken for months," said Darren. "Now it works. Give the beer an hour."

"If you want to hear firsthand about Kapa Kapa, you should meet Basil," Brett said, responding to my questions. I'd heard that the difficult trail had been trekked recently, and wanted to know more about it.

"Basil?" I said.

"Lives here. Actually, he's the guy who owns the fridge that's cooling the beer. He's one of the few people since World War II who's hiked all of Kapa Kapa." Brett pointed to the other end of the cookhouse. Beyond a shack that held the fridge, I saw two men seated in chairs and talking in low laughs.

I walked over. "You'll be Basil," I said, extending my hand. His mate introduced himself as Humphrey, Basil's son. His hand turned into a friendly fist that bumped mine in what I realized was an old antic of his, not an adoption of modern fashion.

"You've been on Kapa Kapa, I hear."

"Two times," said Basil. He looked wily. In his prime, this elder must have been a formidable hiker. He sat back in his chair. "Once I walked it with a man from an Australian company. He thinks Americans will want to trek it." He sighed. "Very difficult. It's not walked much, not by foreigners. Maybe once a year someone does. Not every year. Seventeen days. The jungle's growing over it. Except where locals walk."

Humphrey said, "You know it's twice as long as the Kokoda Trail."

I asked, "And the second time?"

Basil smiled. "Same man, with paying customers. We made it. Steeper steeps than the Kokoda. More dangerous than the Kokoda." He tapped his forehead. "Sixty percent up here." He grabbed his leg. "Fitness forty percent. A tough walk in paradise."

Basil told me he started work as a porter on the Kokoda Trail in 1983, when he was twenty-three years old, and completed his 300th trip years ago. "They mentioned me in the *Lonely Planet* book," he said. "I like the ups and I like the downs. I don't like hiking on the level."

Sensing he was retired, in whatever ways Papuans retire, I asked Basil, "Would you do Kapa Kapa again?"

"I would not do it again," he replied firmly. "We must remember the past but look forward. It should be trekked. Just not by this old man." He laughed. It sounded conclusive, and I accepted that our conversation was over.

"Basil," I said. "Is it possible to get a shave and a haircut?" My beard was scruffy after ten days.

"Haircut, yes."

"And?"

"Shave, no."

"Let's start with the haircut," I said. "Who would do this?"

"Tuksy," said Basil.

"And where might I find Tuksy?"

"He will come to you."

Twenty-four cold beers eventually made their way to our circle, instead of lunch. In the camaraderie that followed, we reminded one another about hill climbs that kept getting steeper and steeper in retelling.

Later, I was in the reading bungalow that doubled as our breakfast and dinner place. It was hot, a day without breeze. We sweat as we sat. There were a dozen books on a shelf and Martin was into one entitled *World War II*. It was large format and each page looked, to my upside-down glancing, to be a collage of photographs, maps, and memorabilia such as letters. There were charts. Martin read a quote about where we'd hiked. "One of the most bitter campaigns of the war, fought in possibly the most hostile terrain and unforgiving climate experienced in any theater."

We digested that.

"Did you know what was going on elsewhere in World War II while the South Pacific was being fought over?" He asked this while shifting the book to face me so I could see it properly. I flipped the pages he'd been looking at. There I saw photographs of Anglo-US troops landing in northwest Africa in the fall of 1942, Operation Torch. That enabled British General Montgomery to blunt the Afrika Korps under German Field Marshal Rommel, known as the Desert Fox. Montgomery's forcing Rommel to retreat back to his base in Tunis is said to have "turned the tide of the war." A page later, I read of the Soviets reversing Germany's assault on Stalingrad in the fall of 1942. It, too, was said to have "turned the tide of the war." All the while, Australian and American troops were taking on the Japanese right where Martin and I sat reading; actions that, along with Guadalcanal, were later said to have "turned the tide of the war."

What struck me while reading this book, and what I did not know, was a paragraph about the Casablanca Conference between US President Roosevelt and British Prime Minister Winston Churchill. In Casablanca, mid-January of 1943, the two leaders took their decisions to invade Sicily, to begin ruthless bombing of Germany, and to increase US troops in Britain as a buildup for invasion of Europe. It was in Casablanca the two agreed their goal was victory that ended with, as the book said, "on Roosevelt's insistence, the unconditional surrender of Germany, Italy, and Japan."

"Haircut man?" This call came from outside, the voice hesitant. The staircase creaked. I turned in my chair. A boy in his late teens stood on the bottom rung. His stance indicated I should go to him rather than him interrupt our space.

"Tuksy," I said, walking over.

"Justin is what I am, if you like."

"I like Tuksy better, if okay with you," I said.

"Yes, Tuksy is name."

He shook my extended hand as much to make sure I didn't stumble the stairs as to seal our business arrangement.

"*Katim gras?*" he said.

"Katim . . .? I beg your pardon?"

"*Katim gras*," he repeated. "I cut hair. Yours."

"Please," I said. Seeing that he was without barber utensils, I presumed we would walk to his shop. "Where?"

"Here." He pulled a plastic chair out of the shade and onto the grass a few feet from the building. He removed a pair of homemade scissors from his pocket. They were saw-toothed in the style used for cutting cloth. He held a razor blade in his right hand. The blade might have been called "old-fashioned," as it would have fit a razor like my dad used in the 1950s. But Tuksy didn't have a clasp for the blade nor a handle. The blade was bare.

"First a shave," he announced.

Sitting in the midday sun, I hoped the building's shadow would move our way. I kept my posture steady and offered a tilted head for his assessment. Thinking this would not take long, I opted against interrupting Tuksy to retrieve my sunglasses.

Chin up and away from him, I readied for the water and lather. There is a form of shaving that is quite special—the soft warmth of a towel folded with hot water, opening the pores, letting the skin give up flexibility; then foam smoothed all over one's cheeks and chin. Once the lather settles on the whiskers, the barber's first round of shaving moves the razor along the neck to take the easiest trims. This allows the tougher upper face whiskers to bathe longer in the foam, softening them. Under Tuksy's approach, that was not to be. There was no water, no soap, and no lather. So why bother with a towel?

Tuksy scraped the semi-sharp blade against my dry cheek. He steadied the razor between his fingers. His nervous hand touched my sideburn. The razor scraped. It tore the stubble loose on the first pass and removed it on the second. Tuksy was methodical. "Keep your face quiet," he said. He scraped away more whiskers with his handheld blade. With every four configured carvings, a square inch of beard disappeared. Given the acreage of my face, it could be a long afternoon. I started to wish I'd gone for my sunglasses. Shadow never came; the sun beat at me.

I was beginning to wonder if this was Tuksy's first time shaving someone. Thinking I'd hint for lather across my face, I asked, "Maybe a splash of water?"

"Yes," he said, and brought me a glass of water to drink.

Smiling, I said, "Like this." I leaned back and poured half the water over my face, rubbing the stubble to soften it. Tuksy nodded, and immediately scraped the blade where it was wettest. Slowly he carved downward. The blade moved like a hoe used in tending a garden.

"It is good," I encouraged.

"I've never done this to a white man," he confessed.

Martin walked over and advised (was he talking to Tuksy or me?), "The goatee stays."

Nearly an hour of scraping passed. Not a nick. "I sing in a band," said Tuksy, when I asked about his non-village life. "It is a Jesus band. We want our faith to share. Strong." He told me the group had five members and a regular run of services and events. Tuksy explained their repertoire included, "Songs we write about us and the Lord." The sun reddened my face. My barber worked diligently and without rest, his blade becoming even less sharp. Which meant it impolite for me to get up, or to question his band's music selection.

When he finished around my face, leaving Martin's recommended goatee, I asked, "Would you sing one of your songs for me?"

"Yes."

Nothing happened.

Tuksy took the cloth-cutting scissors in ready. He scuffed up my hair with his other hand. He brandished the scissors before my eyes. He made decisive cuts. Hair fell away in chunks.

I've a penchant for getting haircuts in out-of-the-way places, such as Tibet or Timbuktu (in fact, one of my books is called *To Timbuktu for a Haircut*). A tenet is to never interfere with what the local artist feels should be your new hairstyle. That + the setting = the experience. Anyway, I've found that the difference between a good haircut and a bad haircut is three days.

Singer, songwriter, and barber Tuksy also carved the author's walking stick with a missionary's message.

Monk came over to Tuksy. "Clip him short. He's become shaggy and embarrassing to the rest of the lads." I wanted to smile a sarcastic thank-you, but Tuksy was working the finish on my face and any move invited a cut. He also used the razor on my hair, slicing at patches that had proven stubborn for the scissors. When Monk left, Tuksy sang. The song was in his language, and I knew nothing of its meaning except the repeated reference to "Jesus." The melody was extraordinary and not at all familiar. Tuksy was done. I was baked. He poured the remaining half-cup of water on my head and face, and rubbed it.

Monk returned. He told Tuksy, "It's Rick's birthday in two days, and you've made him look years younger."

Tuksy smiled at the accolade. I held out my hand with coins, kina, and US dollar bills. He picked among them and took what he felt fair. It was maybe two dollars. I insisted on more.

When you are the out-of-country guests of an entire village, your hosts do not spare any attention. The religious gathering wrapped up midafternoon, leaving us the only outsiders. Villagers returned to the mending of yards and garments. Some prepared our dinner. We were served large platters of fish. The fisherman and boy I'd seen earlier close to shore were feeding the village with their day's catch. We were beneficiaries of a harvest, one cooked over coals until the fish was crisp of skin and tender inside. There was corn on the cob that had been sliced into two-inch pieces and grilled. The potatoes were sumptuous from their time over the flame and a dashing of an herb I could not identify. I wondered if some of the food was leftover from the religious gathering, but Brett told us, "I saw their table cleared into backpacks after lunch. Those leaving took the uneaten displays with them. All of this was prepared specially for us." It was a feast of farewell, as we'd leave them in the morning. The presentation was art on a plate. And they deboned the fish in front of us, taking away the heads and leaving the fins. It was as delicious as any food I've ever eaten, anywhere. They wished only to be remembered as gracious hosts.

When everyone was finished, Monk, Darren, Mark, and I sat around the table as two women cleared plates and platters. They were cheerful in their work, and proficient. They left the table to us. The wick of a kerosene lantern cast enough light for me to make notes and for the guys to read books. Monk thought to ask for a post-dinner coffee, and motioned his cup to one of the women, his smile already saying, "Thank you." She brought percolated coffee. The beans were from the Papuan Highlands, traded here for palm products. In my pre-trek anticipation, I'd wanted Papua New Guinea coffee when in PNG. I did not imagine it would taste so special. I savored the moment as much as the brew. One's smell and taste are memory triggers, and if ever again I have the pleasure of such coffee, it will catapult me back to that evening in Buna. We sipped coffee as would sentenced men, knowing our days in this one-time-hell, now-again-paradise, were almost over.

"I wish more people could come here to experience this," said Monk. Mark piped up: "If too many came, it would ruin the uniqueness." "Might bring needed monies. Help with sanitation and goods," Darren said. We are but passing amusements, I thought. A voice topped the stairs and spoke toward us. "You should find sleep," Basil said. "You will leave early tomorrow."

Basil trimmed the wick in case we didn't get the hint. All was dark when we went down the stairs. Stars shone so brightly they reminded me of our irrelevance. We were guided to the sleeping quarters by laughter from our mates, a few hundred feet across what Basil called their *ples kunai*, the grassy patch.

We were like tired little kids at bedtime wanting to stay up later but no longer having the energy to keep talking. "Tell us a war story, Brett," asked one. Another: "Tell a good-night story, Brett." And finally, "Tell us about cannibalism."

Brett snored.

There would be no story this night, unless I thought myself to sleep reviewing what I'd learned. The word "cannibal" associates with the uncivilized, primitive, inhuman, or savage. It is anathema to modern values, taboo in today's society.

However, soldiers along the Kokoda Track were often short of food during the war. On occasion, there was none at all. Nutrition was vital for the energy of battle, clarity of sight, and fortitude for hand-to-hand combat. Malnourished troops conceded skirmishes because they could not fight adequately or move out of harm's way. One Japanese account recovered after the war explained the quandary when it came to eating anything in order to sustain oneself and one's ability to fight. "Our food is completely gone. We are eating tree bark and grass. In other units, there are men eating the flesh of dead Australians. There is nothing to eat." Paul Ham wrote in *Kokoda* about "the manner in which the Japanese fastidiously prepared Australians for consumption. They cut the flesh in strips from the body, wrapped it in leaves and then dried the neat little parcels—reminiscent perhaps of a plate of sushi—on an open fire." The Japanese referred to meat off a dead Australian as "white pork." If harvested from a dead Papuan, it was termed "dark pork."

Military historian Dr. Peter Williams told me of his interview with Kōkichi Nishimura, the Bone Man. Nishimura said: "It was at Buna that soldiers started eating human flesh. At first, we shot American soldiers close to our position to take the food they carried. At that time, we did not need to eat human flesh. But after some time, the American soldiers did not carry any food at all. In the end there was no way for us to survive without eating human flesh."

Professor Williams also asked Nishimura about Japanese veterans of Buna who say they didn't eat human flesh. Nishimura said reflexively, "If you were there, and you survived, and claim not to have eaten human, then you are a liar. It was the only way."

Eventually, the unimaginable hunger of the Japanese who were penned in on the Northern Beaches without food led to cannibalism of their own. At some point during the battles over the Northern Beaches, the Australians, Papuans, Japanese, and Americans were all cannibalized. It would be two years later before Japanese troops in Asia were officially forbidden to follow this practice in part, and provided with clearance for other aspects by a military directive: "Those who have consumed human flesh—excluding that of the enemy—will be sentenced to death for committing the worst possible crime against humanity." Such a judgmental view sounds as if it was made with a full stomach and a glass of wine handy, mulling over the desperate actions of others you have no way of understanding.

Morning came, an uneasy stomach with it. I was the last out of the thatched building. I sat on the porch. Should I go to the latrine or to the breakfast room?

"You need to whistle up a wind, mate," said Monk, taking his dried clothes from the rope line. "Your face is blanched. You okay?" It was 7 a.m., and all I wanted was to lie down.

Tuksy walked across the field with a staff in his hands. "This is for you," he said, presenting it to me. "I carved last night. Is for your life." Pleased and amused, I accepted his gift of a walking stick. A knob handle was shaped where the branch once adjoined a tree. He had wiped whitewash over it. Near the handle, cut-in lines crisscrossed as tree leafs. Tuksy had carved a message for me along the staff, apparently with the same patience shown while shaving my face. It read: JESUS IS THE ONLY HOPE. On the lower portion: HAPPY BIRTHDAY RICK.

"You can lean on the words," he said. Then he sang a verse of song in his language. The vibes were good. He smiled, turned, and walked away, his singing trailing behind him.

I skipped breakfast, a decision vindicated when I later heard it was sliced green bananas with bacon. Instead, I walked along the beach to give my gut a head start adjusting to the voyage. I love being on a boat and had looked forward to this part of the journey, but something I'd eaten, or maybe exposure to the heat, or maybe a parasite, was roiling my stomach. I watched the village kids and our few remaining porter friends load everyone's gear into the boat. It would go with us for our last overnight further along the Northern Beaches, and then on to Popondetta for tomorrow afternoon's flight to Port Moresby. By 8:30 a.m., everyone was boarding the boat at the beach, me at the end of the line. Nausea overcame me and I dropped to my knees, retching in the sand. I keeled backwards on the beach and closed my eyes. I wished for the politeness of a pail. A boatload of friends looked back. "What's with Rick?" I heard through my stupor.

"I'm fine," I said to the sky. It was a lie; an unknown illness had me in its grip.

With effort, I propped myself up on an elbow. A Papuan I did not know came over to help me. Then another. "You okay, man?" With strong hands, the two of them hauled me up. A third Papuan held out a bottle. "Water," he offered. Bowrie kicked sand to clean the beach of my embarrassment. It was the last time I saw my friend.

There was a shunting around on the boat. I was last on and did not in the least feel unwanted. Room was made so I could sit next to Tori, at her insistence. Bless all nurses. "Wear this," she said, handing me a life jacket. "If you conk overboard we'll want you to float." I felt soothed by her smile. But I did not look her way. Any breath mints? Locals pushed our boat from shore into deeper waters. We headed to Sanananda. I leaned my forehead against Tuksy's carved staff as the motor chugged and belched noxious fumes. I almost heaved again, inboard.

"These," said Tori, without explanation. "Take them." I swallowed whatever pills she'd proffered. I rested my head back on the walking staff, facing over the side of the boat as the horizon bobbed. Gawd, what an obnoxious bob. The boat chucked over the waves. I chucked over the side. It was embarrassing, but unavoidable.

Monk looked my way, right past Tori and her years of nursing experience, and said, with a Westerner's insensitivity: "Rick, maybe there's a witch doctor in Sanananda." Wearily, I locked my red eyes with his blue ones. Bless all mates. Forty-five minutes later, our boat bumped sand as it neared shore. Many of our porters lived here, but none had come to greet us. Our arrival time was uncertain and, aside from that, their tending of our needs had already come to an end.

We had all climbed out of the boat when I realized my sea legs were staying behind. I was unsteady and uncertain. I lay down on the grassy ground a few feet up from the beach. Realizing I was in the sun, I pushed myself along with my feet until a coconut palm brought shadow's gift.

As a gesture of welcoming us, there was food laid out on a table. Monk brought a little over to me. I should try the bread. Shakily sitting up to eat, I made one mouthful, then two. Emboldened, I stood unsteadily as everyone left to walk the village. Monk and Tori offered to stay with me, but I waved them off. Walking slowly behind the procession, I detoured on my own village walkabout, several times introducing myself to villagers who had outhouses.

Exiting one of these outhouses, I saw everyone else not far away, lifting items. I realized these were memorabilia of war—American, Japanese, and Australian. It was the Sanananda-Giruwa War Museum. Open-air shacks. There were helmets of the different armies and military caps. Handguns and rifles were sorted by country. There was nothing celebratory about the displays. They were remnants from the last days of Japan's occupation of PNG.

The sequence of Allied victories on the Northern Beaches was Gona, Buna, and Sanananda. After three weeks of faltered attacks, the Australians controlled Gona on December 9, 1942, making the first crack in the Buna-Sanananda-Gona fortress constructed and defended by the Japanese. Australian Colonel Ralph Honner's message to his commander was as brief as it was definitive: "Gona's gone." It was neither the end of suffering nor the beginning of peace—in fact, it was subsequent to the message that Americans took Buna, after which combined American/Australian forces evicted the Japanese from Sanananda.

Fragmented, as a word, appropriately describes the once-mighty Japanese landing force that retreated off the Kokoda Track back to Sanananda. Five thousand disenchanted Japanese were boxed in at their last holdout, with nearly 20,000 combined American and Australian forces attacking them. Dying Japanese were abandoned swiftly, as was a trove of suddenly useless equipment. The near-dead preferred a fellow soldier's bullet to an enemy's, and asked for it.

Kōkichi Nishimura was in Sanananda during the war's last weeks. Along with depression and disease, Nishimura shared two other things with his fellow Nankai Shitai in the bunker: hunger and fear. American soldiers huddled in trenches not far away, facing Nishimura's fortified hole. The Americans were rattled with their own versions of depression, disease, and fear. The fighting situation was ghastly, primal, and cruel. Soon, one side would rush-attack the other, shooting guns, throwing grenades, and stabbing bayonets.

"The American soldiers were cooking something," Nishimura recalled years later. "They'd been given special rations for the season, maybe canned turkey. Maybe cranberries." Whatever it was, Nishimura said, "Some nice smell was wafting towards us." Abruptly, a Japanese soldier near Nishimura stood in full view of the Americans and Japanese. Slowly he took off his clothes, except his underwear. Then he straggled into the open and toward the American pits. Obviously unarmed and looking to be drunk, he was not shot. Nearing the enemy barricades, he disappeared from his comrades' sight. Not long after, Japanese and American laughter drifted from the American trench and over the no-man's-land between the two positions. Eventually, the Japanese soldier reappeared standing in front of the American trenches, wearing his underwear as before. He walked to where his comrades crouched in their camouflaged hole. He carried an armful of food. Nishimura said the Japanese soldier returned happy, telling them, "We were having a good time eating and drinking, whether we were enemies or not. I got something for you guys, too."

It was Christmas Eve.

With Gona gone, Buna lost, and Sanananda no longer tenable, evacuation by the Japanese was the closing scene of Act III in the Papua Theater of War.

A couple of hours after our boat's arrival in Sanananda, the trekkers returned to shore, where I lay asleep. Monk's foot nudged at me. Tori, more sensitive, lifted my head and tipped a bottle of water to my lips. I heard Rod say to Darren, "Help me lift him." They shouldered me toward the boat, up and in.

An hour's voyage west of Sanananda, the surf pushed our banana boat to shore at Saroda, near Gona. Kids from the village ran into the water, hands out to say hello. They grabbed the gunnels of our boat and hauled us to a stop. There were banyan trees on shore; shade.

"Rick, up and over," said Tori.

"Your feet, not your stomach," Monk said.

I got out of the boat and walked through water and onto the beach with their support. Once on shore, they let me stand on my own, out of politeness. "Thanks. I'm fine. I've got balance," I said. As they watched helplessly, I face-planted in the sand.

"Mate, you're crook'd," said Monk. The Aussie term for "gotten ill" sounded to me like an indictment.

"Crook'd bad," said Michael. The two of them lifted me up like a sack of turnips, and walked me away from Tori and Rod so they could gather their own packs from the boat. Monk slung mine with his.

"We'll get you to shelter," said Monk, who then left me with Michael as he went to the front of our herd to see what he might organize for my resting place.

A grassed-over road, wide enough for a vehicle if there was one about, led off the beach and toward a village. We walked. Homes were set out sporadically on either side of us. Stilts supported the houses. Kids giggled and played in the yards, or under the structures. Were the small fires for cooking or comfort? Women sat nearby them. Those who waved had smiles, and were younger.

Suddenly, warriors raced down our path. Their faces were painted in angry stripes. They shouted at us. Insults? Their spears were raised. "Why now?" I thought. The horde stormed toward us. They strung wide, ready to swarm. A mad spear-carrier made to toss his weapon at me. I wanted to lie down and die. His spear seemed convenient.

Monk was leading our pack. One fearsome warrior thrust a sharpened spear, stopping only an inch from Monk's throat. Monk froze and stared. He didn't budge an inch. Pure guts.

Song broke out. Laughter crossed the war-dressed faces. Then came "Oro. Oro." The kids alongside us squealed, their part in the entrapment a success. Delight swept the roadway like a monsoon. Everywhere was happiness. The warriors were among us, holding us, their spears at rest or shown off. They offered to carry our packs. They walked in friendship. To the kids we were here to travel, or *wokabaut* in Tok Pisin. To the adults, we were *pasindia*, guests.

It was the third time we'd been spoofed by a faux attack. As a practical joke, it was harmless and as much fun for the perpetrators as for the unsuspecting visitors. Yet I had to think that they were playing off the fears and misconceptions they thought we carried with us. All the while and in harmless fashion, they were reinforcing the stereotypes.

Sometime during the milieu, Michael left me on my own.

An aged warrior said to all of us, "Come. We have dance. Much music. We sing. You sing. First though, we sing. You learn our songs. Then you sing."

There were dozens of us in the flow now. It was a parade of warriors, trekkers, and kids. The throng coursed into a field the size of a soccer pitch. Thatch-roofed cottages surrounded it to form a village around a common. Bare-breasted women—the warriors' wives and daughters—greeted us. Any cultural embarrassment was restricted to the trekkers. Draped with what looked to be bark coats or animal skin skirts and many wearing feather headdresses, the women danced and sang. Whatever the words, it felt as though land and society, work and play, friends and family were entwined with, not distinguished from, the lovely setting. Brett said, "We follow them. They've prepared a welcoming performance for us."

As my fellow trekkers moved to center field, I slipped behind. When no one was looking, I dropped back farther. Then I slunk away in search of anything private and horizontal. I had a shirt full of shivers. A Papuan

Dancing and music are very much the Papuan way of daily life, but villagers often put on special performances on the rare occasion that foreigners enter a village.

elder came to me, as if from nowhere. He was wiry and small. Seeing my pasty white face, he asked. "You alright?"

"I'm . . . a little sick. I want to . . . lie down. Right now," I said, pitifully.

"I'll take you," he said. "We'll go slow." He placed my arm over his shoulders and bore my weight. He mumbled something that sounded like a bad diagnosis. Later I found out that his "*I stap gut*" meant "health."

We walked toward an open-air structure at the far end of four buildings. Like the history we'd trekked through, like the mountains and valleys we had looked out on, this room seemed near to us, but was far away. If any of my friends noticed, they would have seen me in good care. None followed, and I appreciated that. Music covered the field of play.

"Up steps," urged my warden, his hand firmly on my forearm, lifting me. There were three steps and a landing. Looking at that climb, I said, "Rest first." The elderly man helped me sit. I caught what warm oxygen I could. Open-mouthed, I swallowed air. "Steps, please," he said, making sure I rose. "Now is best." He kept me upright and moving. At the first door opening, he moved back a curtain. "Mattress," he said, pointing.

I was shaken awake hours later. It was dark. "Mate, you need to take these. Tori said so." Monk gave me water and pills. "You've been gone a long time," I heard him say. Music drifted in. Tribal songs. War songs. Friendship songs.

I slipped away. More hours passed. I was aware of Tori and Rod standing in my doorway. "Water, Rick. Keep drinking." Music came from a dwindling number of voices.

After midnight: "Get up, mate. I've got you a remedy." Monk hoisted me against my willingness and forced me out to the porch. He'd scored a chair, and sat me in it. The field was without music. Everyone else was in bed. A sliver of moonlight shone. "Meet Philipa," Monk said, motioning to a slim woman approaching the porch. She wore a loose dress and a knowing smile. Monk introduced her as, "Cook. Mother. Medicine woman."

Philipa came to me. "You need my help," she said. If I'd thought about it, I would have noticed that this was not a question. She carried a five-gallon pail, aided by a small child in shorts and nothing else. Monk helped them place it onto the porch. Philipa shoved the pail at the base, forcing it over the slats to where I sat. "This is grass. Lemon and other," she told me. "It is boiled with flowers I know. It has garden good. Lean forward."

Philipa climbed onto the porch. She guided my upper body so my head was directly over the steaming pail. Finally, I had a pail. But my crook'd gut no longer needed to expunge. Philipa pulled a large towel from her waistband and laid it over my head. It completely covered the pail and me. Friendly steam swirled beneath the cover.

"Keep with breathe," she said.

Monk said, "I was at the kitchen looking for a snack. I met Philipa and told her you were crook'd. She said you needed her special remedy. It's taken her an hour to prepare this. She says to stay under that cover for ten minutes. You better cooperate." Monk stepped away and down the stairs. Less than five minutes after hearing him leave, I'd had enough of the steam. Alone on the porch, I pushed the cloth from my head. My eyes met with Philipa's.

"Put that back on," she said.

A few minutes later, I heard her dip a washcloth in the warm medicine. She took the towel off my head. "Wash," she said, handing the smaller cloth to me. "Wash all over, or I will." I wiped my upper body, legs, and face. It was a wipe-on massage. Monk returned in time to wash my back, saving Philipa the chore. My lungs felt clear.

Philipa sang a healing song as she helped Monk escort me to the room. She stood aside and Monk let me tumble gracelessly onto the mat. I faded away to Philipa's singing.

My Saroda sleep was a trance. I rolled and lay on my back. Dampness flowed across my forehead, pooling in my eye sockets. The mattress was soaked in sweat. In my dreams, I swam. Away from what? To what? I thrashed the cover sheet away. Cool air crawled in and over my fever.

I awoke with a bounce, and I felt much better. Philipa's potion and Tori's care and rehydrating had brought my health's turn for the better (I neglected, at the time, to think of Monk as enabling any of it). Fresh air seemed to be what I needed next. I was not the first to step out in the morning light. Panther was across the field, headed to the toilets in pursuit of ongoing relief. He pantomimed a question in the air, one of concern for my health. Without thinking to give a thumbs-up, I demonstrated my good health by dancing a jig, my right foot crossing over in front of my left, then alternating. Suddenly I went wobbly, and decided best to stop. Panther jigged in return, a measured two-step, a high step, and a quick twirl. Amazing for a man with the trots.

I heard a shout. "Rick. Rick!" It was Philipa coming my way carrying the steaming bucket, aided by the same child and followed by another woman holding a large towel.

"Morning need. Again," Philipa insisted. I obeyed. Warm moist air sapped at my pores, ridding me of toxins as my head stayed under the towel. Philipa's healing actions were cleansing my lungs and loosening the last shakes of fever.

Our morning plan, according to Brett, was "a walkout to the road a mile away, where a flatbed truck will find us and take us to Popondetta." Flights were organized. Brett encouraged us to leave behind whatever we could. "Don't bother if it needs washing, or if they'd actually like it. That doesn't matter. Here, it will be shared and used." I shed it all. Socks. Shirts. Shorts. Footwear. Monk showed up with his kit bag half empty. He motioned it toward me and said, "For Tori."

Tori had said to all of us, "Leave me with any salves, cloth dressings, or regular medications you have. No prescription drugs. I'll go through all of it with the women here and explain how to use it. You can replenish at home."

Over-prepared, as always, I had not required any of the first aid supplies I'd brought. When I was ill, it was not the chemist's supplies but a stew of local foliage that brought me round. I placed two handfuls of remedies into Monk's bag.

I stepped off the lowest stair and made toward the kitchen, my intention being to thank Philipa. She was walking toward me, preempting my search. Was it anticipation? No. She had no expectation of anything from me. She'd done what she did because I was in her village and needed care. Before I could clasp her hand and shift paper money to her under the guise of a handshake, she reached my way with both hands raised. "This." She stopped after that word, as though it alone was enough. She read the puzzlement in my face. "I made it for you. This morning." She held out a necklace of little shells, strung through and linked by fishing line.

"Philipa . . ." I began. But she shushed me. I was a walk-on actor in a universal play, one about humanity and concern for others. She was wrapping up my cameo appearance in her life.

"Rick," she said, making her voice the one of control, her actions the ones that mattered. She draped the necklace over my bowed head, and let it lie on my chest. There were a dozen shells, each over an inch long, slender and cream of color on one side. The curved inner shell was orange. "It is help with healing. And memory of my village." I was then able to place currency in her hands. She was accepting, but not curious enough to look. It was not in her to be compensated for kindness. Her stance said I should go now. She left to make breakfast.

Food was my enemy. This was made harsher because of my dislike of onions, and the first odor from the breakfast table was of onions embedded in fried eggs. Once, on travels in Mongolia, I had been awakened in a gher with a hangover and been served onion omelets, which I supposed was a trick by my two sons with whom I was traveling. No such antics this morning, only bad timing. My revulsion was immediate. I felt a relapse coming, and stepped away. Forgiven because of my earlier illness, the rudeness of my leaving was overlooked. This put me ahead of the others on a walk to the beach.

I liked the solitary time when I first got to the beach, but it wouldn't last long. When the other trekkers and adult villagers arrived later, a dozen kids materialized from out of their yards. They wanted to match hands with us, snickering at the contrasting skin colors.

Back at the grassy field, two of the villagers waved us over. One held out an offering. Betel nut. His hand was dirty in the way hands that work the land always look soiled, even when clean. As I went to take up his offer, Martin pushed my hand out of the way. "Really, Rick. You capsize on us for twelve hours. Then you revive and take betel nut? We'll lose you for another day." With that, he took the crushed nut from the villager, tucked it in the leaf of mustard root topped with lime powder, rolled and bit. He chewed. Spittle slowly surged through his lips, the result of his gag reflex. The villagers laughed, their red tongues vivid even against their stained teeth.

We walked off with the villagers along, packs on our backs and kids holding our hands. The kids spoke with the joy of seeing strangers. The women smiled as though words did not matter when all those leaving were healthy and well-fed. The elders made tribal talk with us.

A mile later, most of the villagers had dropped back, with other chores to tend. Now, in a messy jungle setting, we waited for our transport, surrounded by truck parts and garbage ready for pickup. We were all out of goodbye phrases and thank-you words. There was no use of "see you again" when it was obviously unlikely.

The dirt road rumbled beneath our feet. A belch of smoke signaled the vehicle's arrival. The Northern Beaches are a reprieve from the rest of Papua New Guinea, the distance saving both villages and villagers from too many visitors of any kind. For the locals, this has meant prosperity from abundant seafood and enough produce to meet their needs, and to share. And with the porters hired from here, and treated well by tour companies who need them along the Kokoda Trail, there is village money for imported goods. That and the setting explains much about the villagers' happiness. The question is whether it will last.

We departed at 1:00 p.m.; trekkers, Brett, a driver, and two kids who hung off the back of the PMV for a ride to town. There was no way to be comfortable, only slightly less uncomfortable. We retraced part of the route that brought us here three days ago. The truck kicked dust, and we swallowed it. Houses stood back from the road, their yards busy with animals, kids, and cooking. They were consistently tidy.

We arrived in Popondetta at the same grocery store we had visited earlier. It was as unwelcoming now as then, and as dodgy in its hangers-on outside the fencing. In a country with so many wonderful people, and openly displayed family values, the minority of *raskols* was instead on show here. It was an unfair representation of the community, but not one easy to shake. The sense of vulnerability was immediately in our conversation, and left an impression we'd each take home. For ten minutes it dominated our view of the population—but did not overtake impressions left by our friendships with the porters and the way they represented their country's personality and future.

To be clear, it was not a town of villainous thieves, but *raskols* have nudged their way to a disturbing prominence. Monk was at a shack exchanging money when a youngster stalked next to him, eyeing the currency on the counter. An older boy pushed him away and took up the position. Monk is strong and clever, and gave them his back while he did the transfer. They eyed him from maddened faces, as though he'd stolen their due. It was disconcerting. We were a corralled group being canvassed for a weak one to cull and pounce. There were none of us they could grift, and so they stood back. We split up among the store aisles. Our purchases were without any coordination and were always in bulk. We returned to the truck with cases of beer or pop, or in my case a dozen ice cream bars that needed to be shared promptly. I gave three to kids nearby, which created tension when no more were left for waiting hands.

There was no need to be early for our 5:30 p.m. flight; no one was queuing. We arrived at the airport with low expectations, having been there to see off our fellow trekkers a few days ago. We walked away from the terminal's single building and through its parking area to an American B-25 Mitchell bomber propped at the entrance. The frame was whole, though dismantled in places. It had been scrounged. At first we thought it a casualty of war, but learned it was left behind in 1943, at the Dobodura airfield that once existed nearby. It gave shade, and we sat out of the sun. We passed around beer. On the plane's nose was the fading name the crew knew her by: *Bat Outta Hell.*

The war was over for us as trekkers; we were done always talking about it. Well, we were almost done. To those of us beneath the old bomber, Brett started a conversation none of us had asked for but which he felt necessary. "The Allies' victory on the Northern Beaches in January '43 coincided with Japanese retreat from Guadalcanal." Monk and Whitey filled in the rest: The American and Australian contingents quickly moved on the Japanese base at Rabaul, and northward. Battle names like Lae, Wau, and the Bismarck Sea made headlines around the world. In '44, MacArthur waded ashore in the Philippines to waiting newsreel cameras. Not long after, Okinawa and Iwo Jima fell to the Allies' momentum. On August 15, 1945, Emperor Hirohito spoke on the radio: "The war situation has developed not necessarily to Japan's advantage."

Anthony wrapped it up: "Aboard the USS *Missouri* in Tokyo Bay, MacArthur signed the Instrument of Surrender which had been signed on behalf of the Emperor." Anthony got to the point he wanted to share. "MacArthur supported Australia's demand to sign the document separately, which was signed on their behalf by Commander Blamey."

The war stories were over. Having had two weeks without internet, phone, or news—or contact with loved ones, we were all curious about elsewhere. Undoubtedly the outside world had revolved okay without us watching it. Indeed, we were aware that any outside contact would have hampered our ability to immerse in the world we'd explored. We boarded a Canadian-built Dash 8 operated by Airlines PNG. Clouds blocked our view of the Kokoda Trail as we flew over the Owen Stanley Range.

Arriving in Moresby, we left behind the happiness of villages and entered the frenzy of growth. Landing and disembarking, we were unnecessarily gruff toward dwellers around Jackson's International Airport.[43] We didn't want hassles when we'd met the best of their countrymen. Even compounds can have cache; one of the nearby hotel properties was subsequently named among the top ten airport hotels in the world. At our hotel we retrieved anything left behind at the start of the journey, and took our bags to our rooms to repack in anticipation of leaving for Australia in the morning.

First, though, there was a final evening of camaraderie. We wanted the fuller choice of their dining room menu, but wished to sit outside at an empty table, one not planned for dinner service. We cut a deal with the waitress: she'd let us sit outside if we would order at the kitchen counter where she was positioned and fetch the plates ourselves. With a tip-anticipating smile, she agreed to deliver our pitchers of beer and glasses. The steaks arrived at our table in the hands of Monk, Mark, and Michael, and were shared around. Chicken platters came next, carried by Brett, though I noticed his face askew as though the smell put him off. He was taking a turn for crook'd. Vegetables followed. We gave our tips in cash, knowing the waitress would not see the gratuity otherwise. "Great meal," pronounced Michael. "They get some things right in this country." Martin's radio voice provided the headline: "Papua New Guinea's best is food." He thought about that a second. "PNG's best is scenery." He self-edited again, announcing, "PNG's best is porters and villagers."

"All good things said, New Guinea is raw," Monk replied. Mark said, "Better beckons." This wasn't offered as a slogan but as a hope, an acknowledgement that progress is rough when your country's profile is associated with dated monikers like headhunting or cannibalism, or hijacked in current times by the *raskols*.

We pondered what had been said, sipping topped-up glasses of beer. Anthony broke the quiet. "You really think that was your old man, Monk? The guy on the plaque at Isurava?" Monk quaffed his beer. The

---

43 Named after Royal Australian Air Force Squadron Leader Johnny Jackson of Queensland, who was shot down and killed at Port Moresby on April 28, 1942.

way he kept the glass to his lips conveyed contemplation. Removing it he said, "I'll find out. I cared when I saw the picture. I think."

When we were on the Northern Beaches, Monk told me he moved his father out of the care facility where he'd found him and had taken him into his own home. The gesture was beyond kind. Was it forgiveness? Not at all, he'd said. Monk simply had the means and comforts his father needed, even if he didn't deserve them. So they lived together in a generosity of spirit that took me by surprise. His father died under a roof of respect that he had not earned in the eyes of his son. Had that now changed in Monk's mind? Had the old soldier earned a dose of dignity by being on the Kokoda Track?

A good journey tests and refreshes one's values. "To mateship," said Michael, his glass raised. For two weeks this group of us had run toward life while walking with ghosts. We pressed our beers together and chorused, "Mateship."

AFTERWORD

Better Beckons

"Let my arrows fly another 50,000 years."
—Kumalau Tawali, Papuan poet

"New Guinea is raw." That comment over dinner the night before we left the island made sense to me overall. It was an observation, not an accusation. The Papuans we met (aside from the Popondetta *raskols*) were hospitable and delightful. Yet their national mosaic was fraying. Mark's observation that "better beckons" for PNG augurs well for a future based upon the country's beauty of land and people, but one wishes the social strife to end.

Acquiring a good reputation takes more than re-branding a country for its tourism potential; it requires a lot of work over time. An official website positioning PNG as "A million different journeys" is but a hint in the right direction. A brand is a promise, not a slogan. Placing an asterisk beside the country's tourism data, many parts of PNG are safe. Visitor numbers, including business travelers, exceed 200,000 a year; more than one third of these are tourists and half of those are Australian. Many who visit do so just once.

Travelers to the island of New Guinea today can visit remote tribes. But in many cases, the "lost tribes" may not benefit by "being found." I cite perspectives from three authors who spent considerable time among such tribes, beginning with explorer/author Mick Leahy's observation in the aftermath of sharing his finding of remote tribes. He said that they unfortunately became "showpieces."

A second observation comes from Peter Matthiessen, who was part of a Harvard-Peabody Expedition that included Michael Rockefeller (Matthiessen's book *Under the Mountain Wall* is dedicated to him). The author reflected upon New Guinea's Kurelu tribe in the 1960s as "a lost culture in all its primitive simplicity and violence." The indigenous peoples went so quickly from "Stone Age to study pool" that it immediately altered habits not changed in hundreds of years. Matthiessen was concerned, "[They] will be no more than another backward people, crouched in the long shadow of the white man."

There are also the Dani (or Ndani), among them the people of Baliem Valley. When Westerners first crashed into their civilization 75 years ago, they were a highly functioning society. The *Nit ahkuni Balim-mege* ("We people of the Baliem") had well-constructed homes, potato farms, and community facilities such as ditching. They had not invented the wheel. Then the Dani were "discovered" and exposed. Missionaries came to Baliem Valley. The profiteers of commerce arrived as surely as trade follows tourism, dissembling an ecosystem that had thrived for hundreds of years. Tribal tensions, leadership development, and community purpose floundered under imposed Western values. New physical diseases and social ones arrived in the valley on the wings of progress.

In his book *Lost in Shangri-La*, Mitchell Zuckoff recounts his visits with indigenous peoples in the early 2000s. "They spoke complex languages—the verb that meant 'hit' or 'kill' could be inflected more than two thousand ways—but had a single word to describe both time and place: *0*. In a world awash in color, they had terms for only two: *mili*, for black, maroon, dark browns, and blues; and *mola*, for white, reds, oranges, yellows, light browns, and reddish purples. They feared the ghosts of their ancestors but worshipped no gods." Today, as described by Zuckoff, "Elderly native men in penis gourds walk through [a village] begging for change and cigarettes. Some charge a small fee to pose for photos, inserting boar tusks through passages in their nasal septums to look fierce. More often, they look lost."

I share these in the context that hosting Westerners has been of mixed blessing for New Guinea, and one wishes the balance to shift toward sustainable culture being on equal footing with commerce.

The number of trekkers visiting the Kokoda Trail has grown from a few hundred a year in the early 2000s, to several thousand each recent year. The trail never felt crowded to us. However, even with two directions of trekking and scheduled departures, days of congested hiking may come. One wonders if, like the Galapagos Islands or the country of Bhutan, there should be a quota of allowable trekkers, a cap to ensure a quality experience for visitors and villagers.

In February 2018, the Kokoda Trail was closed by traditional land-owners protesting insufficient benefits generated by trekkers. Among organizations targeted by complaints was the Kokoda Initiative. The trail reopened after the PNG government committed to a review of the agency. The Kokoda Initiative is a hybrid of Australian and Papua New Guinean administration, begun in 2008. The initiative's mandate is "protection and management" of the area, being mindful of the environmental impact. They focus on responsible tourism. This includes ensuring that communities in the corridor are culturally sustainable. They seek safety for all trekking or hosting trekkers. One of its goals is for villages to develop and maintain better sanitation facilities for their residents, as well as for trekkers. Activities are also aimed at improving health care and education for those living along the trail. All this comes with an expected economic uptick.

Responsibility for the trail falls separately to the Kokoda Track Authority, which encourages trekking companies, such as Getaway Trekking who made our arrangements, to abide by a cooperatively created code of conduct. They also issue permits, collect fees, and facilitate payments to the communities.

As trekking along the Kokoda Trail became established, awareness of World War II stories generated interest in the Kapa Kapa Trail as well. The difficulty and duration of a Kapa Kapa expedition hampers its popularity, though there are trek departure dates set. There's a suggestion it be renamed the Ghost Mountain Trail, with one eye on a more marketable connotation. Also, the Black Cat Track is again open for the rather exceptional adventure it is, more rough than the Kokoda Trail.

PNG's bad rap reputation may be lessened if Westerners didn't exaggerate their experiences and perceptions, and if the media lessened its willingness to sensationalize rumors. Here is one unconfirmed instance, a story that emerged from the Kokoda Trail in recent years: A foreign couple, a woman and her boyfriend, a former reality television personality, claimed to have been accosted by machete-wielding men while hiking the trail. They depicted their assailants as speaking in grunts. According to initial reports, the woman had been assaulted. After the publicity surrounding their reported experiences, there came accounts of a different sort, portraying them as ill-prepared and refusing to hire a guide, ignoring the time requirements for completing a crossing, dressing inappropriately, and being cocky. By not paying fees, they could have been trespassing on private property. Subsequent interviews cast questions on the veracity of their initial accusations. Use of terms like "savages" had garnered headlines, and some saw their stories as salacious and exaggerated, if not possibly fabricated. Yet by the time differing opinions emerged for a balanced investigation, they were insufficient to counter aspersions about a country that could not withstand them. Determining the truth remained elusive. For a society that loves children and respects elders, it is sad to hear PNG periodically portrayed as a place where there is little respect about life.

How might this unfinished country end up? PNG seems set for ongoing perceptions that mining and forestry profit without fair compensation to locals. More negative coverage will flow around proposed independence for Bougainville Island. And, likely there will be more people who disappear-to-be-rescued, such as the British explorer in 2017 who vanished while producing a documentary on a little-known tribe. After he was found safe, the media reporting on Papua New Guinea itself vanished.

On the trek, we held a bias that locations highlighting Australian or American soldiers were sites of more human suffering than those of the Japanese. We only glanced at testimonials about Japanese losses at Kokoda Station, or the Shinto altar in Sanananda. We didn't bother to find Nishimura's home in Popondetta. Nor, at the time, was I aware of a Japanese-funded school built in Sanananda. We were ignorant that, during the post-war years, it was not uncommon for veteran groups in Japan to contact American or Australian veteran groups, as was the case in reverse. Indeed, such associations were often among the first to build bridges of understanding between nations that once warred.

Professor Williams told me how time casts uncertainty over basic facts of past conflicts and former enemies, often out of indifference. The war historian was in a Tokyo bar in the 1990s and had just begun to talk about World War II with a Japanese businessman sitting next to him (not that the topic is recommended as a conversation opener in such a setting). A friend of the Japanese man walked in and joined them. The businessman said to his friend, "This guy is from Australia and we were just talking about the war." With that the Japanese gentleman turned to Peter and asked sincerely, "Remind me, which side were you Australians on?"

It was the better part of a year after our trek before I began writing about it in earnest. I'd kept field notes as a memory jog, but not a journal. I'd written down sentences, snippets, or quotes in the same way Monk or Tori took pictures. Reviewing them revealed the narrative threads I had to work with. One of them was unexpected, and that was about Monk and his father. Once back in Cairns, Monk and I kept up our hikes on Earl Hill and the Blue Arrow. Our "walk across the country" was never far from the conversation. Over beers after one of our hill climbs, months later, he mentioned his father for the first time since we'd returned from PNG.

"When I had the old man in my home during his dying days, he seldom spoke. Our distrust fermented. But here's what I should tell you. When dad abandoned our young family, guess where he went?" Monk wasn't really waiting for my answer. He kept talking to get it over with. "Dad disappeared to Papua New Guinea and hid out there for decades."

Since Monk had raised the topic of his old man, it seemed a good time to ask if he'd gotten around to contacting the Department of Veterans' Affairs to see if that was his father on the Isurava plaque. "I don't want to talk about that bastard," he said.

We had both turned sixty-six during our walk, Monk mere days before we stepped on the Kokoda Trail. I was old enough to know when to respect a mate's decision.

When Monk and I had arrived back to the Cairns Airport after our Kokoda trek, we'd both lost weight, me visibly more so because of the illness. We decided to play this up a bit when exiting the luggage area. We slowly dragged our gear behind us and hunched over our walking sticks for support, staggering. Thinking we were the two funniest men on earth, this seemed a clever way to greet our spouses after being away two weeks on what could be a life-sapping adventure. As we turned a corner and they saw two worn-out characters, both Janice and Wens were taken aback. Before we could stand up and display our tans and evident good health, their lit-up smiles faded to shock. We had returned, literally and spiritually, different men.

Monk

Acknowledgements

I begin with Glen "Monk" Thompson—a man of irrevocable friendship, inspiration, and dogged determination. I say my thanks to him for instigating our escapade, and seeing it through. The first time I saw him after our "walk" across Papua New Guinea I took over a can of Spam: "Monk's *pâté*."

Cory Allyn of Skyhorse Publishing has now been the editor of four books I've written, guiding them through the publication process—with patience and a lot of talent, I should add. His colleagues in New York continue to impress me, and I wish to thank Chris Schultz for the engaging book design, Brian Peterson for creating such a wonderful cover, and Laura Snider for proofreading. I appreciate the professional thoroughness of the index created by Karen Maurice. Drawing the public's attention to an author's work is a craft unto itself, and I wish to thank Oleg Lyubner, Wendy Underwood, Margaret Mackinnon-Cash, Felicia Quon, and Catherine Whiteside for their belief that this author's books should be widely read. It was nice to discover Dr. Andrew Peacock's photographs in his book, *Glimpses of Kokoda*, and gain his permission to use one on this book's cover. I thank Dania Sheldon for her patient assistance as permissions editor, on yet another book.

There are those who spent time with my early manuscript and offered heartfelt critiques, prods, and questions to improve the storytelling. My respect and appreciation go to Darren Johner, Jon Hutchison, Jess Ketchum, and Sonu Perhar for being friends of this book by making it better. A fellow writer asked for anonymity of his edits that encouraged structural revisions of the early draft; thank you, G. The two leaders on our expedition, Mark (Yeoy) Yeomans and Brett Phillips, gave their blessings for content, quotes, and inferences. Fellow trekkers also reviewed the manuscript and contributed ideas to better my telling and to ensure accuracy about our travel companions and the experience we shared—my thanks to Kristy Laslett, Martin Ewart, Anthony Keck, and Michael Bowles. And I thank Tori, Monk, and Michael for access to their photographs. I've benefited from the motivation and suggestions from many others.

I notably benefitted from reviews of the text and maps by the war historian Professor Peter Williams, author of *The Kokoda Campaign 1942: Myth and Reality*, whom I also thank for his keen insights and engaging stories. And I appreciate advice and corrections I received from Peter Gamgee, a member of the Getaway team for Kokoda Trail, and one of only two individuals I've encountered who has trekked Kapa Kapa Trail, resulting in his book *The Kapa Kapa*. Peter reviewed my storytelling with an eye to place-names and to addressing the inconsistencies found between various maps. Through him I learned about names given by Captain Bert Kienzle. In addition to sorting that out for us, Bert's son, Soc, clarified proper references regarding Templeton's Crossing. I also wish to thank Dr. Ryota Nishino, Senior Lecturer, History, at The University of the South Pacific in Fiji for his suggestions.

My friend Garry Marchant provided encouragement and resource material before passing away late in 2017. His wife, Marnie Mitchell, kindly read and clarified the pieces where I'd written about him.

Eric Leinberger created maps that help orient the reader to the unfolding story, as he has for my previous three books. His maps continue to inform the readers' understanding of complex situations in unfamiliar geography.

Sue Fitcher and colleagues at Getaway Trekking of Australia were thorough, conscientious, and demanding when preparing or delivering on our trek expectations, in every way true professionals are.

My agent Robert Mackwood, principle of Seventh Avenue Literary Agency, has nurtured the relationship with Skyhorse Publishing on my behalf.

I've taken to referencing the "Antonson focus group," kin who have become part of each of my books from the incubation stage: my older brother Brian and my sons Brent and Sean. Their candor, sarcasms, and tireless e-nudges have influenced my decisions on everything from storylines to titles, vignettes to consider, and those to leave out.

Janice created a writing room for me in our new home in Australia when this book began to take shape, and then for two years when we moved to Europe where much of this work was completed. She also was the "first reader" of the manuscript once it was ready to be shared. More, though, she enabled our meeting of Monk and Wens, without whom neither the escapades nor the stories would have existed. My heartfelt thank you for her years of support, encouragement, and enabling of this writer.

Our porter friends come to mind often—particularly Bowrie, Winterford, and Woody, from whom I learned much about the strength of individual character, a sense of duty and hospitality, as well as respect for their culture and country.

I've saved room for that qualifier: any oversights or uncomfortable assumptions are my responsibility.

Rick Antonson is the author of the travel narratives *To Timbuktu for a Haircut: A Journey through West Africa*, *Route 66 Still Kicks: Driving America's Main Street*, and *Full Moon Over Noah's Ark: An Odyssey to Mount Ararat and Beyond*. He is the coauthor of *Slumach's Gold: In Search of a Legend*. He was president and CEO of Tourism Vancouver, is past chair of the board for Destinations International, based in Washington, DC, and served as deputy chair for the Pacific Asia Travel Association, based in Bangkok, Thailand. He speaks around the world about the multigenerational philosophy "Cathedral Thinking." Rick and his wife make their home in Vancouver, Canada. You can find him online at www.rickantonson.com and www.cathedralthinking.com.

Sources and Recommendations

Before my journey in Papua New Guinea, and of course afterwards, many books were brought to my attention. Some were gifted by way of orienting me to the land and its people and their phases of history. Others arrived to inform about the broader wartime happenings, origins, and outcomes, several specific to the Kokoda Track. Reading many, I turned each page amazed by the unfolding story. They gave me a sense of place, as well as highlighting personalities invaluable for context about the country and conflict. In early drafts of the manuscript, I wrote at length about individuals or occurrences that did not make the final cut and were excluded from the book, either by myself or on advice of the editors in order to keep my storytelling focused. Nonetheless, preparing those pieces gave me perspective and themes I eventually told in a more straightforward manner. My work owes much to the well-thumbed volumes, as well as to other books in which a favored line or two appeared, and from which I quoted. I've highlighted the following titles from a shelf of books. I encourage readers to find a copy of any that catch your eye—or that flesh out storylines my book hints at but does not sufficiently feed your curiosity.

Anderson, Robin, and Connolly, Bob. *First Contact*. New York: Viking Penguin Inc., 1987.

Brune, Peter. *A Bastard of a Place*. Crows Nest, NSW, Allen & Unwin, 2003.

Campbell, James. *The Ghost Mountain Boys*. New York: Three Rivers Press, Crown Publishing Group, 2007.

Collie, Craig, and Marutani, Hajime. *The Path of Infinite Sorrow: The Japanese on the Kokoda Track*. Crows Nest, NSW, Allen & Unwin, 2009.

Duffy, James P. *War at the End of the World*. New York: New American Library, Penguin Random House, 2016.

Fetherling, George. *Running Away to Sea*. Toronto: McClelland and Stewart, 1998. Reprint. Dundurn Publishing, 2009.

Fitzsimons, Peter. *Kokoda*. Sydney: Hachette, 2004.

Flynn, Errol. *My Wicked, Wicked Ways*. New York: G. P. Putnam's Sons, 1959. Reprint. New York: Cooper Square Press, 2003.

Gailey, Harry. *MacArthur's Victory*. New York: Presidio Press, 2004.

Gamgee, Peter. *The Kapa Kapa*. Australia, Outskirts Press, Inc., 2014.

Ham, Paul. *Kokoda*. Sydney: HarperCollins Publishers, 2004.

Happell, Charles. *The Bone Man of Kokoda*. Sydney: Pan Macmillan, 2008.

Hoffman, Carl. *Savage Harvest*. New York: HarperCollins Publishers, 2014.

James, Bill. *Field Guide to the Kokoda Track*. Lane Cove, NSW, Australia, 2006.

Johnston, George H. *The Toughest Fighting in the World*. New York: Duell, Sloan and Pearce, 1943. Reprint. Yardley, Pennsylvania: Westholme Publishing, 2011.

Kienzle, Robyn. *The Architect of Kokoda*. Sydney: Hachette, 2011.

Leahy, Michael J., and Jones, Douglas E., eds. *Explorations into Highland New Guinea 1930–1935*. Reprint. Tuscaloosa, Alabama: The University of Alabama Press, 1991.

Lindsay, Patrick. *Kokoda Spirit*. Melbourne, London: Hardie Grant Books, 2009.

McDonald, Neil. *Kokoda Front Line*. Sydney: Hachette, 2011.

Marriott, Edward. *The Lost Tribe*. New York: Henry Holt and Company, 1996.

Matthiessen, Peter. *Under the Mountain Wall*. New York: Viking Press, Inc., 1962.

Peacock, Dr. Andrew. *Glimpses of Komodo*, 2014.

Rems, Alan. *South Pacific Cauldron*. Annapolis, MD: Naval Institute Press, 2014.

Schneebaum, Tobias. *Where the Spirits Dwell*. New York: Grove Press, 1988.

Sinclair, Gordon. *Cannibal Quest*. Toronto: Doubleday, Doran & Gundy, Limited, 1933.

Waiko, John Dademo. *A Short History of Papua New Guinea*. Melbourne: Oxford University Press, 1993.

Williams, Dr. Peter. *The Kokoda Campaign 1942: Myth and Reality*. New York, Melbourne: Cambridge University Press, 2012.

Williams, Dr. Peter. *Kokoda for Dummies*. Milton, Queensland: Wiley Publishing, 2012.

Willmott, H. P., Messenger, Charles, and Cross, Robin. *World War II*. London: Dorling Kindersley, 2004.

Zuckoff, Mitchell. *Lost in Shangri-La*. New York: HarperCollins Publishers, 2011.

Searching for indigenous writing out of Papua New Guinea may lead one to The Crocodile Prize Competition (crocodileprize.com) with its contemporary offerings, and its recognition of new voices. Those writers will add to a base established in the latter part of the last century by writers such as Albert Maori Kiki and his *Ten Thousand Years in a Lifetime* (Cheshire, 1968) and Kumalau Tawali's poem *The Bush Kanaka Speaks* (1970). Those are among the writings I've not acquired. The country's market is small, and the reach of PNG publishers is not as wide as the writers deserve. I've recently ordered *My Walk to Equality*, edited by Rashmii Amoah Bell (Australia: CreateSpace, 2017).

If you'd like to travel into the wilds of New Guinea with other Western writers during other times, I would recommend beginning with Tim Flannery's *Throwim Way Leg* (Grove Press, 1998). But don't stop there. Five remarkable books are based on women and their journeys, often solo, frightening, and thrilling in their encounters: Two young American artists—Caroline Mytinger and Margaret Warner, travelled there in the late 1920s, as told in Mytinger's *Papua New Guinea Headhunt* (Macmillan, 1946). Christina Dodwell's *In Papua New Guinea* (The Oxford Illustrated Press, 1983) is, literally, a captivating read, as is Inez Baranay's *Rascal Rain* (Angus & Robertson, 1994), though for other reasons. Isabella Tree's *Islands in the Clouds* (1996) is fascinating for its anecdotes. Kira Salak's *Four Corners* (Counterpoint, 2001) tops off the chronological order, but you could start with it.

In the world of online research it is easy to skip from one tracked-down site to another, then another so quickly that even a more diligent researcher would be hard-pressed to note each and all, such is the spontaneity of interests and variety of leads offered by videos, blogs, photographs, and writings about the Kokoda Trail or the country that hosts it. Yet such a trackless trip on the Internet is informative and to be encouraged. There are videos available in Australia (though not always in formats useable in other countries), and among those I found fascinating are the feature *Kokoda* by the Australian Broadcast Corporation (ABC), *Parer's War* (also ABC), and Damien Parer's *Kokoda Front Line!*

If you search for travel information you'll conveniently find well-credentialed Kokoda Trail companies, and can always source more information through www.papuanewguinea.travel.

Permissions

Index

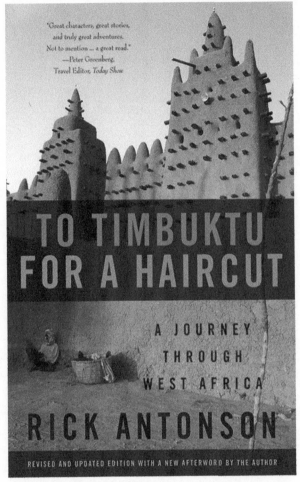

"Great characters, great stories, and truly great adventures. Not to mention . . . a great read."

—Peter Greenberg,
Travel Editor, *CBS News*

"*To Timbuktu for a Haircut* is a great read—a little bit of Bill Bryson, a little bit of Michael Palin, and quite a lot of Bob Hope on the road to Timbuktu."

—Professor Geoffrey Lipman,
former Assistant Secretary-General
of the United Nations World Tourism Organization

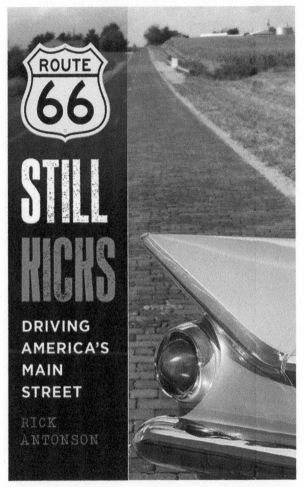

"An excellent read. Two guys went in search of Route 66 and found America . . . Highly recommended."

—Bob Moore,
coauthor of *The Complete Guidebook to Route 66*

"Reading Rick's account of his time spent on the road is forever etched in my mind and showed me things that I did not know. Antonson's book will make you feel it, live it and love it—for make no mistake, this is solid proof that Route 66 'still kicks.'"

—Jim Conkle, director,
Route 66 Pulse newspaper and TV

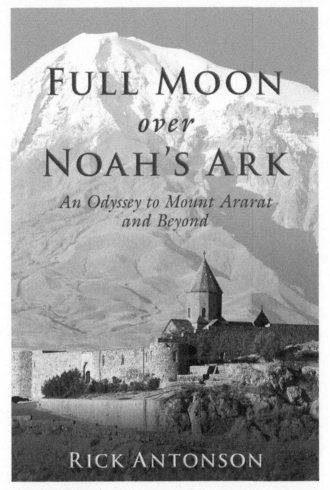

"Packed with historical facts and anecdotes, enhanced by excellent maps and photos, this is a fascinating travel adventure to one of the most ancient areas of the world . . . A reader's feast that is not to be missed."

—John A. Cherrington,
author of *Walking to Camelot*

"An educational, amusing and inspiring tale told by an experienced and worldly traveler . . . a fabulous weaving of adventure and research."

—Shannon Stowell,
president of Adventure Travel Trade Association